SATELLITE INVASION OF INDIA

SATELLITE INVASION OF INDIA

S. C. BHATT

GYAN

GYAN PUBLISHING HOUSE

NEW DELHI-110 002

Satellite Invasion of India

(Mass Communication, Information and Broadcasting, Journalism, Advertising, Culture)

ISBN : 81-212-0483-6
Library of Congress Card No. 93-900331

Published 2008 in India by
Gyan Publishing House
5 Ansari Road
New Delhi 110 002

Vishal Kaushik Printers Delhi - 110093

To my wife

RAMA

Who died while this book was being written

Preface

The problems of television as well as the other mass media have been engaging the attention of subject specialist and layman alike for quite some time. When TV began to penetrate Indian homes and until much later there was no competition as the government-owned and government-run Doordarshan alone catered to their visual media needs. Except in the areas close to the borders with Bangladesh and Pakistan the people could not receive any other signal and DD was without a rival for long.

All this underwent a sea change as first the cable people appeared in almost every nook and corner with their daily offerings of feature films and later they facilitated the advent of foreign and other channels from far and near. With that began to spread myths in our print media and among the viewers of the foreign channels.

This book deals with the issues thrown up by the satellite programmes being beamed to Indian TV owning homes both from outside and inside the country, by the courtesy of the cable operators. How the national network came up with an answer and served Indian TV watchers and the radical changes wrought in the media scene has been delineated in detail. The pros and cons of the penetration have been examined threadbare. What should be the future scenario of TV in India has also been gone into. Since the related issue of a possible print media invasion has also cropped up in recent months, a chapter has been devoted to it.

The book is offered to serious media students as well as the intelligent viewers of TV to help them appreciate better the complex issues in perspective. While projecting a point of view, it has been my effort to tell this story with adequate documentation and the sources of information have been identified and quoted extensively. A number of people helped me to gather authentic data without which the endeavour would have been incomplete. I cannot thank Y S R Murthy of the Press Information Bureau adequately for his help. He provided me with a wealth of data and arranged for me to interview a few top people in the Information and Broadcasting Ministry and Doordarshan. Some of them were not particularly forthcoming nor available (after fixing an appointment) but some others were willing to discuss with me in detail the issues involved.

This led to unlocking valuable information on the technological and programmatic aspects of the foreign penetration. In this context, my special thanks are due to P S Sundaram, the energetic and enthusiastic secretary of the Broadcast Engineering Society (India) and to M P Lele, Deputy Director General, DD, who first told me of the society and its excellent work. Dr N Vijayaditya of the National Informatics Centre spared some of his valuable time and his colleagues explained the backroom work of the NIC in collecting and disseminating election results with lightning speed with the help of satellite Insat I-D.

Thanks are also due to the Indian Institute of Mass Communication and its Director, Dr J S Yadava, for the useful and relevant information they provided. Mrs Roop Sharma, President of COFI, Cable Operators Federation of India, talked to me at length on the role and problems of the cable operators. My friend, author and journalist G N S Raghavan, went through the manuscript and made several useful suggestions, besides making valuable material available on foreign newspaper penetration. The Registrar of Newspapers also gave some information. Journalist Rajat Sharma, currently Director, News and Current Affairs, Zee TV, answered my questions and also provided me with an informative folder on his organisation. The Star representative in India, Siddhartha Ray, received me at short notice and provided information about his organisation.

To all of them my grateful thanks. They are, of course, not responsible for the views expressed and the ideas conveyed which are my own. I sincerely thank Birendra Singh Rawat for his unstinted help in preparing the typescript with care and devotion.

S C BHATT

Contents

1

1993—Year of Consequence for Indian TV

In more ways than one, the year 1993 was an eventful year for television in India. For one thing, satellite TV, beaming signals *via* a satellite to the thousands of cable operators and their dish antennae and through them to hundreds of thousands of TV households, became firmly established. India's own government-run Doordarshan(DD) itself launched as many as five satellite channels to beat off the foreign and foreign-inspired and supported Indian competition.

For another, the Metro channel of DD, operated both as a terrestrial service in the four metropolitan cities of India—Delhi, Bombay, Calcutta and Madras and later Lucknow—as well as a satellite channel, the Entertainment channel, for the rest of the country, came to occupy a prominent, if not a dominant position in the world of TV entertainment.

While competition also grew, the primary channel of DD, the real money-spinner for the government, strove manfully to hold its own against such competition and against DD's own baby—the Metro channel. Zee TV completed its first successful year but before the year 1993 ended it almost became the 101st media company of the media moghul Rupert Murdoch. Born an Australian but now a naturalised American, Murdoch had, earlier in the year, brought controlling interest in Star TV, based in Hong Kong which was the main foreign challenger to DD, with its latest claim of over seven million TV homes which "can view star programmes".

The Indian newspaper media, always decrying the craze for things "phoren" but themselves falling a prey to it with great ease, continue to sing Star's praises even after Rupert Murdoch had arrived and gone, and kept on running down DD. That Murdoch had already entered India through the Star backdoor had not caused the print media to lose any sleep but when he made a right royal main gate entry by taking almost 50 percent of the Zee shares the thin end of the Murdoch wedge was patently evident, alas, not to the newspapers whose own existence one day Murdoch could be threatening.

The cable operators continued to thrive. Their number was estimated to have climbed to a hundred thousand but some put the number even higher. Apart from bringing the latest Hindi movies, alongwith a lot of old ones, to their audience, their mainstay and their *raison detre,* the cable people have been the only vehicle of the satellite TV channel. If you are viewing Star or Zee or any other satellite channels it is *courtesy* your local, small cable operator.

For the first time the government also recognised their existence and sought to regulate the operators, activities, which incidentally would also give us some authentic information on their numbers, among other things. Registration would be compulsory for the operators. But the bill, introduced in Parliament in its 1993 monsoon session, could not be taken up for detailed discussion after its amendment by a committee of Parliament even in the 1994 budget session. Such vital media function has remained totally unregulated, while everywhere else in the world the cable operators have to have a licence from their government.[1]

The cable channels were used for the first time during the year for electioneering. Although DD. and its older but now much faded version, All India Radio AIR are under Government's control and virtually under its thumb and are much maligned for their servile attitude, they have generally not been used as agents of the ruling party. Now for the first time the ruling Congress(I) party used cable TV for putting across its point of view and asking the voters to choose its 'hand' symbol on the polling day during the assembly elections in the four former BJP(Bharatiya Janata Party) - ruled states—Uttar Pradesh, Madhya Pradesh, Rajasthan and Himachal Pradesh—and in the national capital of Delhi.

For hours together, the cable people beamed programmes asking the people to vote for the Congress(I) party and were paid for doing so. The rival party, the BJP, did not lag behind either. It had, in addition, at its disposal the services of the Jain satellite TV beamed *via* a Russian satellite.

There were other developments too. The ATN(Asia Television Network) channel, known to many cable viewers through the 'Gold' Hindi feature films, now acquired a multinational image. It entered into an agreement with the British news agency *Reuters'* TV, the Thames Television of London and the American TV network, ABC, *American Broadcasting Company,* whose programmes (including *Reuters* TV news) could now be seen in India. Yet another satellite channel went on the air in the form of the Asianet TV with its Malayalam channel to attract the Malayalam speaking people of India's Kerala state and the Malayalees in the Gulf countries in West Asia. Not to be outdone, DD also beamed regional languages programmes, including those in Malayalam, in the spare time of the satellite channels.

In DD the hardware was running much ahead of the software as its time slot scheme went awry with some leading newspapers, now in the TV business, not a phenomenon peculiar to India, frustrating DD and its time allotment scheme with court writs. All the same the year was of great consequence for DD because what could have been accomplished only in two or three years was achieved only in a matter of months--its five satellite channels.

The rivals did not have much to worry about satellite hardware as readymade transponders could be hired. But as Zee TV learnt to its cost even the hiring could be a painful process. Its sub-lease of a Star transponder could and did result in nearly half of the company's shares being acquired by the main lessee, the Star TV, now owned by Murdoch.

All these channels operated from abroad. The viewers would hardly know that Zee TV's video cassettes are airlifted daily to Hong Kong and are aired through Star TV's studios and *via* the Asiasat satellite they reach Indian TV viewers *courtesy* the local cable operator, and likewise its audience in other countries where Hindi is spoken or understood, as claimed by it. The same applies to the other channels. Only in the case of the TWI, Trans-World International, a multinational company, the broadcaster was allowed to generate his own signal on Indian soil and beam it straight from India to a satellite *via* its own earth station put up by it from wherever it was televising the Hero Cup cricket matches in November 1993. The uplifted signal was flashed back to India *via* Star's Prime Sports Channel. This was under a court order and if this precedent is cited in future the same facility and right could be availed of by another party, Indian or foreign. Mercifully the permission was on a one-time basis.

For years Indian TV (and earlier radio) audiences had few options. Radio listeners at least had the short wave facility and could reach out to foreign stations beaming programmes to India in Hindi, English and other Indian languages. But the TV signal can hardly travel any worthwhile long distance. Except in the border regions where Pakistan or Bangladesh TV could be watched the TV audiences had no access to any non-DD telecasts until first the cable arrived with Hindi movies and later, through it, the programmes of foreign satellite channels and some Indian channels using foreign satellites.

The year 1993 was thus a watershed. It brought several options to Indian audiences, apart from the continuing service of the staple diet of Hindi movies through the cable services. The foreign and Indian satellite services became an established fact, a *fait accompli*. The national network rose to the occasion by opening additional channels and offering through them alternatives.

In September 1992, for the first time, the Indian government swerved from its monopolistic and paternalistic viewpoint and recognised that it alone could not provide all the entertainment the viewers wanted and which had to be given to them if foreign competition was to be met successfully. The time slot scheme was born of this search for a countermeasure. Indirectly the government recognised that the private entertainment industry could make a valuable contribution if only DD threw open its channels to them. The time slot scheme which was then conceived could not be implemented as planned but the Metro Entertainment channel, alongwith its satellite version, became a reality and offered the viewers a major alternative with a number of lively programmes.

The TV medium is a medium of the three E's—Entertainment, Education and Enlightement, the last including news and other informational programmes. Education has, of course, to be conceived in the broadest possible terms to cover education of the people in health, sanitation, good manners, citizenship, civility, immunization and good upringing of children, the small family norm and the rest of it.

News has to be fair and objective, factual and accurate. But, above all, TV is watched because it brings to the people right in their drawing rooms enjoyable and entertaining programmes - feature films, other filmbased programmes, serials of comedy, soap opera, detective stories, thrillers, song and dance.

Doordarshan's decision to open its channels to private producers of entertaining programmes was essentially a recognition of the need to step up the entertainment component of its fare. It ultimately resulted in a complete channel of entertainment being born. This, of course, raises some vital issues whether the emphasis or overemphasis on entertainment subserves the larger interests of the Indian viewers. Standing up to foreign competition is all right but are you, in the process, sacrificing something vital and are you letting consumerism loose, is an excess of entertainment encouraging public inertia, deadening their individual and collective sensitivities, and are you, while outdoing the competitors practising oneupsmanship. 'what you can do we can do better, if you bare the legs we can expose the top, most of it'.

These are frankly questions of great import and relevance in the context of our cultural ethos of which the foreign competitors and their Indian sidekicks are blissfully unaware or about which they bother the least. They could not care less if Indian children are immunised or not, or the Indians eat iodised salt or not or the chocolates served up by the multinationals contain lead or not.

That is the difference between a national network and pure entertainment channels, whether they are based in Hong Kong or Bombay. While DD has to care and be answerable to public opinion and Parliament the foreign satellite TV and its Indian counterparts are only concerned with advertisement revenue. The Indian print media conveniently close their eyes to this vital point.

Television, for all practical purposes or until a national crisis faces us, is identified with entertainment. The fact that the viewers now have a set of options and signals are being beamed to the Indian homes from all directions and many countries is in a large measure due to the rapid advances in technology. Doordarshan's monopoly would not have been broken otherwise, since it was left unchallenged on the ground. Nobody seems to have tried to set up a terrestial station in competition with DD and none tested the provision in the Constitution of India guaranteeing freedom of expression, now bandied about by all and sundry. The overwhelming force of technology made it possible for TV signals *via* the satellites to reach your homes and wrought a mini-revolution in the business of audio-visual communication.

Not only that. The frontiers of technology are getting enlarged at a fast pace and digital technology may make it possible for a number of channels to be brought within your reach and even direct broadcast signals may be flashed and be received by viewers. So, while many countries, including China and Malaysia, have banned Star and other foreign satellite channels (and similar demands have been made in India too) they could still be knocking at your doors.

The question of relevance of the programmes coming to you from across the skies would, of course, be there. Apart from the language of the telecast which you may never be able to understand and, therefore, be in no position to enjoy the programmes broadcast in that language, the problem whether the contents appeal to you or go over your heads cannot be evaded.

But already many of these channels seek your attention in your own tongue. The fact that the British Broadcasting Corporation (BBC), which never tires of speaking of its altruistic motives, is at loggerheads with the Star channels of Rupert Murdoch over the former's plans to launch a round-the-clock Arabic service (of "News" and current affairs) shows that you are being approached not by one but two or even more channels with programmes in your own languages. The question whether they would still be relevant to you would persist.

One may well ask; why should the BBC or Star be laying on a whole channel in Arabic? But then one may also ask: why are so many multinationals rushing to make their toothpastes or soft drinks available to you? And if Coca Cola comes, can

Rupert Murdoch be far behind? Not merely his TV channels, but his newspapers too. In the process the TV channels are also spreading a culture alien to your country and are encouraging such cultural forces which have already found a home in your land. The harbingers of a hybrid culture and of trends not in accord with your cultural ethos are gleefully welcoming the satellite invaders.

Mahatama Gandhi, who had thought about many questions besides the freedom of India of which he was the architect, had told us not to be swept off our feet by the cultures of other countries although he said our doors must not be stuffed and Indians should be exposed to the cultures of all lands. Now we are facing the issue in all its nakedness. Daily and nightly the glitter of America, a country where more than a third of the marriages end in divorce, invades the drawing rooms often along with false pictures of family cohesiveness.

Satellite TV got firmly established in India in 1993 throwing up this and other questions of vital importance to the nation. How have we faced them or failed to face them is the theme of this book.

A big effort was made and it was also rewarded with a substantial measure of success although the question of warding off foreign influence has not been faced squarely. Some of the invaders were, however, in a mood to climb down at the end of the year. The beginning of 1994 saw them trooping in one after the other with Rupert Murdoch, as expected, in the lead. Gestures to soften the attitude of the Indian government and make it feel that the foreign channels meant well by this country were also made and joint venture proposals were put by major foreign broadcast organisations like the CNN (Cable News Network, New York), BBC (British Broadcasting Corporation, London) and others[2].

A government wedded to liberalisation, meaning thereby open arm welcome to the multinationals, could perhaps enter into such deals.

2

State Monopoly of Radio and TV

Nearly a century and a half (147 years to be precise), after the first newspaper made its appearance in India[1], radio broadcasting began on a regular basis in 1927. Thus this the latest, electronic medium of mass communication came to India just five or seven years after scheduled broadcasting of programmes became a reality in the advanced countries of the West, the United States and Britain[2]. But while the press has always been in the private sector, the radio (and later television) grew up under the governmental umbrella and both remain state monopolies to this day.

Surprisingly, it was not so when broadcasting was launched from Bombay on July 23, 1927 by the Indian Broadcasting Company, as a private commercial venture. It inaugurated its Calcutta Station five weeks later, on August 26 the same year. Although it was a commercial undertaking, the promoters had the requisite vision.

The company chairman, Sir Ibrahim Rahimtoola, speaking at the opening of the Bombay station by the Governor General, Lord Irwin, said, "One of the greatest problems in India is that of distance and the constant difficulty of maintaining efficient communication between her component parts. It is the recognised merit of broadcasting that it annihilates distance . . .. With the advent of broadcasting there is nothing to prevent, in time the farthest confines of Kashmir. Sikkim or of Travancore simultaneously receiving the news of the moment"[3].

The founder spoke not only of linking the remotest corners of the country, including Travancore (a princely state now part of Kerala), but also of news being communicated to them simultaneously thus helping the process of unifying the country. The same sentiment was voiced by the Managing Director of the company, Sultan Chenoy, in his speech at the commissioning of the Calcutta Station:" ... parts of Bombay Presidency have of late been visited by disastrous floods involving the complete isolation of large tracts of Gujarat and Kathiawar (now known as Saurashtra, part of Gujarat State) and letters have since reached us which says that the only news of the outside world received by the flooded areas for a week was through the Bombay broadcasting station"[4].

The Indian Broadcasting Company received much financial support from the British government in India in the form of eighty per cent of the radio (BR, broadcast receiver) licence fee and a cess on the purchase of radio sets. Surprisingly, commercials were not thought of by the IBC as a source of revenue and had to wait for the next 40 years to be broadcast over the Vividh Bharati channel of All India Radio, AIR. Perhaps the unhealthy state of India's economy during that period of the economic depression which was then hitting most parts of the world prevented the company from tapping that source.

The company was in the red before long and had to wind up. The revenue from BR licences was too inadequate to meet the company's expenses and the number of sets was by no means going up by leaps and bounds. There were less than 7,000 radio sets in the whole country in 1928 and the number had gone up to 8,557 in 1933, whereas the number of TV sets jumped from about 35 million in 1992 to 40.3 million in 1993. As many as 11.5 million colour TV sets were bought in just one year, 1993.

The British government, which was only too happy to see that a private company had taken up the vital task of bringing radio to India, was most reluctant to take over the IBC and run broadcasting as a state enterprise. After much hesitation and taking into account public opinion, which strongly wanted broadcasting to continue somehow, the British rulers took over the job and pumped some money into it. Delhi and six other stations came up and a brilliant and highly educated person, Lionel Fielden, was brought from Britain to head the organisation, first called by the cumbersome name of Indian State Broadcasting Service but renamed, at Fielden's instance, as ALL INDIA RADIO.[5]

Came the Second World War and the British now found the state-run broadcasting, which they had unwillingly acquired and grudgingly developed on a modest scale, a powerful medium of mass communication at its disposal to provide a counterpoise to the nationalist propaganda through the press. Large sections of it supported the cause of freedom, with the exception of British owned newspapers, like the *Times of India* and the *Statesman*, which were out of sympathy with the freedom struggle. Not only were broadcasts started in a number of Indian languages and news bulletins were launched in many of them but a network of External Services was also created to reach the uncommitted or partisan listeners in East and West Asia, then called the Far East and Middle East.

When freedom dawned and with it came the partition of the country, there were six stations, Delhi, Bombay, Calcutta,

Lucknow, Madras and Tiruchirapally (in Tamil Nadu), which remained as AIR Stations in India, and Dacca, Lahore and Peshawar which became part of the newly created Radio Pakistan, later called the Pakistan Broadcasting Corporation. The government of independent India was quick to realise the value of broadcasting in carrying its message of nation building and national unity across the vast areas of the country. If gradually expanded and strengthened the home services and also expanded the External services.

The 1991 census tells us that there are 120 million radio households in India out of a total of 152 million households. So, although the voice of AIR, also known as Akashvani, the voice from the sky, now reaches 96.2 per cent of the population and 86.1 per cent of the area of India, the number of those who can actually listen to AIR is somewhat limited by the availability of radio sets.

AIR has a network of 149 stations, including 141 fullfledged centres, three relay stations, two auxillary centres and three exclusive Vividh Bharati centres. There are some thirty Vividh Bharati Stations apart from the exclusive centres and commercials have been broadcast even from AIR's primary channel on some 60 stations fetching AIR a revenue of Rs. 52.73 crores (527 million, or $18 million approximately) in 1991-92. The Vividh Bharati services, which broadcasts mainly film and other light music and some skits, plays and features, is on the air daily for 13 hours and fifteen minutes, with an additional half hour on Sundays.[6]

The External Services network of AIR, which is on the air almost round the clock, broadcasts in 24 languages of which 16 are foreign languages and eight Indian, spoken both in India and abroad. The foreign languages used by AIR include Chinese, Tibetan, Arabic, Persian, Pushto, Indonesian, Swahili (the language of some African countries) Russian, French and Burmese. Its Urdu service is heard both in India and Pakistan, consisting of music and news bulletins.

Interestingly, AIR has been using the Indian satellites, I-D and 2-A, and has been doing so since well before Satellite TV became a dominant force in TV programmes. Insat-1D is being utilised for the relay of programmes (including news bulletins) from Delhi. The Department of Telecommunications' earth station at Sikandarabad (in Uttar Pradesh) is used for uplinking the signal. The major stations at Bombay, Calcutta and Madras also use the satellite with uplinking facility for their regional services. Additional uplinking facilities exist and are being used through Insat-2A which links Delhi with a number of stations.

The important point to be noted is that while AIR made a substantial contribution to the popularisation of Indian classical music and light-classical music, brought literature in various Indian languages to the people's doorsteps and promoted an Indian consciousness and national unity, it has remained a state monopoly. There has never been a radio station in India other than an AIR Station since independence. AIR was the one and only radio medium.

There have been at the same time, various attempts at conferring autonomy on AIR but all of them ended in failure. Through the Director-General of AIR and the Director-General of News of AIR, the Information and Broadcasting Ministry of the Indian Government has exercised effective control over the contents of the news bulletins and the policies governing the dissemination of other programmes. The control is wielded mostly through oral and word-of-mouth orders, conveyed in official briefings of the top brass of the medium or on the telephone when urgent instructions are required to be passed on. The Prime Minister's office is another source of control through its spokesman or the PR adviser to the Prime Minister.

The other important point of note is that there has been no serious challenge to this situation. Political parties vow to make AIR (and its TV counterpart, Doordarshan, DD) autonomous when they are out of power and forget the pledge as soon as they occupy the seat of power or forget to implement the promise. The Congress(I) party claims it wants the two media to have "internal or functional" autonomy but oral orders on what to broadcast and what not are the order of the day.

The Janata Dal Government of V.P. Singh had come to power with a commitment to freedom of the media, meaning freedom from government control, but in effect his Minister of Information and Broadcasting made no pretence in 1990 of being any different from his Congress(I) counterparts of the past. The Janata Dal, however, did get a bill passed by Parliament on creating autonomous corporations for AIR and DD, subsequently called the Prasar Bharati act, but fell before it could find the time to implement it. The two succeeding governments have never really tried to implement it. After nearly four years of the enactment the Prasar Bharati remains a dead letter.

When television came to India[7], first as a purely experimental service in 1959, and later in 1965 as a regular daily service, DD was actually a part of AIR and had a common boss. Even after the umbilical cord was cut in 1976 and a separate directorate general of DD, with its own DG, was set up, the organisation was made a cog in the wheel of the I and B Ministry. Its Headquarters in Mandi House in New Delhi, close to the commercial district of Connaught Place, has always been subservient to Shastri Bhavan which houses the I and B Ministry. More about the growth of Indian television in the following chapter.

The Constitution of India provides for freedom of expression as one of the fundamental rights to which a citizen is entitled and which he can enforce by approaching a High Court. It is contained in article 19(*i*) which says: "All citizens shall have the right - (a) to freedom of speech and expression".

This freedom of expression has been interpreted by the Supreme Court of India as inclusive of the freedom of the press and, indeed, often the newspapers have gone to court with writ applications challenging this or that action of the Central or State governments as violative of their fundamental rights and often the pleas are upheld by the relevant courts. But, surely, freedom of expression should include not merely the freedom of the press but also the freedom of the other vital media, the radio and TV which, on the one hand, would mean a radio and TV outside the dictates of the Government and on the other, freedom for its citizens to establish radio and TV stations, subject, as always, to reasonable restrictions.

This, however, has not been seriously tested in the courts and to this day state monopoly of the two vital electronic media has remained unchallenged. The votaries of satellite TV have found a convenient way out of the dilemma and the availability of satellites have facilitated their task of challenging DD's monopoly without setting up terrestrial services. In this task, the fact that satellite services are available in foreign countries has been a godsend to them. But imagine what would happen if the services of Asiasat in Hong Kong or Statsionar in Moscow or similar services in other countries were not at their disposal or there was a law or legal provision against such services being used. Or imagine the Indian government had reciprocal arrangements with the countries concerned not to allow programmes to be beamed to India *via* their satellites. Or consider what would happen to Asiasat after 1997 when Hong Kong reverts to China, which has already banned foreign satellite services in its own territory. Can China then allow Hong Kong, a part of the People's Republic to be used as a base for satellite TV services to invade India?

Of course, the Indian government has declared more than once that it has no intention to ban foreign satellite services and has perhaps never approached a foreign government to prevent the use of a satellite under its control or being operated from its soil for telecast of programmes addressed to India. The satellite TV operators in India are not in possession of facilities on the ground to uplink their programmes from Indian soil. They, like Zee TV and Jain Satellite TV and others, have to fly their cassettes of serials, film-based programmes or other sponsored programmes to Hong Kong, Moscow or other centres from where they are uplinked *via* one or the other satellite.

In effect, AIR and DD have had no challenger on the ground. AIR had to contend with foreign short wave (and some medium wave) broadcasts and now DD faces satellite competition.

3

Origin and Development of TV in India

Doordarshan, India's national network, has 31 major Kendras (stations) with studios, production facilities and regular programmes originating from the stations, and 550 transmitters. Some 83.6 percent of India's vast population (now over 900 million). are able to watch DD's programmes, signalled to them through a nearby relay transmitter. For such an imposing network, DD's origin was not only humble but also unpretentious and almost insignificant.

On September, 15, 1959, a Pilot Television Centre went on the air in the posh Parliament street area of the capital[1]. Located midway between Broadcasting House, the nerve centre of radio broadcasting, and the adjoining Akashvani Bhavan, housing the administrative and controlling offices of the Directorate General of AIR, was the Akashvani Auditorium of radio. This commodious hall was used mainly for live broadcast of music concerts by great masters like Pandit Onkarnath Thakur who would be heard with great reverence and rapt attention by the cognoscenti among the invited audience and often simultaneously by the listeners at large. There were galleries overlooking the hall which would be thrown open to the guests if there was an overflow from the main hall below.

It was here that Indian TV was born. Since TV was considered only an extension of radio broadcasting it was natural that the baby be born in the mother's own house, almost in her lap, and grow up under her care, only to overshadow and dwarf the procreator when it grew up.

The Akashvani Auditorium was converted into the studio from where the regular programmes of Indian TV were put on the air although the first experimental programmes were telecast from a makeshift studio in Akashvani Bhavan. The service itself was known as a Pilot project, aided by UNESCO (United Nations Educational, Scientific and Cultural Organisation), because the programmes, put out on a mere two days a week, were intended to be experimental in nature to test the efficacy of this (TV) medium in carrying relevant and useful messages of social education to the poorer sections of society.

Teleclubs were formed in different neighbourhoods where people would gather on the two evenings of the week in front of a community set. Not more than 21 sets in Community Centers in middle and lower middle class areas were provided for the viewers. After watching the programmes the audience would also take part in a discussion led by an organizer, on the relevance and appropriateness of the message thus reaffirming the principle "tell them what you have told them." The extreme inadequacy of resources did not deter the engineers and programme persons from providing live coverage of Republic Day and Independence Day celebrations in 1960 without an OB(outside broadcasting) van.

This went on for two years after which another experiment in educational TV was launched. This time real instructional TV was used as programmes relevant to school children of Delhi were broadcast. Since word had gone round that Indian TV was educational, even instructional, in nature the general public was not much bothered about it. Even those who could afford a TV set had not acquired one since thee was not any "worthwhile" programmes to watch. But some sets were slowly infiltrating the households, specially sets brought in as accompanied baggage by Delhites returning from trips abroad. Many of them had seen TV programmes while visiting advanced countries and even otheres since TV as a status symbol was being fast acquired by many developing countries too, irrespective of the use to which it was being put nationally. In some houses in Delhi, the parents' curiosity was aroused by the reports that their children brought about the TV programmes watched by them in their schools.

For all these people wanting to see real TV programmes, Indian TV had an answer, not a fullfledged one but still an answer, when a regular one-hour service was started by DD in Delhi on August 15, 1965. The Fifteenth of August is a date invested with special significance in the Indian calendar as it was on that day that India became a free nation in 1947. The day was chosen even later for launching Indian TV's new phases again and again.

It would be another nearly four years before the one-hour service was increased to two hours in May 1969 but in between TV had made a significant impact on the minds of the dwellers of Delhi. Specially interesting was the Hindi movie telecast in two parts, first for an hour on Saturdays and the second instalment on Sundays. It was customary for neighbours and children from a number of homes in the neighbourhood to invade your homes on both days, a custom which has lingered in some form despite the deep penetration of homes by TV sets.

The daily output of programmes was raised to three hours in July 1970 and another half an hour was added in December that year. By now, TV had acquired a definite personality for itself although it was still the poor relation of radio and it was not yet taken seriously by many people. One reason for the rather slow advance registered by television was the extreme paucity of financial resources and the Planning Commission which allocates funds and sets priorities had assigned a low place to TV in its scheme of developmental priorities[2]. It insisted, rightly in the eyes of many people, that TV was essentially a medium of entertainment which should wait while the vast network of radio which had been built up in India must be first put to use for nation building and other socially relevant programmes like family planning.

There was thus no question of Indian TV acquiring colour and none for providing a countrywide network of TV which would bring this new, enchanting medium to the doorstep of the people in remote areas. All the same, the country's second TV station came up in Bombay in 1972. Bombay was fortunate to go ahead on its own steam, away from the AIR umbrella, and have its spacious studios in Worli in Central Bombay quite some distance from the radio's premises in South Bombay.

India is a country where not only the politicians, media busybodies and the culture vultures act as pressure groups in the formulation and execution of media policies but she has also to contend with regional and other forces which have their pulls. This worked to the advantage of TV's expansion and regional centres came up in Calcutta, Madras and Lucknow in 1975, and in Srinagar(Kashmir) and Amritsar(Punjab) even earlier in 1973.

Centres had thus come up in different parts of the country and TV had become an established medium although it was still only the affluent classes and those who had some foreign connection who could afford a set. There were some community sets provided by the Central and many state governments but not enough to cover all the villages of India - and, of course, many big and small cities were still unable to receive any TV signal at all.

It was at this time, on August 1, 1975, that the SITE (Satellite Instructional Television Experiment) was launched for a year in six states - Rajasthan, Karnataka, Orissa, Bihar, Andhra Pradesh and Madhya Pradesh[3]. It was an American satellite ATS-6 which was used for direct reception of programmes. The experiment was carried out in cooperation between the

American NASA and the Indian Space Research Organisation, with the active involvement of AIR, of which Doordarshan was still a part. The programmes on agriculture and social education were in the respective languages of the regions and were watched with much interest by the rural audiences in 2,400 villages, for whom they were meant on community sets, receiving signals direct from the satellite with the help of a dish antenna.

The SITE programmes only emphasized the educational role of TV and the people working in Indian TV remained for a long time under the spell of the formula that TV was a medium for the upliftment of the people not for their entertainment, or mainly for it. However, the commercial aspect was not neglected and in 1976 the first commercials were put out from some of DD's centres. Although DD, as we have seen, was not oriented towards making money out of entertainment programmes, it earned Rs. 7.7 million in the very first year, 1976-1977. In that year, DD was separated, "delinked" as people in Doordarshan would say, from its progenitor, AIR, and acquired its own DG and a separate headquarters in Mandi House.

The general view that TV was an expensive medium which a poor country could not afford and, in any case, there was more than enough infrastructure of radio which must be first put to good use, still prevailed and TV's growth was somewhat stunted[4]. There was as yet no effort to link up the various centres and a national channel was far from the thoughts of the planners. All the same, the first linking of the four Metros - Delhi, Bombay, Calcutta and Madras - was achieved in 1980, on the eve of Republic Day when the citizens of the four cities could watch a common programme of music simultaneously. Until then, Bombay's programmes, mainly interviews with film personalities, were telecast as a recorded event by the other centres and similarly different centres would exchange their programmes in the form of video cassettes.

When Indira Gandhi came back to power in January 1980, after nearly three years in wilderness, her second son Sanjay, who was not in the government but wielded tremendous authority (referred to by the media as extraconstitutional authority) over the affairs of the government, was a great votary of colour TV and of rapid expansion of TV in the country. In the then minister of I and B he had an equally enthusiastic champion of the cause of TV. Under that dispensation, TV flowered in India as never before and the old inhibition evaporated. With commercials now flowing in, TV was also generating substantial revenue.

On August 15, 1982, the National Programmes was introduced when all the TV centres would be linked every evening at prime time for the news in Hindi and English and for some soap operas, comic and detective serials, programmes of music and, of course, feature films and film-based programmes. The commissioning of the INSAT-IA, the first Indian multipurpose satellite, about that time, came in handy as the linkage would not have been otherwise possible and microwave linking would have been difficult, often faulty and costly.

Thereafter India has been launching a number of satellites of her own almost regularly and they have helped in linking up the centres for both the daily national programmes and for special national programmes, covering special telecasts, including live coverage of major sports events of national and international significance.

In 1983[5], a massive programme of opening LPTs (low power transmitters) was launched mainly with an eye on the elections which were due in the end of 1984 or early in 1985. The engineers of DD put in long hours as the Indian hardware manufacturing units worked overtime to produce the equipment which they put in position and later in 1984 an LPT was coming up every day. The LPTs carried the Delhi programmes, which meant a mixture of entertainment, news and information and education, *plus* a lot of government propaganda. But in the process TV reached the far corners of the country much ahead of any planned expansion under the five year development programmes would have ensured.

From the ruling party's point of view also the expansion helped to achieve its target. Although Mrs. Gandhi died and her elder son Rajiv Gandhi, who had been groomed by her after the tragic death of Sanjay in a plane accident, took over, the elections were held as planned in December 1984. The nation-wide TV coverage of the mother's funeral after her assassination helped to project Rajiv to the national electorate through the newly built LPTs dotting the Indian countryside.

From the date the National Programme was launched on DD, colour was also introduced and the first nationally telecast programme in colour was the Prime Minister's address to the nation from the ramparts of the historic Red Fort in Delhi on the 35th anniversary of freedom, August 15, 1982. For all his 17 years in office, Jawaharlal Nehru had addressed the people of India from the same spot but his speeches were heard only on the radio through AIR. Coverage on the television came much later but now for the first time people could see the Prime Minister, the surroundings of the fort and the school children and others in the audience in their colourful dresses.

From that time DD did not look back. Doordarshan itself created the first Indian soap opera, *Hum Log* and that archtypal serial was on the air as the first sponsored serial on July 15, 1984. A succession of serials followed and in 1987, again amid much criticism, DD began transmitting programmes in its morning breakfast service. In another two years, on Republic Day 1989, the Indian TV began transmitting its programmes in the afternoon also. By 1992-1993 its annual income from advertisements had risen to Rs. 360 crores. The number of TV households in India rose from a mere 649 in 1965 when a regular one-hour TV service began in Delhi to 40.337 million in 1993[6]. Of these 12 million sets are in the villages and 28 million in the urban areas. Besides there are 64,600 community sets in the country.

By 1992, the challenge from foreign and foreign-supported Indian satellite channels, as well as the mushrooming cable operators, was also becoming a severe headache for DD. How this challenge emerged and how DD has been facing up to it is dealt with in detail in the following chapters.

4

Foreign Competition—An AIR Experience

In the Western World and Japan, television made its appearance in the early 1950's, although elaborate scheduled services began later in that decade or the following one and the radio reigned supreme. In India, as we have seen, it was radio raj until much later when Doordarshan's network had spread far and wide and the national programme was launched in 1982. This brought the entire country under a common TV umbrella when AIR, once the progenitor of TV, actually became its poor cousin. Until then, AIR had no competitor in India, specially on the ground, and DD does not have even now a terrestrial competitor.

The radio, however, had to contend with long distance broadcasts on the shortwave from foreign stations which sometimes were boosted, as in the case of the British radio, BBC, through ground relay stations built in other lands because of old imperial connections, economic inducements or arm-twisting of the weaker nations by the powerful nations of the west.

These shortwave programmes were, however, of limited duration and did not pose any significant threat to AIR's listenership, except in later years when blatant partisan propaganda over AIR to serve the ends of the ruling Congress(I) party made a section of the radio audience turn to foreign stations for news. In the fifties, however, there was a threat of a different kind, direct to AIR's appeal to its home audience. It arose from the light (mainly film) music programmes of Radio Ceylon, as Sri Lanka was then known, based in Colombo, and Radio Goa in Panaji, then known as Panjim.

Both offered to the Indian audience popular Hindi film songs over long hours together with commercials which were then a novelty for listeners in India. AIR was then looked upon by the powers that be as a vehicle of culture and in the eyes of Dr Balakrishna V Keskar, who was I and B minister under Jawaharlal Nehru for ten long years, from March 1952 to March 1962, it meant classical music or khayals with a sprinkling of light classical music like *thumris, dadras* and *ghazals*, or *bhajans*. Classical music is generally known as *Pucca* (or hard) *gana*, music. Film music some of its based on classical *ragas* was also broadcast but in selected small doses to underline its subordinate status.

There is little doubt that AIR rendered yeoman's service in propagating and popularising classical music and admirably took over the role of patron for the ustads and pandits after the decline of the princely class, but it was unwise to try to thrust classical music down the throats of the bulk of listeners.

Radio Goa and its Ceylonese counterpart presented film music on a platter, morning, afternoon and till late evening. And the audience could never say, 'enough, enough'. Denied their quota of entertainment over the national network, many listeners lapped up the fare from the two foreign stations.

So much was the popularity of these stations that people going out to buy a radio set, itself an event those days, would often ask the dealer whether 'Ceylon comes on it' or 'Goa comes on it', meaning can Ceylon be heard on the receiver, can we get Goa on the set.

Of course, only those who lived close to Panaji or Colombo could receive the programmes on their medium wave sets. Others had to go in for a shortwave receiver and in those days not every radio buff could afford the price.

The two services were, however, popular and those in Broadcasting House and in the I and B ministry were quite worried at the loss of a section of the audience of AIR. By now AIR had acquired more than one channel in several stations and Vividh Bharati, the light music channel, was born in 1957 as a solution to this challenge. It was to become gradually a film music channel and, allowing for the slowness with which governments move, the first commercials were broadcast in the light music channel in 1967. By and by more Vividh Bharati stations were added (now there are 32 of them) and Hindi news bulletins in the morning and evening hours were also introduced. The bulletins in the primary channel were relayed by Vividh Bharati.

Goa was liberated from Portuguese rule by the Indian army in 1961 and the threat from Radio Ceylon had also receded. The Vividh Bharati service gradually became so popular that for many Indian listeners that was the real AIR, Akashvani, the voice from heaven. So when Vividh Bharati went off the air in the afternoon hours many listeners would switch on AIR Delhi's Urdu service, directed to Pakistan on the shortwave but heard by Indian audiences alike, and would say, 'now let us listen to All India Radio'. Under the notion that an Indian name like Akashvani would not go down well with the Pakistani listeners, many of whom have been regular listeners to the Urdu service because Indian film songs have been quite popular yet remain banned from Pakistan radio and TV, AIR would call itself by its original name in that service.

All good communicators know that the audience is never captive. If there is no option, a listener or viewer would just turn off the set the moment the programmes fail to interest him, or pay no attention even while the set is on. If he has any option in listening or watching he would switch channels. Audiences are also sensitive and if the foreign programme is offensive they would not watch that channel for a long time to come. Once, those watching a Pakistan TV live relay of a cricket match (in both countries people are crazy about movies and cricket) the Pakistan TV people thought it fit to broadcast some worthy's anti-Indian speech and that was the end of watching Pakistan for the viewers. The Pakistani programmes forgot the tenet 'respect your audience'.

The viewing of programmes from an alien culture may result in cultural distortions but that issue will be examined later. The fact remains that the audience is always in search of options and alternatives and has no particular resistance or inhibition to programme originating from an alien source provided the programmes is interesting and attractive and not repulsive.

AIR itself had many loyal listeners in Burma (now Mynmar), Indonesia, Iran and elsewhere at different times. Its external services in their languages were quite popular for a variety of reasons. When the Indonesian leaders, including the first President, Dr Soekarno himself, were jailed by the Dutch colonial government early in 1949, AIR's Indonesian service was very popular in that ancient land of many islands. I wrote the daily commentary in those days and it was translated into Indonesia from English by an officer of the Indonesian mission in Delhi. (India had granted diplomatic status to the mission even before Indonesian became a fullfledged, sovereign nation.) Years later when I was AIR's South East Asia correspondent and visited Jakarta in 1968 I met him as a senior staff member of Foreign Minister Adam Malik. Of course, when the Indonesian leaders were released from prison later in 1949 itself and once again given charge of their country prior to complete transfer of power, the Indonesians had their own radio service and the popularity of AIR's external services declined considerably.

The point made is that the audience is always looking for options. The newspapers in India are a lively lot, despite their many failings, and strive to be ahead of their rivals among the contemporaries because there is keen competition to capture the attention of the readers which is the only way to build up circulation. It takes many things, including substantial financial resources, well recognised editorial skills and dynamic management, to make a newspaper click and become acceptable to the readers. If, however, there were to be no alternative and the reader was obliged to buy the only available (perhaps state-sponsored or run) newspaper, it would become complacent, hidebound and sluggish in its reaction to developments and would be inclined to take the readers for granted.

Competition is thus the soul of the print medium and those running the dailies and periodicals know it too well that if they lag behind they would slide down and the paper could even face closure. Competition must, likewise, be the soul of the electronic media too, both in respect of news and current affairs programmes as well as entertainment. If AIR had not opened a light music channel in the late fifties and sixties(and happily it thrives to this day) it could have led to a total erosion of its popularity in the country and its credibility. This problem did arise, as we have seen, in a different context when AIR found the audience slipping through its fingers, but to see that happen over the issue of your ability to entertain them is indeed galling.

Incidentally, Vividh Bharati helped to underline an important media point. By opening the channel and building it up, AIR provided itself with in-built competition. The light music channel was the real AIR to many listeners, offering competition to the primary channel. It was an option to those who had no cultural or intellectual pretensions and were happy with their daily dose of film and other light music and some news, skits and plays which came over the service in the midst of sponsored or other film music programmes.

It is a matter of great regret that AIR never built up nor (the government) allowed any competition outside to come up in the area of news and current affairs. AIR thus remained a monopoly and gradually it came to be accepted by many in India that the electronic media have to remain a state enterprise.

5

No Competition for DD for Long

For a late starter in the TV business, DD made up for much of the lost time in the eighties. As we have seen, the process of expansion and modernisation was inspired by politicians who overcame the inhibitions of the Planning Commission and rode roughshode over the largely accepted view that the nation's scarce resources must not be expended on an expensive medium like television and, in any case, the infrastructure of radio must be first fully used for social education.

Now this outlook underwent a sea change, at the instance of the ruling coterie, and in the middle of 1983, an unplanned allocation of Rs. 68 crores was made available to DD to instal 180 LPTs (low power transmitters) all over the country by the end of 1984. The date was to coincide with the national elections expected to be held in December that year or near about that date.

Of course, the stated object was to link up the whole country, or most of it, and make it possible for any TV household in the country to receive TV programmes for long hours as well as watch the National Programmes every evening. This was on the air since August 15, 1982. The unstated object was to place a network in the hands of the ruling party and its top leaders by the time the country went to polls to elect a new Lok Sabha (lower house, or House of the People, of Parliament). The radio had been used in 1977 to this end, with disastrous consequences for the ruling party, but few people learn from experience.

Anyway, the country acquired a grand new TV network in the process (which also served the requirements of the ruling party in an unexpected way). In expectation of the network coming up and to meet the people's growing demand for entertainment, the I and B secretary called in some writers and radio playwrights to find out whether they could undertake to write a serial or two. The archetypal Indian soap opera, *Hum Log,* was thus born. Writer-Journalist Manohar Shyam Joshi was among the invited script writers and took up the challenge to produce a serial which became the pace-setter soap opera with few parallels all these years. A joint venture of DD and a private producer, a former DD hand himself, the 116-episode serial, aired twice a week on the DD network, *Hum Log* focussed on the problems of the middle class, their aspirations and failures. With a powerful script and scintillating dialogues the soap opera captured the attention of the viewers and earned their affection. Its repeat exhibition some years later could still attract audiences and sponsors.

The serial faithfully followed the principle 'tell them what you have told them' and managed to enlist the services of the thespian Ashok Kumar for the purpose. Most of the actors were new to the small or even the large screen of the cinema but turned in attractive performances and went on to become professional TV actors and actresses and some even got recognition in the films.

Followed a number of serials, good, bad and indifferent, soap operas, situation comedies (called sitcoms in the popular press), detective serials, all telecast at prime time between 8 p.m. and 10 p.m., and most of them sponsored by multinational and Indian companies. DD has a number of failings but most of its critics in the media, some of them ill-disguised PR men and women of some Indian or foreign outfit, ignore its many successes.

Among them are some memorable serials like *Buniyad* (penned again by Manohar Shyam Joshi) *Yeh Jo Hai Zindagi, Ramayan, Mahabharat, The Sword of Tipu Sultan, Chanakya, Kakkaji Kahin* (Joshi again), *Nukkad, Circus, Talash* and other serials by Hrishikesh Mukerjee, Basu Chatterjee's detective serial *Byomkesh Bakshi*, the best detective serial on DD so far, some serials based on literary works like *Rag Darbari* of Phanishwar Nath Renu, and Sharad Chandra Chatterjee's *Charitraheen* (commissioned by DD), and another Bengali novel-based serial *Mujrim Hajir Hai.* Hindi writer Sharad Joshi, alas no more, had a hand in *Yeh Jo Hai Zindagi* and penned an entire serial for the afternoon transmission, *Devi.*

There were some memorable Sunday morning serials until the Sunday morning show lost its prime time status, partly because of DD's attitude. The Hindi feature films on Sundays or later on Saturdays and Sundays have been always popular and so have been the film-based *Chitrahaar* programmes and the similar Sunday morning *Rangoli* presentation. All these film and film-based programmes constitute the most widely followed TV programmes in India. This is true despite the stiff competition which DD faces from several other channels, including its own DD Metro Entertainment channel.

Mention must also be made of the regional programmes in major Indian languages like Tamil, Bengali, Marathi and Gujarati, both film-based and non-film programmes, which have earned DD considerable revenue and the gratitude of the viewers. In fact, some of the serials in these languages have been more popular in the respective areas than the corresponding Hindi serials.

Look at the number of prominent cinema artists and producers or directors who had their first innings on the small DD screen - Raj Babbar, Kulbhushan Kharbanda, Shah Rukh Khan, Meenakshi Seshadri, Sai Paranjpe and a host of others. Shah Rukh Khan acted in DD plays, then in DD commissioned serials like *Fauji* and *Circus* by which time he was noticed by Bollywood. Some writers have stupidly asked why these people left DD at all. They had better ask why some talented colleagues of theirs left their newspapers and joined others in search of fresh and greener pastures. DD has to be given the credit for unearthing such talent.

Credit must also go to DD for some lively social action programmes in the midst of many dull, boring and usually pro-government current affairs programmes. It called for a great measure of latitude, guts and imagination to take DD cameras to a dying Shalini Malhotra in a Delhi hospital where she was admitted after severe burns, a case of alleged dowry death for which her husband and in-laws are standing trial in a court. The matter is *sub-judice* and not much can be said on that account but the DD video is itself part of the evidence.

Only a channel devoted to the people's interest, not merely interested in making money for its shareholders, can think of such a programme. In those days, the DD cameras also went to the homes of Delhi's prostitutes and gave us a peep into their wretched life.

The *Janavani* programme of the eighties often resulted in some senior ministers' discomfiture in front of an invited audience and the TV viewers at large as they failed to come up with satisfactory answers brought up by the audience members. Rajiv Gandhi, who was the Prime Minister then and had not yet succumbed to the temptation of misusing the DD medium for his party and personal ends, had himself asked DD to put out the programmes and some of his ministers who were later sacked owed that fate to their failure on the *Janavani* appearance.

A number of well designed quiz programmes should be mentioned in the category of credits. School and college students and even adults have keenly watched these programmes and a TV personality of Siddhartha Basu's ability grew out of them. His health quiz programmes scaled great heights and showed that DD's competitors had nothing similar and relevant to offer. A TV personality so pleasing and yet so competent at compering is something difficult to find elsewhere. Incidentally the quiz programmes have all been in English and relieve the monotony of Hindi shows one after the other. The children's cartoon serial *Jungle Book* must also be entered in the credit list.

The credit list is quite long but so is the debit list, even longer. The conscious and unconscious attempt to build the personality of the dominant political figure and fostering the personality and family cult, failure to make the newscasts true, factual and fair, apart from the inability to make them lively, putting out of a succession of dull and unentertaining programmes in the name of children's and women's programmes, mercifully relieved by the presence of entertaining serials in the evening or afternoon hours, the bureaucratic and hierarchical approach (a general Indian failing), stifling initiative and creative talent, not being able to tell the minister of I and B and other ministers and the secretary of the ministry where they get off, punishing some subordinates at their instance while not encouraging the talented ones, generally behaving smug and self-satisfied, are among the failures.

One of the professional failings has been not being able to think in the visual idiom. Many of the early programmers, programme officers and producers, came from the older medium of AIR (even now the programme, news editorial and engineering cadres are common to DD and AIR). Those who came over thus brought with them their experience in another mass communication medium like scheduling and production of programmes which was all to the good but many of them could not shed their audio approach.

The sense of economy displayed by the early people must be commended. In Bollywood and in Madras and Hyderabad where Tamil and Telugu films are made, it is customary to take a dozen or two dozen takes of a shot or a scene. 'Cut, retake' is the order of the day. In DD's early days, they would rehearse and rerehearse the entire scene and shoot it in one go to avoid wasting film. This was praiseworthy but the radio habits died hard and the pattern of a presenter introducing a subject, followed by some outside scenes and then a panel discussion was routinely followed. There was no innovativeness and imagination displayed and some of the radio comperes ill fitted the new medium. The producers themselves relied a great deal on words and sound rather than let the camera speak.

The result was that some of the programmes could well have been broadcast by AIR rather than being televised programmes, except that the faces of the participants could be seen. A good programme, like *Jan Hai Jahan Hai* on medical care, is being presented even today almost as a spoken word programme without any visuals at all. You can follow what the eminent specialist is saying with your eyes closed and miss nothing.

With such presentation of programmes the wizards of the Ministry of Finance who control DD's purse strings were not easily inclined to sanction any equipment and expenses on visuals. The news bulletins were the worst sufferers for which the sluggish approach of the editors and their bosses must also be blamed. For lack of competition they were content to present bulletins without any attractive visuals.

The only pictures or films you can see in these bulletins are VVIP-oriented film coverage of seminars, conferences and *goshthis* opened by the worthies mostly in Delhi, or the arrival and departure of foreign dignitaries and the guard of honour given to them in the forecourt of Rashtrapati Bhavan. There would, of course, be foreign visuals often as irrelevant to Indian viewers as the news programmes put out by the foreign satellite channels. Such foreign visuals are easily accessible since the multinational visual agencies are always knocking at DD's doors with their footage.

A serious rail or air accident may take place anywhere in the country but the visuals would appear only on the second or third day after the minister or chief minister has found time to visit the site of the accident and comfort the injured in hospital. All these must find a place in any bulletin but first the accident visuals must be shown. If, however, there is a fire in Delhi DD would go to any a extent to show it and some critics would go into ecstacies over the coverage. Only, they forgot Delhi was not the whole of India and visuals of such happening outside Delhi could be seen two or three days later, if at all.

All this goes to emphasise the need for competition. By making the DD newscasts visual in content, speedy, almost first with the news, fair and truthful by giving all sides and not merely the government's point of view, DD can render the foreign newscasts even less attractive than they already are. By competition, we mean Indian competition not the services of foreign satellite stations or foreign-aided Indian channels. The competition has to be genuine like in the Indian print media, based on Indian soil and Indian in outlook, terrestrial if possible but operating by satellite if necessary.

In both Japan and Canada, there is a peaceful coexistence of a national, public-financed network and a very large number of privately owned and operated stations, all terrestrially based and run. This applies to both radio and TV in these countries. The Japanese and Canadian public have the best of both worlds, in terms of both news and entertainment and public service programmes, like immunization of children, the literacy campaign as on DD, which do not seem to worry the DD competitors at all. The networks in Japan and Canada are not dependent on commercials but because of the competition from privately owned, commercially motivated channels, they come up with excellent programmes and the people have any number of options.

Japan has both the NHK[1], Nippon Hoso Kyokai, or Japan Broadcasting Corporation, with its headquarters in Tokyo, several regional headquarters and over 60 stations of its own, and some 3,000 privately owned and operated TV stations throughout the country. Canada[2] likewise has the Canadian

Broadcasting Commission (later called Corporation), operating both radio and TV services, and hundreds of private stations. Even the British model, much admired by some of our media specialists, provides for a public funded BBC with its elaborate network of TV and radio services in the British isles and the rival Independent Television which has a cluster of private stations. For the BBC's external services there is no domestic rival and it is funded by the British Parliament through the Foreign Office.

Curiously in India, both parliamentarians and the media people, including many culture vultures and busybodies, have never favoured a similar coexistence of a national network and privately owned stations. The Verghese Committee which was appointed by the Janata Government of Morarji Desai in 1977 came up with a report[3] on the autonomy of the two electronic media, on which the 1990 Prasar Bharati Bill and Act[4] of the Janata Dal Government of V.P. Singh was largely based, but it could not visualise such coexistence.

Autonomy yes, but competition no, seems to be the attitude of some of these gentlemen. The Prasar Bharati Act envisages a fully autonomous (of government) corporation to run both AIR and DD and the Act gathers dust in Shastri Bhavan. But it offers no panacea for Indian broadcasting because there would be no competition even if it is finally taken out of the mothballs and implemented, which is hoping against hope.

Even under that Act, TV and radio would still be a monopoly, a kind of oligarchical monopoly of hopefully good men appointed by a committee of wise men in the government.

The advent of satellite TV has not only raised the issue of the primacy of entertainment programmes on TV but also of living with competition. But should this competition be confined to foreign-originating programmes aimed at capturing the Indian audiences and their purchasing power and finally their minds or should there be Indian competition to DD? Japan and Canada have possibly no fears from satellite TV because the audiences there have enough of competing fares from within their countries themselves.

6

What is Satellite TV

The launching of artificial satellites into outer space began in the seventies and now there are around 300 satellites[1] circling the earth. For the ever increasing needs of man the earth has been growing too congested and as technology has advanced the scientists have looked for a safe habitat for basing communication and like facilities to escape overcrowding and pollution and the constant interference in terrestrially-operated facilities. All users of radio and TV and, of course, the engineers who strive manfully in backrooms to make free-of-trouble transmissions possible are aware of the danger of unstable sound and picture signals when they are dependent on earth-bound facilities.

Satellites have come to be used in three main areas: (a) Telecommunications (telephones, telegraphs, fax and so on); (b) meteorology, daily and hourly pictures of the earth (particularly your own region or country), to study cloud formation, wind conditions and so on to be able to tell this evening's, tomorrow's or the next season's weather, and (c) audio and video communication for better and almost foolproof radio transmission and TV pictures.

India has not been lagging behind the world and had launched her first scientific satellite, Aryabhata,[2] in 1975 which still goes round the globe. Aryabhata and the successful implementation of India's space research programme owed much to the vision and drive of Dr. Vikram Sarabhai who pioneered the space development programmes in India the same way as Dr. Homi Bhabha did in nuclear research.

After Aryabhata, India has been successfully launching a series of other satellites, like the remote sensing satellites. What the people know more intimately is the Insat (Indian National Satellite) I and II series of which I-D, 2-A and 2-B are now in orbit and are providing telecom, weather and mass communication facilities on a big scale.

The first Insat satellite, Insat-1A, was sent up into space on April 10, 1982 and within a few months transmission of TV pictures in colour became a reality. What is more, on Independence Day 1982 DD was able to link up all its transmitters in the National Programme, thanks to the satellite. The next satellite in the series, Insat-1B became operational in October 1983 and, thereafter, with some hiccups and moments of anxiety when an operational satellite was about to finish its life-cycle and another was yet to be launched, India has kept her head well above water in the vast lake of satellites looking down on the earth.

Insat-2C is now in the offing. The Indian Space Research Organisation, ISRO in Bangalore, fabricates the satellite which is a highly complicated, scientific endeavour. A Technical Advisory group of the Department of Telecommunications, AIR and DD, and the Department of Meteorology advises the ISRO scientists as users on what they expect the satellite to deliver.

The actual launch is done with the help of the French or Russians, because India is still in the process of developing launching capability and building the elaborate facilities needed for putting a satellite into space costs a great deal of money. In India the entire work from the planning and fabrication of the satellite to its control and operation is done by Indian engineers and scientists in the public sector. The satellite industry around the globe, however, is fast developing into a private industry.

Even the Russians have formed a private company, the Global Information System Inc.,[3] which operates Globostar, an international satellite system. Although there are rich dividends to be had, neither has Indian big business thought of coming forward to put up a satellite nor would Indian public opinion as yet permit such a development.

The Asiasat, through which Star TV invades Indian homes, *courtesy* thousands of cable operators (cable systems as some experts would say), is actually owned by a company called Earthvision. Star TV's Hindi arm, Zee TV comes through to Indian viewers *via* the same satellite of which a single transponder has been leased to Zee.

Some Indian engineers hold the view that Zee or other Indian satellite channels need not look to Hong Kong or Moscow for uplinking their TV signals if only the spare capacity of the Insat satellites is thrown open to these people. But, in that case, the question whether anyone other than AIR and DD can uplink their radio or TV signals from India will have to be settled. Of course, during the controversial Hero Cup one-day cricket matches in November 1993, such (one-time) uplinking facility was allowed to a multinational company, Trans-World International, at the instance of the Cricket Association of Bengal, a part of the BCCI, Board for Control of Cricket in India. In any case, senior scientists are of the view that the Insat satellites have this capacity and valuable revenue is lost by not utilizing it. They, in fact, believe the optimum capacity of these satellites has not been determined.

In terrestrial TV, as is the case with DD's primary channel with which most Indians are familiar, the TV signal comes direct to your TV set from the nearest LPT or HPT transmitter. In satellite TV such signal comes to you with the intermediacy of the satellite. The signal first goes out from the TV transmitter to an earth station, whether in India or in a foreign country, and is bounced back to you set *via* the satellite and then a cable operator's dish antenna to be relayed by his simple cable system to your receiver. Your set has multiple channels so you are able to view not only DD's primary channel (and its Metro channel if you live in Delhi, Bombay, Calcutta, Madras or Lucknow), but also any of DD's satellite channels or Star, Zee, ATN, Asianet or Jain or any on other satellite TV, which your cable operator deems it profitable to bring to you.

Satellites, more particularly transponders which are part of them, are described by engineers as mirrors which reflect and throw back at the denizens of the earth the TV signals beamed to them from an earth station. Or they help to establish telecom connectivity. "A satellite is like sunlight, which you cannot keep out, try what you will," opined a highly placed DD engineer.

Communication technology has advanced by leaps and bounds in the past few years and, while it has posed many a socio-economic and political problem, it has broken national boundaries and made transnational television a reality. What shortwave radio had done in the age gone by, satellite TV has done in a much more effective and satisfying manner because while the shortwave signal is often disturbed by atmospherics and other causes the satellite TV signal is absolutely clear and can be watched hours on end.

There is no other way to describe this phenomenon than calling it an "invasion" across the skies. No wonder several countries like China, Malaysia, Singapore, Vietnam and some Gulf nations like Saudi Arabia have disallowed dish antenna which make the viewing of satellite programmes possible. Whether such bans are effectively implemented there is no reliable means of knowing but it is significant that many countries have felt threatened by the commercial ventures taking advantage of scientific advances and exploiting people's curiosity and hunger for entertainment. Indian Government leaders have said they will not ban the satellite services but the government and DD had to find other ways to counter the competition from abroad as we shall see later.

The technological possibilities are immense[4] and kind of mind boggling. There is what is called DBS, Direct Broadcast Satellites, so that you do not need a very costly dish antenna to receive the TV signals from a foreign station. You can get them straight from the horse's mouth, that is the satellite, through which the signals are flung at you.

There is also what is called the digital[5] compression system which would make the use of several radio and TV channels possible instead of just one at present *via* a transponder.

There are, of course, software or programme implications which the engineers and scientists have not figures out, like whether the foreign station would be always broadcasting programmes in the language you know and whether they would be at all relevant to you. There is also the question whether governments will not be able to find a way to smother the DBS also, if they feel threatened by the foreign invasion.

The satellites are beneficial in yet another way - data transmission - as has been seen in the election results coverage over DD in the past four years. Beginning with the Tamil Nadu assembly elections in January 1989, DD was able to bring to its audiences election results, almost instantly, as in the Lok Sabha poll the same year later, mid-term poll in June 1991 and the major state assembly elections in November 1993. The results came extremely fast and a picture of the emerging trends was afforded to the viewers many hours ahead of the actual declaration of results, sometimes by a day or two. The coverage enhanced manifold the joy of knowing what was going to happen.

All this was made possible by the National Informatics Centre,[6] located in the Lodhi Complex of offices in New Delhi, cooperating with DD and New Delhi TV of Pranoy Roy who did an excellent job of bringing the results and presenting a coherent picture to the viewers. The NIC has offices , some 600 odd, throughout the country, including all district headquarters.

In normal times, these District Informatics Centres feed data of developmental significance like prices, progress of projects, agricultural production and so on. Each of them has a small earth station which beam the information to the satellite Insat-1D which then flashes it back to the headquarters of the NIC in New Delhi.

For the election results, the computers of the NIC and its district centres were wired to flash the results and trends in just *ten seconds* from the time they became available to the district centres from the returning officers under whom the counting centres were functioning. In the DD studios in the Kendra at Delhi, the graphic generation would be done and the results would be telecast on the TV screen, almost as soon as they were announced in places hundreds or thousands of km away. Intelligent (and not so intelligent) analysis or comments by leaders of the affected political parties would then follow.

The NIC was giving the same results to the DD newsroom and to the Press Information Bureau in New Delhi and a new leap was taken in information dissemination. Gone were the old hotlines and the endless calls back and forth to find out the results and crosscheck what was coming through. The NIC network had done a lot of groundwork before the results were declared so that they were ready to transmit the data on six leading candidates listed by them on the basis of their knowledge of the electoral contest, with possible adjustment to include a seventh candidate also. The district officers had prepared themselves to be able to get the results and feed it into their computers without any loss of time.

We have explained this data transmission which according to TV engineers is only a fraction of the video's transmission task, at some length because people have greatly admired the presentation of the election results, without knowing much of the backroom satellite work behind it.

7

Cable TV Appears

By the middle of the seventies, TV had arrived in all the metro cities of India and in other cities and towns too. But DD's programmes were on the air mostly in the evening. After TV had spread to the whole of India, its morning transmission began only in 1987 and the afternoon transmission another two years later.[1] Many people in the urban areas had time and money hanging on their hands. They had been bitten by the home entertainment bug after watching TV but the DD network was not providing them the opiate they were now getting used to, not in sufficient quantity and not at the times they wanted it.

The arrival of the VCR (Video Cassette Recorder) had further whetted the appetite. Brought in at first by urban Indians returning from foreign trips, the VCRs came handy for Sunday or holiday watching of Hindi, Tamil, Telugu, Malayalam or Kannada movies of which cassettes were also available in the market. Soon enterprising dealers sprang up to hire out VCRs for those who did not own one, alone with colour TV sets for customers who owned only a black and white one or none at all, together with cassettes of films, of course. There were all night sessions at which not one but two or three films would be viewed by a group. The activity was not confined to the homes of the wealthy or even the middle classes. Even the humble dwellers of the hutments, *Jhuggi-jhonpri* clusters, in which nearly a quarter of urban Indian humanity now lives, came together to hire VCRs for such nightlong sessions now and again.

From watching films on VCRs at home to community viewing with the help of a cable was only a logical step. That was taken by some dynamic operators in Bombay in 1984. Instead of a home VCR watching, a small group activity, the Cable TV brought you a film or two every day for a monthly payment of around Rs.150 and a one-time payment of Rs.400 or 500, as a security or installation charges.

From Bombay the cable business spread to other parts of India, but only gradually and it took six long years[2] to reach even a major metro like Delhi. The prime cause for its success was the leisure at the disposal of the urban people, the money that they could afford to indulge cable viewing and the absence of any DD programme in the late morning and afternoon hours. When DD finally got round to telecasting programmes in the morning and during the day, they were at first the usual interviews, women's and children's programmes and programmes on cooking which begin to pall after you have seen them once or twice. It was only later that DD realised the need for putting out real entertainment programmes, films or film-based song and dance sequences in the familiar Chitrahaar pattern, by then the cable habit had taken deep roots. In any case the cable audiences also took advantage of DD's entertainment programmes provided the film was not a C grade movie or one that had never been released in the theatres.

After the United States war against Iraq in February 1991, which the CNN, an American outfit, carried in its channel and some five star hotels, catering to American and other foreign guests or affluent Indians on the move, showed the programmes on their closed circuit TV systems, the cable people, now spread out in many small towns and even some rural areas thought of relaying the satellite channels. To the attraction of films was added the temptation of watching foreign TV programmes. DD had always shown some English films and even some serials, like *Lucy,* in its National Programme and other transmissions but there was nothing like a continuous English channel on DD with a succession of foreign serials, nor, indeed, pop music session round the clock, although, again DD had not been lagging behind in showing such musical programmes mostly with Indian performers.

We will see in later chapters how DD has come up with alternatives to meet this challenge, but there is no denying that cable penetration and the relaying of foreign and foreign-supported Indian satellite programmes by the cable operators has been a serious and significant development. That does not mean that the exaggerated accounts in the English print media have to be taken at their face value nor the picture of a cable or satellite TV in every home painted by them has to be accepted as true.

Cable activity in many foreign countries is often a community inspired effort to help the community to view a number of TV programmes which may not be within their technological or financial reach otherwise. In India, however, a cable operator mainly signifies one who brings you the latest along with a lot of old movies, and since the middle of 1991, when the first satellite relay came over Indian TV sets, one of the satellite channels.

In many ways, satellite services and cable operators are in a mutually complementary role, with a "I scratch you back, you scratch mine" relationship. Cable got a big boost in terms of a large increase in its clientele when it brought to the English speaking homes and their young ones, who sway like mad to foreign pop singers' tunes and dances, the programmes of Star TV and the American MTV relayed by it, and later to the others the programmes of Star's Hindi arm and other channels carrying Indian language programmes. The satellite people, of course, rode piggyback on the cable because, even as Star's India representatives, admitted to me when I met them in their Delhi office, 99.9 per cent of their viewers get the Star channels *via* the cable operators.[3] The Star's periodic viewership surveys invariably speak of TV households which "are able to view" its channels. This ability is brought to them by the cable people. Only in a strictly limited way, like some housing complexes in Bombay which are served by a common dish antenna there are a few non-operator cable organisations showing their members satellite and other programmes.

In the cities and even smaller towns and perhaps in the rural areas too, wherever the cable has proliferated, some seven or eight satellite channels (sometimes fewer) are brought to the subscribers by the operators. These may also include a Doordarshan channel and in many cases the popular Metro channel is laid on, despite some problem with the size of the antenna dish. Obviously, many non-Metro viewers who win prizes in the numerous Metro programmes are drawn from these non-Metro cities and towns because they are able to get it through their local cable man. Otherwise they could not be seeing the Metro programmes and winning prizes.

When the cable business got under way the operators had to make an initial investment of around Rs. 5 to 6 lakhs on the dish antenna and other equipment and on hiring a large room from which to operate, according to Mrs. Roop Sharma, President of the Cable Operators. Federation of India (COFI), in Delhi. Mrs. Sharma was among the first four cable operators in Delhi. "We had heard about cable but never seen how it works and did not know much about the business. Some of us went to Bombay and studied the cable operation at first hand and then launched it in Delhi", she told the author.

After the mushroom growth of the cable business, a virtual cottage industry has sprung up from which the local police does not forget to collect its *hafta*,[4] whether it is Delhi or anywhere else in India. The equipment manufacturers working overtime to meet the demand found it economical to sell the equipment at prices much below what the pioneers paid. Now the initial investment has come down to as little as Rs. 2 to 3 lakhs.

Many operators in the intital stages showed copyrighted film without acquiring the rights and there was a kind of chaos for some time. Since the unscrupulous operators showed such films the ones who cared for the rights also had to indulge in these practices. Some even showed the uncensored material (and do so even now) and perhaps totally pornographic films but this could not be a widely prevalent practice because the main clients have been families of TV households and they would not easily countenance resort to it.

Gradually the copyright problem was sorted out by the producers and big companies came up in Bombay which acquired the VCR rights of feature films from the producers and sold them in turn to the distributors in different cities and towns who claim to be the custodians of these rights. The distributors have a whiphand over the small cable operators and extract a high fee from them for the VCR copies they make available for telecast over the cable network. Distribution has apparently become lucrative business for some politicians to dip their hands into it. In Delhi, the son of a top BJP politician is said to be connected with a distributor outfit.

The cable operators are sometimes raided by the local police mainly at the instance of a distributor and this accounts for the propensity of the police to demand *hafta* and the tendency of the cable people to pay it as protection money. The cable business is now well organized, at least in the matter of respect for copyright, and those which are fairly well established would not think of showing any programme which is not cleared in every respect.

Apart from the subscription paid by clients - a good cable operator has an many as five hundred subscribers, but others may have only a couple of hundred or a hundred - the operators make some money over local advertising relevant to the area of city in which they operate or by way of telecast of some local sponsored programmes, like the 1993 electioneering propaganda, as we shall presently see.

But to think of the cable in India as a community service would be making the wish father to the thought. True, some operators in Bombay or Ahmedabad, both cities where cable has made a substantial dent, carried *Dandiya* and *Garba* programmes live but these are only exceptions to the rule that the cable is a passive small time business, a typical cottage industry which now may be employing more than a million people. There has been little effort to put out any programme save the sponsored ones. In any case, *Dandiya* or *Garba* is more for one's active participation and involvement rather than just watching like a TV serial.

It is amazing that until the government brought in a bill to regulate the cable business in August 1993 (yet to become law), nobody thought of putting this vital activity into some kind of regulation. Nowhere else in the world is cable business as free and as unregulated as in this country. A licence is a must and cable operation is a well organized business run by people who have technological and organizational resources at their disposal. The Hutchison Cablevision, the forerunner of the Murdoch-owned Star TV in Hong kong, was a cable company in the British colony. In 1989 it was among a group of television companies and financiers which had submitted to Hong Kong's British rulers proposals for expansion of TV in the island and the adjoining Kowloon mainland (also part of the British colony). At that time, Hutchison Whampoa Limited, the managing member of Hutchison Telecommunication, had claimed that it was investing HK $30 billion in the colony.

In the United States[5], there are sevntyeight cable network services available to the cable systems around the country numbering more than 11,000. The cable industry spend as much as $3.8 billion on programming; by comparison Indian cable operators who should now number 100,000 spend on an average, no more than Rs. 4,000 a month on paying the distributors of film VCRs, about $170 million a year. The amount could be even less as the payment of Rs. 50,000 a year in Delhi by each cable operator to the VCR suppliers may not be true of the whole country. The cable in the United States serves 61.5 per cent of TV households and the subscribers receive as many as 30 channels, as against eight or less on the average, in India, and pay as little as $19.08 (by American standards) for the cable service a month, against Rs.150 a month paid by this Indian counterpart. The payment in India may vary from Rs.100 a month in some towns to Rs.200 in some places, plus a one-time installation or deposit fee of around Rs.400.

That the cable industry in the US must be doing well by itself can also be seen from the figures of their revenue. In 1992 it generated a total revenue of 21.4 billion dollars (approximately Rs. 64,200 crores) made up of $12.4 billion in basic subscriber contributions, $5.1 billions as pay subscriber charges (they insert a coin to watch a programme for a limited duration) and the remainder by other services. The Indian figures could be around Rs.1,000 to 1,200 crores, or $400 million at most from the subscribers alone. These are only estimates as the cable industry has so far been almost entirely unorganized and no figures about its number and their earnings or expenditure are available in an authentic manner. If the regulatory bill becomes law, at least the number would become known.

All this should make it clear to people in India, specially those interested in the development of the electronic media, that cable is a much more organized and well developed service in most countries and a government licence is absolutely essential to the existence of a cable operator or network. Those who made a hullabaloo over the Cable Regulation bill of the Indian government ought to have taken this fact into account. People who enjoy unlimited freedom of the skies all over India are at present answerable to none and a kind of free-for-all prevails of which unscrupulous elements like the *hafta* collectors and the overloads in the VCR distributors business, and, indeed, many operators are able to take full advantage. The cable people, of course, make a decent living and provide an essential service to the viewers. They also find jobs for many young men, at the rate of at least ten persons per operator; upwards of a million people owe regular work to cable.

It was to infuse some orderliness, and, of course, to have a measure of control over their operations, that the I and B ministry introduced on August 3, 1993, in the Rajya Sabha (upper house of the Indian Parliament) the Cable Television Networks (Regulation) Bill, 1993. After some discussion the Bill was referred to the Standing Committee on Communications of both houses of Parliament by the Speaker of the Lok Sabha (lower, popularly elected house), in consultation with the Chairman of the upper house, who also happens to be India's Vice President.

The Committee took evidence, including some from the cable operators who, by now, had organized themselves into representative bodies, like COFI of Roop Sharma. The operators had already met the I and B minister, K.P. Singh Deo, before the bill was introduced in Parliament and were heard by the Standing Committee which, in its modified version, gave some weight to their viewpoint. Unfortunately, the expedition with which the Standing Committee, which presented its report to the presiding officers, on August 23, did not percolate to the two houses which are yet to find time to discuss and pass the main bill. The ministry of I and B has apparently a low priority in the scheme of things of both the government and Parliament, and has not been able to come up with a revised bill either in the remainder of the monsoon session in which the original bill was introduced or the winter session in December 1993, nor in the budget session in 1994.

The text of the bill and the recommendations of the Standing Committee can be seen in the appendices. The bill seeks to regulate the cable industry, make registration of the operators compulsory, a provision which would give the operator an identity and legal status which he would not mind, and make him responsible for the programmes his cable carries to his subscribers, which he is not happy about. It would make it obligatory for each operator to relay one of DD's channels (of his choice) and keep an account of the programmes he relays from the VCRs and from the satellite channels. Typical of any bureaucratically drafted measure, the bill lays down severs penalties and confers powers on the Group One (formerly called Class One) officers to seize the operator's equipment if he is found to violate the provision of the bill relating to relay of communally sensitive programmes.

Among other provisions of the bill may be mentioned those relating to the standardisation of the cable operators equipment to conform to the standard laid down by the Bureau of Indian Standards. This was seen by some political elements as a government device to compel the operators to change over to a larger dish antenna required for relay of DD's satellite channels *via* the Insat satellites. However, the I and B officials, who appeared before the Standing Committee, said the DD channel need not be a satellite one, even a terrestrial channel could be relayed by an operator. In any case, the matter is not one of principle because under subscriber pressure some operators are already showing DD's Metro Channel which is a pure and simple entertainment service.

Political elements and some constitutional pundits thought that the obligation to relay a DD channel could be a cover for the government's intention to use the cable network for its own propaganda. This is a rather narrow view since the entertainment channel which many subscribers would like to see carries hardly any propaganda programmes; it is almost entirely entertainment plus two or three news bulletins. The Standing Committee, which heard all the objections of the cable operators, did not find any force in this plea. It felt that the operators who merrily show foreign channels could surely include one DD national network channel in their offerings.

But the bill still is hanging fire and even in the long budget session of Parliament in February-May 1994 time was not found for consideration and passing of the bill. The operators are not against registration but would like the fees for registration to be uniform. They are against the penal provisions and also plead that they could not be held responsible for the bias, anti-

Indian sentiments or even the communally provocative programmes of any of the satellite channels they may be relaying. The bill would hold them responsible for all relays. They are also against the elaborate procedure of keeping registers of each and every programmes laid on by them, against their equipment being seized for not conforming to standards, and so on.

The COFI led a delegation to the Secretary of the I and B ministry in November 1993 after which the operators felt satisfied that their viewpoint had registered on the official mind. The ministry chose to keep quiet on the meeting but the operators thought they had reached an agreement to protect their interests in the event of the bill becoming law. In particular, they felt that their demand for treating cable as a service, rather than a commercial activity, had been accepted. Indeed, the Standing Committee had reacted favourably to it. They also claimed that their demand, that the satellite channel putting out anti-Indian programmes be warned first by the government and its programmes banned if necessary, was agreed to.

Their impression that the ministry would hold the distributors responsible for any violation of the copyright of the VCR films was not confirmed when I met the Secretary of the Ministry. However, the picture should be clear when the final version of the bill comes before Parliament.

The important point is that the disorganised cable industry is being subjected to a measure of regulation without interfering with its right to relay programmes of its choice, except for one DD channel, out of some eight or less, the cable operators are already relaying. The penal provisions would be softened to the extent possible and the equipment standardised without interfering with cable business and without any economic or other impact on the operators.

The cable people's quarrels with the local film distributors would still persist. Those who talk loftily of the freedom of expression and say the cable is relaying satellite channels which the people want to see are perhaps not aware that the Hindi movies, and the south Indian language movies in the south, are the main attraction of the cable. Within ten days of the release of a film in the theatres, its video version is in the hands of the cable operator and although at least a month should elapse between the release and its cable exhibition the audiences of cable TV are able to see the new releases in a matter of days. Some operators are able to show the films in a couple of days after you could possibly see it in a theatre. Such is the hold of Bollywood and its southern and other counterparts on the Indian audiences that cable operators move heaven and earth to show a new film first and the audiences are keenly looking forward to it.

The distributors who control the home-viewing rights of the VCR films (which is supposed to include the cable rights) are, according to the cable people, the real villain of the piece. They are able to get the police to raid some cable operators' premises and seize the equipment for alleged violation of the copyright. The cable operator loses not only face but also some of his business when this happens, although the law ultimately comes to his rescue if he is not in the wrong. Sometimes, a couple of distributors (in a city like Delhi there are three or four) hold the right or claim to hold it to the same film and a cable man who has bought the VCR from one distributor is held to ransom by the other distributor.

Even the Zee TV fell[6] foul of the cable operators in December 1993 when the exhibition of a film relayed by some operators in the Zee service was claimed by a copyright holder not to have been covered by exhibition rights of the cable operators. The matter seems to have been sorted out pretty soon but not before Zee was threatened with a boycott by the COFI and some individual operators and newspapers came out with reports adverse to Zee TV.

The cable operators have, therefore, been demanding that the onus of ensuring conformity with the programmes and advertising code, to be laid down by the government (in accordance with the bill), must be borne by the originators of the programmes. They seem to look upon themselves as mere purveyors (so much for freedom of expression). They would like the government to tackle the distributors and producers of films on the one hand and the satellite channels on the other for any wrong committed by their respective programmes and leave the cable people alone. How can such total abdication of responsibility by people who claim to perform a great media task and make a living by it be accepted by the government or any other agency?

For the first time in the assembly elections in October-November 1993, television was extensively used in the process of electioneering, not DD but the cable TV. For reasons of the Election Commission's guidelines and its own code of keeping off party propaganda of any kind, DD's news bulletins and other current affairs programmes steered clear of electioneering. DD only put out some inane election broadcasts by all the recognised parties on different days on an equal time basis (a scheme incidentally introduced by the Janata government in 1977-79). So, even the ruling party, the Congress(I) which has DD at its beck and call could not use it for putting out its election appeal.

The times had also changed and mere newspaper publicity, wall writings and public meetings, the mainstay of all election propaganda even now, were not considered enough to impress on the voters that they exercise their franchise in favour of one party. The elections were being held in the four former BJP-ruled states, UP, Madhya Pradesh, Rajasthan and Himachal Pradesh, where the BJP was in power until December 1992 when its governments were dismissed by the Central government after the demolition of the mosque in Ayodhya, and in the capital region of Delhi where the first assembly under a modified scheme of provincial autonomy was to be elected.

The Congress party is stated to have approached seven million voters in UP, Madhya Pradesh and Rajasthan through 1,000 cable operators with 45 minutes of video programmes specially created for an appeal to the voters to choose the party's hand symbol[7]. In fact, a pro-Congress(I) newspaper, *The Times of India*), which carried these figures, forgot to mention that even in Delhi the cable TV was freely used by the ruling party which failed to win Delhi. Hindi film stars of yesteryear, like Sunil Dutt, not to be confused with his son Sunjay Dutt, the current no. one or two among Hindi cinema's leading men, Vyjayantimala and Rajesh Khanna, all ardent party loyalists, compered most of these programmes which also adopted some film and TV names like *Dekh Bhai Dekh*, a big draw on DD's Metro channel.

The BJP was not to be outdone, although it lost UP to the combine of the Samajvadi Party and the Bahujan Samaj Party(BSP), and Madhya Pradesh and Himachal Pradesh to the Congress. It barely managed to retain Rajasthan and, of course, won handsomely in Delhi. It used a number of cable outfits and also had at its disposal the experimental Jain Satellite TV Channel (which had also offered its services to anyone on payment). The Jain TV showed huge BJP crowds listening to the top leaders of the party like L.K.Advani and Atal Behari Vajpayee, and the former's latest *rathyatra*, and their thundering speeches. All of this was of little avail as the party lost in three of the four states which were earlier under its rule.

Whether the TV medium was effective in converting former BJP voters to the Congress(I) or the SP-BSP combine would have to be studied by media researchers to find out the efficacy of such patent propaganda on the TV medium. What should interest us here is that the medium was extensively used and that the cable people were found useful for the purpose. No wonder, a number of politicians are not quite enthusiastic about the cable regulation bill. They would like cable to be "free" so that they could use it again, but tie DD hand and foot through government and parliamentary control.

Except for the payments they have to make to the distributors of VCR films, the cable men have everything free (by way of programmes). That is, they make no payment to any of the satellite channels they are relaying and because of which their business has been thriving. No satellite service has so far thought of levying a fee on the cable people.Their gain is, of course, the audience they command through the cable subscribers and, also thanks to enthusiastic newspaper publicity which brings them substantial advertisement revenue from sponsors and spot buyers.

Only Asianet, the Malayalam channel in Kerala, has tried without much success, to extract some payment from the cable operators for its south Indian films and other film-based and non-film programmes. According to a report in the *Times of India* (December 18,1993)[8], which said Asianet managers were having "troubled slumber", only 28 of some 1,000 operators in the state had joined its franchise scheme of a deposit of Rs. 2 lakhs (about $6,000) and a monthly payment of Rs.180 for relay of its programmes. The Asianet's offer of providing Star and other services was hardly able to attract the operators who knew they could get such services free by just a switch of their dish antenna.

What about the extent of the cable penetration in the whole of India? The COFI president told the author there were as many as 1,500 operators in Delhi (in December 1993) and about a lakh (100,000) in the entire country. An enthusiastic writer has estimated the growth to be as much as 120,000 in 1993. The Star people in India, quoting a survey carried out by an agency commissioned by them, put the figure of TV households, which "can view Star services" at 7.278 million. This survey was done in all Indian cities and towns with a population of 50,000 and more (some 632 of the urban areas) in October 1993. To impress their advertisers, apparently Star commissions an Indian agency, engaged through the Hong Kong-based Frank and Small, to gather data about its penetration.

Considering that Star reaches the TV households only through the cable men, the number of operators could, therefore, be more than a lakh by the end of 1993, allowing for some exaggeration in the Star claims. This caution is necessary because, according to a survey quoted by the *Independent*,[9] a *Times of India* group daily from Bombay, the Star audience in Calcutta was extremely small, hardly six per cent of the TV viewers for all satellite channels in the largest metropolis in India. Interestingly, the survey conducted by MARG, showed that the DD's primary channel (74 per cent) not the Metro (58 per cent), was the most viewed TV service and would remain so for some time to come.

Incidentally, the household viewing of DD Metro alone is claimed to be seven million, about the same number as the households having Star connections, although many TV houses have both connections.

The cable operators first appeared in Bombay in 1984 and it was in Maharashtra and adjoining Gujarat States that they were able to make a significant dent. A survey carried out by MRAS-Burke, quoted by DD's study, "Cable and Satellite Television -- A Status Report" in 1992, shows that Bombay city had as many as 472,000 TV households hooked to cable, out of a total of 1,851,000, or 24.1 per cent in December 1991. For Maharashtra State as a whole the percentage was 15.9, the highest for any state except Gujarat where the cable percentage was as high as 29, with 5.8 lakh sets linked to cable out of a total of 15,38,000 TV households in the state. The Ahmedabad Kendra of DD was not allowed to carry the Delhi LPT channel, except for the National Programmes and Network relays. Some of the Gujarati serials of DD Ahmedabad were extremely popular but other programmes were indifferent so cable would capitalise on the situation.

That study had found the penetration of Gujarat, Maharashtra and parts of Madhya Pradesh quite high but surprisingly the cable had made only marginal impact in the other Hindi speaking states and in states like Tamil Nadu, Karnataka and Orissa it was moderate.

It is the advent of the satellite channels, since the middle of 1991 and more impressively since the later part of 1992, that the cable network has expanded to meet viewer demand for satellite services. The DD's Metro Entertainment channel from April 1993 created a strong counterpoint about which we will speak at length later. Suffice it to say that the cable became a real factor in Indian TV scene in 1991 and 1992. We have already seen the latest picture of the CTV and Star effect and found that while it is considerable in some states it is only a small portion of the total Indian audience.

The enforcement of law is lax in most parts of India and, by and large, cable operators have got away by spreading their cable lines at random. The connivance of the police and the governmental agencies, combined with the general apathy of the people and the enthusiasm of some cable viewers, has helped them to lay their cables over large parts of urban India.

What the cable people do is rewire your set so that you get a number of satellite services which would most probably include DD Metro but certainly not DD-1 and, of course, the film-showing local cable outfit. If you wish to watch DD-1 on your set, you have to take the trouble of disconnecting the heavy cable fixed to the set by the Cable operator's mechanic and plug in your old antenna wire. Not everyone would take this trouble and watching the films and all that day after day you may also become an opium addict yourself. DD-1 is thus sought to be obliterated from your reach.

8

Satellite Invasion Begins

The cable framework, or network if you prefer, was already in existence in many parts of the country by 1990-91 for the satellite services to enter millions of Indian homes. As has happened often in India's long and chequered history, the invaders from outside had friends and collaborators within, a kind of "Fifth Column," to help them spread their tentacles[1].

The cable industry's curiosity in satellite business, had been aroused by the Gulf War coverage in February 1991 by the American outfit, CNN, which was relayed by some of the five star hotels in Bombay and Delhi. They did it for the benefit of their affluent foreign and Indian guests on the closed circuit TV system. Those who know little or nothing of news, and some who should know better fell for the propaganda gimmick of the foreign media that news was being brought to the audience as it was happening. If the assertion is true, CNN ought to have shown its viewers in January 1994 the earthquake in southern California - declared a disaster by the US President - live. Not merely the damage, the wounded in hospitals and the relief measures but the earthquake as it occurred, with the highways cracking up, houses crumbling and people dying.

Unfortunately for these media innocents, earthquakes do not serve notice of their advent on TV networks. It was easy for the United States expeditionary forces in the desert, marching out against a small and comparatively insignificant enemy, in the company of "allies", including several Muslim nations like Pakistan among the group, ready to do the bidding of the American general, to invite the CNN cameras to march along. In 1971, when the Indian army's might was ranged against Pakistan in the Bangladesh liberation war, I was the second-in-command in the Press Information Bureau in Delhi. I remember we used to send any *bona fide* Indian or foreign journalist who wished to cover the war in the eastern or western sector on his way within hours of his application. India knew that victory was hers. Thanks to elightened political leadership and highly competent military top brass an open media policy was followed. The publicity war was won even while the Indian armed forces were marching into Dhaka (then still called Dacca) to accept the surrender of more than 90,000 Pakistani soldiers and their commanders.

But in the difficult war, forced on India by Pakistan's in filtration into Kashmir in 1965, this media policy could not have been followed for a variety of reasons. For that matter did the United States take the large American media corps, gathered in strength in Saigon during its disastrous war against the Vietnamese fighting for their freedom in the sixties and early seventies, into the many battles it fought and lost and it its B-52 bomber planes which laid the Vietnamese countryside waste. Many of the mediamen would be seen in the girlie bars of Saigon every evening those days. (I was in Vietnam in 1969 as AIR's South East Asia Correspondent). Were the US media present at the My Lai massacre and other atrocities committed by a nation which now considers itself the custodian of human rights everywhere in the world. Incidentally, the BBC which prides itself on its fair coverage called the Vietnamese fighting the US by the abusive and derisive term "Vieteong".

Going back two decades or more, would the United States have taken its media corps into confidence before it unleashed the atom bomb on the sleeping Japanese city of Hiroshima and later Nagasaki, the only instance of a nuclear weapon being used by any nation? If news, as it happens, can be televised or even filmed for a later telecast, here was an unparalleled occurrence which deserved that treatment. But could any forerunner of CNN have been in Hiroshima or later in Nagasaki, to tell humanity in sound broadcasting what the innocent citizens of Japan were being subjected to?

The Western media have just to coin a phrase for their admirers in the third world to swallow it, hook line and sinker, and repeat parrotlike what the former have said while pretending to be learned in the process.

In July 1993, the P. V. Narashima Rao government in India faced the most potent threat to its existence in Parliament as the entire opposition was ranged against his minority regime over a non-confidence motion. The large media corps in Delhi, and many from outside, were in force in the press gallery of the Lok Sabha, Lower house of Parliament, to record the historic event. So many were there that it looked as though the strong sixty-year-old structure would come down. But even if TV cameras were permitted to go inside the house(they were not), the real news was taking place somewhere else in semi-darkness behind closed doors in the houses of MPs whose loyalty to their party was being subverted to buy their support for the Rao government. They voted for the government and the motion was defeated. Only the formality of the favourable vote could have been televised, which was not the real news.

But CNN cannot be denied the credit for the instant coverage of the United States forces action against Iraq and some resistance by that country which had queered its own pitch by its attack on the much smaller Kuwait. (CNN, Cable

News Network is owned by Turner Broadcasting Systems of the US). In any case, the satellite relay excited the curiosity of many cable people in Bombay and Delhi and later elsewhere in the country, and the next step was relay of the programmes; first the BBC World Television Service began to be relayed in May 1991. The British organisation had (and still has) an arrangement with Star for relay of its 24-hour service and if the BBC could ride into India in its backseat why could not the front seat riders not be seen by Indian audiences. From September 1991 Star's other services then began to be seen, although the Hong Kong-based network opened its Indian office in Delhi only in October 1992.

Satellite Television Asian Region, STAR for short, has five arrows to its bow, Star Plus, a channel of serials and other English entertainment programmes, Prime Sports, supposed to be a continues sports channel, which carries for long hours golf and baseball sports events, which are not the most popular in India, the American Music TV MTV channel for the young lovers of pop, a Chinese language channel, which has few takers in India, and, of course, the BBC.

The Hindi arm of Star, Zee TV, became operational in October 1992, using a leased transponder of Star's Asiasat satellite.

Who is behind Star? According to its own publicity handout bearing the same title, "Who's Behind Star TV", the Hong Kong-based Hutchvision group operated the Star TV service. That was before Rupert Murdoch bought controlling interest in Star in July 1993[2]. Until then, it was a joint venture between Hutchison Whampoa Limited and a company controlled by Li Ka-shing and his family. These two parties provided the equity to finance Star.

Hutchison Whampoa is a Hong Kong-based multinational, mainly local Chinese and British corporation, which had a variety of businesses besides telecommunications, like property, retail trade, container terminals and energy. Its interest was thus clearly to make money for its promoters, which is a perfectly legitimate object, rather than mere professional broadcasting. In 1990, the corporation had an annual profit, after paying tax (much smaller in this kind of tax haven) of American $1.5 billion. Li was also the chairman of Hutchison Whampoa besides being deputy chairman of the colony's powerful British financial institution, the Hong Kong and Shanghai Banking Corporation.

For those in the Indian media who jeer at the fairly innocuous Cable Regulation Bill, we should say that Star began to operate only after Li's company received a licence from the British government in Hong Kong to start its satellite multichannel service beaming its programmes to some 38 or more countries.

The arrival of Rupert Murdoch made a big difference to Star which soon lost its boss. Its Chief Executive Jim Griffiths was sacked to be replaced by a Murdoch man, Gary Davey in December 1993.

There are several dimensions to Murdoch's acquisition of Star which spells a great danger to the Indian media, although many English newspapers in this country are still uncritical admirers of Star's different channels. Murdoch paid US $525 million to Li Ka-shing for taking over 63.6 per cent of the stake in Hutchvision, while Li and his family retained the balance 36.4 per cent minority interest. Li made a big profit of 400 to 500 per cent in selling Star to the media Moghul who already owns Hong Kong's leading English daily, the highly valued and successful *South China Morning Post*. (At one time, Murdoch also owned the Weekly *Far Eastern Economic Review*, which is now owned by the *Wall Street Journal* of the United States. Such is the international link-up today as Indian newspapers are themselves threatened by many of the American and British Giants).

Murdoch also gave the Li family a 2.7 per cent interest in his flagship broadcasting company, News Corporation, which owns the satellite Sky Broadcasting operating in Europe. Murdoch owns a majority of Australian newspapers and has in addition a TV station in each Australian state. He acquired

American citizenship some years ago to facilitate his acquisition of American TV stations (Those in India who see nothing wrong in foreigners coming in to own newspapers and TV in this country have something to think about here). Murdoch owns the prestigious *Times* of London besides tabloids like the *Sun* and *Star* (one *Star* attracts another!). For all his American connections, the Australian establishment would like to look upon Murdoch as one of their own.

Murdoch has worldwide media interests which makes many in India see in Star the thin end of the wedge as Star services extend their tentacles in this country. One of the first thing Murdoch did after his Star takeover was to acquire a 49.9 per cent interest in Zee and in achieving that objective, he quite possibly twisted Zee's arm[3]. A vacant transponder of Asiasat, leased by Star, had been sub-leased to Zee by Hutchvision and this gave Murdoch a big handle to beat down the Hindi service which went on the air in October 1992. It has done quite well in the first year, during only the latter half of which DD's Metro channel had been coming up.

Why should Murdoch take any financial or other interest in ZEE? But then he would not be Murdoch. He owns scores of TV stations and newspapers round the globe, except Africa and Latin America. A person who has so much at his command is now arriving in India in a big way, so much so that his physical arrival to meet top politicians and media people in February 1994 was the subject of a front page write up in the *The Times of India* on January 20. Murdoch owns a Chinese language newspaper in Hong Kong and is on record as saying Asia offers a big market. India has already opened its doors to multinationals of every kind and Murdoch could now stage a right royal entry into this country unless the Indian media world take notice of the danger he poses to us.

In the country of his adoption he owns the Fox Broadcasting Corporation, which is trying to rival the three established American networks, CBS, NBC and ABC besides the Hollywood company, Twentieth Century Fox (will it be renamed Twenty first Century ?).

In any case, he has more than a foothold in India, first through Star, which has a potential audience of six to seven million TV households, through the cable connection, and his financial interest in Zee which he could possibly convert into a controlling interest by making the owners of Zee in India an irrestible offer. Zee claims to have made Rs. 24 crores in the first year of its existence (from October 1992 to September 1993) when it was on the air 12 hours a day, with 18 hours of programmes on Sundays. It had plans to be a round-the-clock service in the second year of its operation and although the Metro channel of DD now offers stiff competition to it and most of the established film and TV producers, like B R Chopra, Ramesh Sippy, *Hindustan Times* TV and other have come on the Metro channel, Zee could still be making considerable money. Murdoch thus could not be uninterested in Zee's operation, besides the Indian connection it would give him.

Not many people know that yet another satellite service, ATN or Asia Television Network, based in Bombay, has entered into an arrangement to carry Thames TV International's programmes. Thames is owned by Murdoch. So the footfold is widening.

Zee is owned by Zee Telefilms Limited[4], of which Subhash Chandra Goel in Bombay is Chairman. A transponder of Star was taken on lease by a group in Hong Kong, said to consist of some Indian NRIs (non-resident Indians), Ranjan Issac, Mohan Tolani and J D R Malhotra among them, who formed a company called Asia Today Limited (ATL). The year 1994 is only the second of the five years for which Star transponder is leased to ATL and Murdoch has plenty of time in which to twist Zee's arm a little further. But he will have first to make peace with the Chinese government which has banned[5] his Star TV's Chinese channel and which is going to take over complete territorial and other control over Hong Kong from the British in another three years, in 1997. Already Star is trying hard to persuade Beijing to let its channel be viewed in the mainland. Recently, China is said to have entered into an arrangement with the Australian Broadcasting Commission's ABC Television, under which the latter's programmes are to be relayed by local Chinese Channels. Murdoch may find Beijing a harder nut to crack than the regime in Delhi, although both are sold on liberalisation at present, for the simple reason that there is more softness in the Indian state.

On October 16, 1993, China's Vice Minister of Radio, Television and Films, Wang Feng said in Beijing that uncensored foreign TV signals raining down on the Chinese people was an issue of national sovereignty. A *Reuters* report carried by Indian newspapers the next day said, "Foreign television broadcasts which include media tycoon Rupert Murdoch's Star TV programmes will be virtually blacked out in China under new control on satellite antenna"[6]. According to Wang, rules issued on October 8, forbid individuals, residents and work units to receive foreign satellite broadcasts.

China, however, exempted residences, hotels and workplaces for foreigners from this ban. In other words, the vast number of TV viewers in China have been barred from watching foreign channels, including Star next door in Hong Kong.

Not many other countries affected by the Star, BBC or CNN invasion look favourably upon their broadcasts. Malaysia and Singapore, otherwise considered as good countries by the western world and their media, have taken steps to keep foreign satellite broadcasts out. Along with Vietnam, these countries "are seeking to hold foreign broadcasters at bay by continuing to ban private ownership of satellite dishes (or dish antennae)", said a report in the *International Herald Tribune,* reproduced by the *Observer* of Delhi[7]. (Saudi Arabia is the latest to impose a ban).

Malaysia and Vietnam followed Singapore's example and introduced a subscription service of pay TV, with participation by state agencies so that there would be effective check on the kind of foreign programmes the viewers would be able to receive. The Malaysian Prime Minister, Dr. Mahathir Mohammed, one of the senior statesmen in South East Asia, has openly accused western broadcast organisations of "undermining progress in Asia".

Why should such economically progressive nations consider themselves threatened by the satellite invasion? Dr. Mahathir was not speaking in a Kampong (village) in his country but addressing the United Nations General Assembly. The harm the hourly dissemination of western permissive culture can do to Asian minds is thus viewed seriously by major nations like China, Malaysia, Singapore and Vietnam, and has prompted them to seal off the broadcasts from the satellite channels run by people who could not care less about the fate of the Asian people in the pursuit of their mercenary goals and the other goals of Murdoch. He openly says that he would keep control of his News Corporation, the holding media company, in his family so that he could run the over one hundred media companies as deemed best by him, that is in his own interest.

The 62-year old media baron lost no time in buying Zee TV's shares after he bought Star. The Asia Today Company, owners of Zee's hardware, which has leased Star's unused transponder sold nearly half the shares of Hindi channel which was even earlier identified with Star as its Hindi wing. Zee TV's Subhash Goel was hard put to explain why at all Murdoch should have been given as much as 49.9 per cent of the holdings. Goel denied there was any arm twisting but other key people quoted in the Indian media said there was an attempt by Amitabh Bachchan's Asia TV, which operates mainly in London, and the *Times of India* group to take over Zee TV in a subordinate relationship with Murdoch. This was averted but Zee's attempts to put a brave face on the deal and its apologetic explanations that Murdoch did not take over control of the company was itself evidence that things were not going well and the Murdoch danger could surface again. Incidentally the *Times of India* newspaper has continued to show a soft corner for Murdoch.

Perhaps its owners, Bennet Coleman & Co. would make another try at Zee *via* Murdoch or be linked with his proposed Hindi channel.

For the present Zee has been allowed by Murdoch to run its affairs under the present team. Zee came to the media scene in India at a time when DD was in a kind of dazed condition, almost in doldrums, not knowing what it should do to face the growing cable and foreign satellite challenges. This will be examined in detail in later chapters but suffice it to say that there was a growing vacuum in entertainment and while the film-fare dished out (on the dish antenna) by the cable outfits was playing its role there was an urgent need felt by the audiences for attractive serials and other TV programmes. These Zee offered and their efforts were amply rewarded in terms of advertising, making its very first year a memorable and money-spinning one for its organisers.

The phenomenon of print media branching out into TV is not something typically Indian but what is peculiar to India is the big stick which the same newspapers having a TV axe to grind wield while pursing their TV interests or seeking to build a TV business. In the campaign the major English newspapers have conducted against DD in courts and outside they have used their news columns to butress their interests while pretending all the while as though they were doing that in the public interest.

Significance attaches to the fact that of the five litigants in the case of time slot allotment by DD for its satellite channels four were leading newspapers - *The Times of India, Hindustan Times,* both of which have considerable TV interests, and *Hindu* and *Indian Express* which obviously are angling to enter TV business. Nothing wrong again, but the public and the media watchers ought to know what is what.

Star must be given credit for pursuing its Indian interests in a systematic manner, apart from making it crystal clear that its service is aimed at India, among other countries, by showing

Indian Standard Time in all its programme captions. Through a Hong Kong Firm, Frank Small, Star has been conducting a series of surveys among Indian audiences to find out the extent of its penetration. The first known viewership survey was conducted in 1991-92 by MRAS-Burke after Star obviously gathered through its sources and the gushing reports in the English media in this country that it was having a sizable audience among Indian TV watchers. As we have seen, viewing of Star's channels-Star Plus, Prime Sports, MTV and the BBC service - began in the middle of 1991 and regularly by September in that year. The Chinese channel, the fifth string to the Star bow, is of little interest to Indian viewers and Zee, which went on the air in October 1992, has always been known as Star's Hindi arm even before the formal tying of the knot with Murdoch in December 1993.

According to the first survey, the Star service was received regularly by September 1991 in the four Metro cities of India and in Bangalore the fifth largest city, where the survey was carried out. It was, of course, through the instrumentality of the cable operators that the viewing had been made possible in the English speaking homes. The standard formula, "households able to receive Star", was forged in the very first instance. The number was 1,282,000 TV homes, and the survey spoke of a total of 22,419,000 million urban TV households. So, the viewership was just above 5 per cent at a time when the English dailies published reports as though Star had captured the Indian audience and DD had gone completely under. Actually, the total number of rural as well as urban, sets, quoted by Doordarshan on the basis of an advertising agency estimate, was 34,858,000 million at the end of 1992. So, the Star viewership was only between three and four per cent of the aggregate Indian audience.

But there was still a significant number of viewers, mostly drawn from the more vocal English speaking class, and the print media which catered to them began writing of Star as though it had replaced DD in India. The MTV channel carrying pop round the clock, somewhat adjusted by Star to suit what it considered was the taste of the Asian viewers was watched, according to the survey, by 37 per cent of the Star audience. The figure appeared to be plausible because only the young would like to sing and dance to its tunes while the elders would prefer the English serials or some sports coverage on Star Plus and Prime Sports.

Star has had several more surveys done, the latest of which was the one carried out in October 1993 in 636 cities and towns of India with a population of 50,000 or more. The number of possible Star viewers, *courtesy* cable,[8] was estimated by this survey at 7,278,000, a sharp increase in just two years over the modest 1.28 million viewers uncovered by the first survey referred to above.

Cable again remained the only channel for the Star audience but by the end of 1993 the total number of sets in India had gone up to 40.3 million. It must be clarified that television receiver licenses were abolished by the government in 1984 (in developed Britain they are still in force) and thereafter reliable estimates by major advertising agencies and survey outfits including the Audience Research Wing of DD or by other professional organisations, are the main source of this information. These estimates[9] put the total viewership in India in 1993 at 40,333,000, TV homes with 12 million sets in the rural areas.

DD put the Star audience at 6.2 million in August 1993, again based on ad agencies or other estimates of households, "able to receive" the Star survice. With the growth of the cable industry in the country the Star audience has risen. Its audience has grown from just 0.41 million in January 1992 to 6.2 million in August 1993, according to DD, and 7.278 million in October 1993, according to Star.

The DD audience has also grown and, it should be noted, many Star or cable households switch on the DD primary or Metro channel on Sundays and Saturdays, a fact which Star's own surveys have revealed. Now that Metro is on the air for hours with attractive programmes even on the other days of the week the same viewers could be hooked to DD Metro. There are some 34 million homes with TV sets but without any cable or Star connection, only DD for them. Now the Metro's appeal is grudgingly recognised by even those who were earlier, out of their ignorance, running down DD and writing it off. But those who knew what was what in the TV world did not mind laying their ad money on the primary channel and when the Metro came they turned to it also in a big way.

An advertising agency man, R. S. Naman of Chaitra Leo Burnett of Bombay, told the *Week* magazine in September 1993 that "the depth of Doordarshan is unimaginable. Star TV and other satellite channels cannot match DD's reach."

At the same time, it must be recognised that in many English speaking homes the Star channels are keenly followed. By English speaking homes we mean families which speak only or mainly English or those where both parents know and mainly use English and the children are in English medium schools and colleges. Star Plus is viewed by most members of such families while the young swing to MTV. Prime Sports is viewed only when there is live coverage of sports and games popular in India, like cricket, football, tennis and hockey (one can seldom see hockey on Star). Its substantial showing of golf, baseball and basket ball, all in far-off lands, is hardly designed to make Prime Sports popular among Indians.

The BBC of course, was known to Indian audiences, or a section of them, through its radio service. What one sees on the Star is the BBC World Service Television (WST) which is a subsidiary of the BBC. It was set up in March 1991. According to the BBC's WST's Asia boss[10], "whereas the BBC's domestic services are funded by a universal licence fee in the United Kingdom and the international radio service are funded by British government grant-in-aid, BBC World Service Television Ltd. has no recource to such funds. It is a commercial broadcasting venture."

So the BBC, fancied by some people, comes to you by courtesy of John Major (or whoever heads the government in Whitehall in London) but some advertiser has to pay for the BBC Television show, unless Murdoch succeeds in his efforts to introduce pay TV which would force all fans of Star and the BBC to pay for the pleasure of watching them. We will see later how the BBC and Murdoch are already at loggerheads on some other issue.

The BBC claimed in 1992,[11] according to an in-house audience research survey in 38,000 households in 24 Indian cities with a million-plus population, that it had more than 11 per cent "penetration" (the word used by the BBC) of TV households. BBC also claimed that this was more than twice that of the American CNN, which it considers a rival. As for cable penetration, the BBC survey said 86 per cent of the networks (read operators) received the BBC while only 5 per cent brought CNN to you.

The BBC Television service's impact on Indian viewers is even more exaggerated than either the Star's or the BBC's radio bulletins. The BBC radio service has, no doubt, built up over the years a steady and significant following which has gone up at times of stress for India like the Emergency rule of Mrs. Gandhi when AIR (there was little of DD then) looked a little more credible than the newspapers which had meekly accepted the official censor as their friend, philosopher and guide. The BBC TV news is, however, largely irrelevant to viewers as the news items are of little or no consequence to the viewers, except media professionals. The relevant ones are mostly against India.

Despite all the constraints of political and bureaucratic domination and interference, the professional inadequacies of the media bosses and lack of requisite resources for visual coverage of home events, DD's newscasts bring you every evening the happenings in Parliament (when it is in session), reports of gas prices (or other prices) going up, of who is dead and who is appointed or dis-appointed (or sacked), of elections and their results and so on.

The Indian Institute of Mass Communication,[12] IIMC, conducted a survey in September-October 1992 of TV viewing and found that as many as 26.2 per cent of the respondents were of the view that the BBC's bulletins were "mostly irrelevant" to Indian viewers. Some 32.8 per cent could not give any opinion (and must be written down as TV watchers who do not understand much of news) while only 41 per cent thought that the BBC newscasts were not irrelevant. As against 25.6 per cent who thought the BBC was biased and lacked objectivity in covering issues pertaining to India, only 34 per cent did not agree.

So, apart from bias which is a major issue (the BBC generally calls All India Radio New Delhi Radio), there is the issue of the relevance of the news. The so-called international news is so often news of Britain and its leaders that one can draw John Major with one's eyes closed. Of course, the BBC is a status symbol with some Indians and you could meet people who would say they watched the BBC news that morning or evening, without being able to recollect a single news item or its visuals. The British TV news agency, Visnews, plays a supportive role by rushing to the BBC visuals of British significance and flash them to DD also as a subscriber. So you would find in a coverage of an international conference the British representative prominently focused and the poor Indian Minister not shown at all or shown *en passe*.

Both the BBC's radio service and TV newscasts have been known to lean towards Pakistan in matters on which the two nations are at cross purposes, which is quite often. Even when the Kashmir militants were holed up in the Hazratbal mosque in Srinagar the BBC found excuses to blame India in a show of evenhandedness. A reader complained to the *Indian Express*, Delhi, on October 27, 1993:[13] "While listening to the BBC's 'Newshour' programme at 1300 hours on October 10, I was surprised to hear that the programme presenter called up Shaharyar Khan in the Pakistani Foreign Office to know the Pakistan government's view on the action being taken by the Indian authorities at Hazratbal in Srinagar. Then the suggestion that followed by the presenter was absolutely shocking that the

Indian authorities had taken this action at this juncture because the political situation in Pakistan was fluid. It seemed that the presenter was acting like a mouthpiece of (the) Pakistan government instead of acting in an unbiased independent manner."

Hazratbal is a holy shrine on the outskirts of Srinagar, summer capital of India's Kashmir state, where the Muslims believe a sacred hair of Prophet Mohammad is preserved. A number of Kashmiri secessionists had been trapped in the shrine by the Indian security forces after they were found to be repeatedly sheltering inside the holy place. After a 32-day siege and extremely patient vigilance and without a shot being fired, the Indian forces compelled the militants to surrender. This was, if anything, an internal matter of India and which deserved to be lauded by any dispassionate observer inasmuch as the misuse of a shrine was prevented and not a single life was lost. Religious places are meant to be frequented for worship, not for the shelter of armed terrorists.

If, for example, some IRA (Irish Republican Army) gunmen had captured the Westminster Abbey in London and had been operating from inside that holy place, would the British government wait for 32 days for them to come out, would the BBC call up the Irish Foreign Office in Dublin and invite it to offer comments and would it accuse its own master of a diabolical move in taking on the terrorists?

It is one thing to report in a fair and balanced manner the views of the Pakistan government or its Foreign Secretary if a statement on the Hazratbal incident were to be made by Islamabad although strictly speaking this was a purely Indian affair. But to go out of the way and goad Saharyar Khan to make an anti-Indian statement amounted to patent bias and a desire to be overly friendly to Pakistan. Of course, the *Indian Express* reader wrongly attributed the bias to the poor news presenter, not knowing that he had merely to do what was laid down by the news editor and other backroom bosses at Broadcasting House in London. Incidentally this letter in the paper was followed by another a few days later in which the BBC was called the British Brainwashing Corporation.

This is only one example of what goes on at the BBC day in and day out. If Pakistani Prime Minister Mohtarma Benazir Bhutto (actually Mrs. Benazir Zardari) is interviewed by the British organisation she is generally not asked to comment on the Indian charge that her government is aiding and funding the Kashmir terrorists in India, a charge which the United States and even Britain accept, although President Clinton snipes at India from time to time on Punjab and Kashmir. The western world, whether it is the President of the United States or the holy cow of the BBC remember that India needled them enough in the past to deserve to be at the receiving end now. The Indian government and people fighting insurgents at home can hardly find the time to speak of the problems of the world and so the west can fashion it as it wishes. So they figure.

Of course, the western world is far from united, specially where the self-interest of one section is in conflict with the entrenched interests of another. So, the BBC found itself at loggerheads with Rupert Murdoch over its plans to launch an all-day Arabic news service. A London *Financial Times* report,[14] reproduced by the *Times of India*, Delhi, referred to an increasingly bitter row between the BBC and the News Corporation of Murdoch over the expansion plans of both to grab a share of the global news market. Murdoch's lawyers threatened the BBC with cancellation of its ten years (from 1991) contract with Star to carry its World Service Television over its network. The BBC would obviously like to exploit its old contracts in West Asia (called the Middle East by the Americans and British) but that would reduce the chances of the people there watching the Star and other Murdoch services. Those who know the ways of the media world were not surprised that the strange bed-fellows found each other at opposite ends of a court dispute.

In the fast moving media scene, the BBC-Star war resulted in March 1994 in the London-based British World Service Television being thrown out of the Star network by Murdoch.

Not entirely, because its coverage of India, Bangladesh and Pakistan would still continue to be *via* Star but it was out of China, Hong Kong, Korea, Taiwan and Mongolia. The British channel then began looking for an alternative satellite by which it could reach these countries. China is out of bounds even to Star, but perhaps it has worked out an arrangement for giving a package to Beijing of its Chinese programmes, which would still not be available to the people of China through the dish antennae. Only in India, everything seems to be freely available, *courtesy* the cable.

What about CNN(Cable News Network), whom BBC considers its arch rival in the Indian region, regarded by both as their preserve? There is little doubt that CNN made many in this country aware of and interested in satellite TV and it is only because of CNN's Gulf war coverage that the Indian cable industry woke up to their immense potential for entertainment and for them to make more money. But now CNN has been left way behind by Star and the BBC in the race for a big slice of the Indian cake. First Star came in in a big way in 1991 itself, the year the United States fought its Gulf war and the BBC rode in on the Star bandwagon while CNN was still making plans to cash in on its reputation. BBC being already known (for good or bad) in this part of the world, CNN remained somewhat of a phenomenon to be admired from a distance.

But CNN has not given up trying. It almost struck a deal with DD in 1993 before the realization of the implications of an American organisation entering India dawned on the political leaders and the enthusiastic bureaucrats rushing to reach an agreement with CNN were restrained. Cooperation, like giving Star a feed of the Republic Day marchpast and cultural pageant in January 1994, is a good thing and there could be more of such give and take in future. But to permit any foreign organisation to acquire permanent foothold in India, and that too with the active participation of DD would amount to a surrender of Indian rights. If DD were to do such a thing, like entering into collaboration with CNN, how could the private parties wishing to effect similar or closer arrangements be blamed at all?

The number of Indian entrepreneurs in the TV medium is sizable, almost always with some NRI (controlling) participation and this could grow, what with the cable not at all regulated and anyone being able to beam TV programmes without as much as a licence. Of course, the financial problems like those faced by Asianet in Kerala where the cable people shrank from shelling out money for getting services they could get free would almost certainly have to be faced by them.

ATN, Asia Television Network, mainly a Hindi feature film channel operating from Bombay, introduced in 1993 ATN-One, an English service with the collaboration of the American ABC, the British *Reuters* news agency's television service and the Thames Television of Rupert Murdoch. It has an NRI god-father, AUN, Asian United Media Ltd., in London. It uses the Russian STATSIONAR (ST-21) satellite at 103 East, said to be reaching 84 countries around the globe.

All the Indian satellite services, whether Zee, ATN, Asianet, or the Jain satellite TV based in Bombay, Delhi or Trivandrum (Kerala), use foreign satellites and have to fly out tapes everyday to Hong Kong, Moscow or London. No uplinking is allowed from India except to those who have taken out a licence under the Indian Telegraph Act, 1885. Many call this an archaic law but there are several laws of the old days still in force and thanks only to this archaic law the cable chaos has not filtered down to satellite TV. The DD monopoly must be broken, but not by foreign media or some Indian agencies acting in close collaboration with foreigners. Even now the viewer does not know that his favourtite programme over Zee comes across from Hong Kong, not from Bombay.

Jain TV, owned by Dr. J.K. Jain, a BJP Member of Parliament, operated on an experimental basis in 1993 and became a regular service from the beginning of 1994. During the election campaign for the state assemblies on October-November 1993 this channel played a significant role in putting across the party's message to the electorate, *via*, of course, the cable. Jain offered his services, on payment, to all parties but the BJP's flags could be seen in plenty along with the massive rallies it organized in Madhya Pradesh, Uttar Pradesh and elsewhere. Only the voters in both UP and MP were not convinced. Jain now offers his channels to all religions and parties but has to fly out his cassettes everyday to Moscow to uplink his programmes from the same Russian satellite which also serves ATN, Statsionar (ST-21), from where the signals are picked up by the the cable in India.

A sympathetic newspaper, quoted Jain on January 6, 1994, "The problem can be solved if I am allowed access to uplink facilities from India itself." This was in the context of his difficulties referred to by the paper in the previous paragraphs: "I am a partisan political activist but here's an RSS man with the first TV channel to propagate Islam through television for the first time in India." However, the articulate and ambitious mediaman (note, not medical man, which the good doctor is) was highly critical of the government policy on direct broadcast service - including satellite television - for not making the relevant amendments in the Act (of 1885), forcing him to fly a trusted executive daily with "video cassettes of the next day's programmes to Moscow and then travel another 300 miles to beam them."

There is a genuine problem here. But would such channels agree to some kind of state or parliamentary control? For any lapse on the part of the DD, there can be an uproar in Parliament or the print media, marches can be organised to Mandi House or Akashvani Bhavan, the respective headquarters of DD and its Delhi centre, and some poor programme officer or producer made to bite the dust. Did Jain TV encounter any such problems in its coverage of the BJP in the run-up to the assembly poll during which the most serious charges against Prime Minister P.V.Narasimha Rao were made by the BJP leaders (which many in India may consider to be true) without any reply or refutation. At this rate, another satellite channel could be identified with another political party and the Congress(I) with the tremendous money power could buy up more than one. Freedom can then degenerate into chaos. The near chaotic conditions now prevailing in the cable business would then be extended to the satellite channels. And the foreigners would certainly find the situation favourable to them.

If you do not find the harmless cable bill to your linking and would not brook any legal restrictions on uplinking and yet would use your programme channels the way you like it, can you still speak of freedom of the media? More of it later.

Incidentally, the Act referred to above is the Indian Telegraph Act, 1885, which comes in the way of Indian or foreign satellite channels doing as they please. Some people called it archaic when it was used to prevent uplinking by a multinational, TWI, during the Hero Cup controversy. But the Prasar Bharati Act, 1990, specifically refers to the act in section 12(1). So the law is not archaic after all and is far from dead. The Prasar Bharati Act was passed with the enthusiastic support of the BJP and others amid general acclaim in the country.

9

DD Surprised, Gropes in Dark

It would not be wrong to say that while the satellite challenge was growing fast DD was still resting on its terrestrial oars even in 1991. More and more cables and dish antennae were sprouting in the urban areas and some rural areas too. The cable people had woken up to the possibility of satellite services boosting their business and they were falling over each other to link up their operations with the foreign and foreign-supported Indian satellite channels.

DD's achievements so far had been remarkable, no matter what the English print media, tradionally adversary to the electronic media, said about it. It had under its belt megaserials like *Mahabharat, Hum Log, Buniyad* and a host of others which had created TV history. Its network on the ground was extending to all parts of the country and into the remotest corners. While DD's feet were firmly planted on the soil of India, the skies were being encroached upon from all sides. Others may be moon (or satellite) - struck, we have hundreds of terrestrial stations, was still the feeling in the DD kendras and in Mandi House as the satellite challenge became visible.

The terrestrial growth was indeed something to boast about. In 1989-90, 184 new transmitters were put up, which was a record by itself, and during a part of that year a transmitter was coming up every day. As usual in this country, regional demands, voiced by politicians having an eye on the next election and jingoistic linguistic groups, were goading the planners in Delhi to fulfil them. For the people of different regions, often neglected in the past, the arrival of local TV was a satisfying development, even if the transmitter were to relay programmes from Delhi most of the time.

DD's print media critics could never realise that the regional growth of television is a matter of local pride. The satisfaction of a cultural want cannot be measured in terms of ad revenue, the criterion adopted in the metros. Those who are guided by what the young ones in their own homes are dancing to (mostly the tunes of MTV) or themselves lapping up foreign serials can scarce realise that a vigorous Ao (Naga) dance or graceful Manipuri opera means a lot to the north-east viewers of DD's North-east service. This is brought to all parts of the strategic north-east region by linking the stations and transmitters in the region (May 1993). Earlier the Panaji station of DD came up in Goa (June 1990)[1]. There is as yet no satellite channel in Konkani or Portuguese for Goa and all Oriya speaking TV centres and transmitters were linked to Cuttack (September 1991).

Likwise, Calcutta formally became the mother-station of all Bengali areas with their transmitters linked to the eastern metro in November 1991, and the Gujarati speaking areas were brought under one umbrella at Ahmedabad in December 1992. More fortunate regions, like Maharashtra, had been similarly linked to a major centre in the state even prior to 1990.

Such laurels easily cause smugness to set in and DD was no exception. The hardware successes have always produced an euphoria in Mandi House and in Shastri Bhavan, of which the launching of five satellite channels in 1993 was the most recent example. That the hardware gains were not matched in programme terms of software was evident in 1993 (as we will see later) but it was evident in the earlier years too.

At the centres of control in Delhi, controversy over the allocation of time to serial producers was bogging down the programmers and files were moving up and down. The CBI, Central Bureau of Investigation, was taking a hand to look into incidents of corruption which was spreading, not exactly like the proverbial wild fire, but it an alarming pace. Questions in Parliament only further unnerved the political bosses and decision making, always a funny and tardy process, tended to become even more complicated. Several hundred proposals for serials were in cold storage.

But the English print media, already swept off their feet by the foreign serials and MTV's musical hits, played an unintended beneficial role at this juncture by reminding the I and B bosses that DD was facing a challenge for the first time. A powerful and attention-catching rivalry had come up in the skies. Not that the I and B and TV bosses themselves were unaware. They were privately watching on the ultramodern sets, supplied free to them by the government, the programmes which the English speaking homes were also enjoying viewing.

The fact that the satellite services had been brought to the viewers by the cable people and the latter themselves were increasingly posing a threat to DD was also simultaneously brought home to the political and bureaucratic masters. The need for the regulation of the totally unrestricted and almost chaotic cable business was thus felt, while the government grudgingly acknowledged that the satellite services were causing it some loss of sleep.

The word "invasion" was bandided about and some intensive thinking was on for a solution to prevent erosion of

DD's audience. There is no doubt DD had a vast territorial advantage and it had a real network, unlike the cable and the so-called hastily put together programmes of some TV services or even the foreign satellite channels with their appeal to a section of the total Indian TV audience. But even a giant has to be aware of the rise of potential and real challengers who may appear to be pigmies in the beginning but become strong rivals in the not distant future.

On October 1, 1992 the government announces its time slot scheme. Actually earlier in July that year the cabinet had approved the plan for leasing time to private producers on the Metro channel and the FM channel of the radio but the actual legal framework was provided by a *Gazette of India* notification on October 1[2]. The scheme was later to be bogged down by a variety of factors as we shall see and only the radio part of it was implemented and private producers were ushered in and given a much larger measure of conceiving and producing their programmes presentations.

This July decision was the first acknowledgement of the fact that TV was essentially a medium of entertainment, that there had been a growing vacuum in this regard as DD had taken its audiences for granted and wasted too much time in the so-called sectional programmes (women, children, youth, industrial workers) paternalistically believing that entertainment for a couple of hours in the evening was all that the captive audiences should get while the other time was devoted to heavy government propaganda.

We have seen that the audiences is never captive. In 1991 the satellite channels had opened up new vistas of entertainment and the cable was coming through in a big way.

What was so different about the time slot scheme? So far, the serials and other entertainment programmes were being brought to the viewers by the sponsors and DD pocketed the money generated by commercial spots because of the attractiveness of the programme. Now, for the first time, the time was to be sold to the private producers for a fixed amount of money paid by them and they could settle their deals with their sponsors and also take away the spot revenue. As, however, happens often in this country the scheme of time slot allocation got mixed up with controversy thanks to pressure groups of one kind or another, seeking to lay down the law, bureaucratic bungling and political ineffectiveness.

How this scheme finally took shape and what was DD's real answer to the new challenge would be seen in the next chapter. The announcement of October 1, 1992 was, however, the first indication that something had to be done to meet the challenge and DD's inhouse, commissioned or other sponsored programmes did not offer all the options which the viewers looked for. In his inaugural address to a seminar on satellite and cable television, organised by the Indian Institute of Mass Communication in November 1992, in New Delhi, the then I and B Minister, Ajit Kumar Panja, made some significant remarks. He showed complete awareness of the satellite challenge and the issues which had been raised by it and indicated how the Indian government proposed to deal with it.

Panja reiterated the government's commitment to freedom of expression as enshrined in the Constitution of India, article 19(i)(a). We cannot do better than quote from the "Proceedings of the Seminar" as follows:[3]

"While inaugurating the seminar, Mr. Ajit Kumar Panja said the government is committed to freedom of thought and expression (the Constitution refers to 'expression') and it is enshirned in our Constitution Article 19(A) [actually 19(*i*)(a)]. With the advent of communication satellite technologies, international broadcasting has come to stay. However, in the present context the freedom of expression tends to be largely that of powerful multinational media like CNN and BBC. There are no specific national or international laws under which the beaming of TV programmes across nation-state boundaries can be stopped. *And we in India have no intention of banning any satellite broadcasting.* (emphasis added) Banning, in any case, is neither desirable nor pragmatic. It involves enormous efforts and resources which could be better utilized for providing facilities like tubewells to the rural people.

"In the circumstances, the media freedom should be utilized by those who are not only knowledgeable and wise as otherwise it might lead to adverse consequences. The recipient countries in the the context of satellite transmission should have the right to be heard and the media companies should be sensitive to the feelings, cultural values and ethos prevailing in those countries. The recipients of the satellite programming should have a right to be heard and there should be some commonly agreed forum like UN or ITU where the complaint regarding undesirable telecasts could be heard and meaningfully resolved.

"Freedom has become the property of the developed countries alone. They decide what is freedom and what is good for India and other developing countries and beam TV programmes accordingly. Are we going to succumb exactly as we did 250 years age to gunpowder? The gunpowder was brought in and we lost our freedom. Now the electronic gadgets are being brought. We have to stand up and face the onslaught from the skies by evolving suitable policy responses and compete with CNN, BBC etc. with quality programmes of our own". Notably, Panja was bitter about the invasion but extremely pragmatic in seeking solutions.

In a cabinet reshuffle effected by Prime Minister Narasimha Rao in January 1993, a couple of moths later, Panja lost his coveted I and B portfolio and moved over to Coal. He was replaced by K.P. Singh Deo whose pronouncements against the cultural invasion have been, if anything, stronger.

However, the Indian view that satellite TV would not be banned has prevailed, although the tall hope that the foreign satellite channels could be persuaded to mould their programmes to suit the cultural ethos of the recipient countries would always remain unfulfilled. Typical of the wooly thinking of some Indian politicians was the point made by Vasant Sathe, a distant predecessor of Panja but one with the status of a Cabinet minister (Panja was only a minister of State as is Singh Deo). Speaking at the same seminar on the same day Sathe said that "leading foreign satellite companies like Star, CNN, BBC and others should be associated with and drafted to evolve a model code for satellite broadcasting keeping in view the sensitivities of programme receiving countries in the Asian region so as to dispel the misgivings created in the minds of certain sections that these media are being manipulated for harming the national interest."

There could not be a more pious hope than that. Imagine Star, CNN, BBC *et al* putting their heads together to fashion a model code of broadcasting to honour Asian sensitivities. They would rather utilize that time and those resources to make more attractive audience catching programmes so that their ad revenue could go up.

Of course, like all people aiming at the minds of men they would try to understand what their audiences want and how much of the foreign stuff they could bear, like what the traffic could bear from a purely commercial point of view. Messrs Sathe, Panja and their ilk could meanwhile evolve a model code which nobody would bother to honour.

Of course, China, Malaysia, Singapore, Vietnam and Saudi Arabia have already evolved their responses, as we have seen before, and they have demonstrated that, by and large, it is possible to keep out the foreign satellite broadcasts. India, however, has definitely ruled out the banning option and there Panja's categorical statement at the IMC seminar has been sustained by policy pronouncements of his successor.

Singh Deo has not spared the foreign media and once even called their programmes "diabolical invasion from the sky"[4]. That was in his address to a seminar of the All India Newspapers Editors Conference in Delhi in December 1993. But he has made it clear that there would be no effort to ban these broadcasts. At the same seminar Singh Deo said that there would be no jamming or banning of foreign satellite channels.

But what was the DD answer to the powerful challenge from foreign media coming through the skies, to this "diabolical invasion"? We will see it in detail in the next chapter but suffice it to say here that arriving at some understanding with the foreign media to prevent them from foisting a foreign culture on unsuspecting Indians has remained a part of the official Indian hope. That nothing concrete has been done to achieve this goal is a different matter. The I and B Ministry's permanent Secretary, who was speaking at a seminar organised jointly by the Press Information Bureau of the Indian government and an organ of the US government in Delhi in October 1993, said, *inter alia,*: "Asian nations are wary of foreign TV broadcasts as they fear ideological 'subversion' and a loss of control over information. Perhaps a time has come when we start looking for agreements - bilateral and multilateral - for the beaming of channels to various counters".[5]

So, that is a kind of policy or hope favoured by India- no banning, no jamming, but bilateral and multilateral agreements to make the foreign media behave, and a number of Indian options would constitute a real policy.

DD also tried in 1992 to meet the entertainment needs of the audience by increasing the film contents of its programmes. The afternoon transmission, which came on the air at a time when cable's video films were drawing substantial urban audiences, was expanded and recast to provide several film based programmes and a full film on Tuesdays. These were palliatives at best.

10

Answer at Last

The realization that TV is essentially a medium of entertainment, which indirectly influences the lifestyle of the viewers, and that DD by itself could not provide all that stuff had now dawned on the nation's TV bosses. The time slot scheme, approved by the Indian cabinet in July 1992, was evolved after that.

Controversy dogged the steps that were to be taken before the scheme could be given shape and substance. Although a high level committee was at work, with a former technologist - bureaucrat heading it, the typical Indian situation in which there are always too many fingers in the pie prevented anything worthwhile emerging out of that exercise. Meanwhile the tension in DD was mounting and the success of Star and now Zee, *plus* the continuing threat from the cable industry, was exerting psychological pressure to impel the network to come up with an alternative soon.

While the bosses were looking in every direction for an answer the awareness that there was a second TV channel in the four metropolitan cities - Delhi, Bombay, Calcutta and Madras - came as a godsend.

The second channel, known variously as Delhi Two, Bombay Two, Channel Seven and so an, was the neglected baby of DD. It was used mainly as on outlet for disposable programmes which could not be allowed to crowd the main channel and secondarily as a minority language channel, like Punjabi programmes in Delhi, while the primary channel was a Hindi one. The linguistic minorities actually appreciated that some attention was paid to their culture and language. Also, some forgettable programmes were televised on the second channel. Like interviews with the local public utility bosses, ostensibly to question them about the problems faced by the users but really to enable them to speak of their achievements.

There were other regular programmes too but the only one, apart from the linguistic minority programmes, which had a following was the regional news bulletin. Supposed to be a newscast presenting local developments, akin to the 'Pradeshik Samachar' of AIR stations (some 42 of them) this bulletin had virtually become a replica of the national bulletin which used to come up an hour later. Only some VIP-oriented visuals, in typical DD news style, were thrown in to lend a local or regional colour to the bulletin. In any case, viewers, would switch on the second channel for the news in this bulletin so that later on they could watch their programmes of their choice (including, of course, DD's primary channel).

The second channel also came handy to DD for continuing the live coverage of major sporting events like a cricket test or an international one-dayer, whenever the relay on the main channel had to be interrupted for the news bulletins or other governmental priority items. Often, the rest of India (outside the four metros) complained bitterly and cursed DD that they were denied the live relay but the programmers had no option.

If the second channel was thus virtually lying in a dustheap in the *barsati* (a room on the roof), it was now to be put to great use as DD Metro, which soon became a household word even in homes wedded to Star or Zee in the major cities and elsewhere. Later christened the Entertainment channel and from February 1994 or DD two, the name Metro became popular and stuck. The Metro actually rescued DD in the urban areas, and in the eyes of the English media, which grudgingly acknowledged its appeal to the viewers in special colour features.

An alternative channel offering a variety of options to the audiences was now a reality.

We have seen how the software in DD has lagged behind hardware (much to the chagrin of the engineers who strive manfully to commission a channel or transmitter after another at short notice). Although the Metro came up in just a few weeks, its beginning with the Sports Hour, from 6.30 p.m. to 7.30 p.m. on weekdays, was somewhat unpromising and virtually lacklustre. There was not much worthwhile material in DD's kitty and frantic appeals were made to schools, colleges, unverisities and other institutions to favour it with capsuled coverage of sporting events. Coverage from the DD stations were obtained and sometimes some gems like the Indian hockey team's thrilling performance in the Poznan tournament were also shown.

But the Sports Hour never really took off and even now under another nomenclature, it only features old, almost ancient events and personalities, mostly on the basis of some foreign TV agency stuff. It had never had any commercials or sponsors and often the same dull voices and unpleasing faces could be heard and seen by sports enthusiasts.

What is significant here is that this was the first Metro Hour programme of DD, launched on Republic Day (January 26, 1993). With the cooperation of NFDC, National Film Development Corporation, a sister organisation, which was known to many only as a financier of good non-commercial films, DD, however, went ahead[1] and programme producers in

Bombay, sometimes referred to as creative people, came forward with serials.

Among the first to book as much as a full hour was the programme *Superhit Muqabla,* which has now run a full year and is still going strong with its ten top Hindi film songs of the week, supposed to have been selected by the viewers who write in their preferences to the producer. The value of the programme is enhanced by slick presentation by popular comperes and sometimes beautiful locales, and, of course, prizes to viewers which has become a regular feature of many other programmes too.

By that time, Minister Singh Deo had made a statement in Parliament and had announced DD's satellite channels. Metro in the beginning could be viewed only in the four metropolitan cities but soon DD announced it could be seen in the whole of India with a dish antenna. The satellite channel of Metro launched on All Fools day, April 1, 1993, later known as the Metro-Entertainment channel, could be seen with a proper dish antenna anywhere in India. Several producers took advantage of the time slot scheme and most of them made good money for themselves while they brought interesting and lively entertainment programmes to DD's viewers.

The policy clothing for the new DD approach to TV programmes was provided by Singh Deo's statement in Parliament on March 23, 1993. He said (in parts):[1]

"The honourable members are aware that several foreign satellite TV channels have started beaming their signals to this country and we are facing what is described by many as a *cultural invasion* (emphasis added). In order to give a befitting response to this challenge, government propose to start a few more channels using the spare time on the transponders (on Insat-1D and Insat-2A). These TV signals, uplinked, through the transponders on Indian satellites, can be received through appropriate TV receiving equipment, commonly known as a dish antenna, and can be further distributed by the cable operators....

"It is proposed to start these channels in a phased manner from 1st April, 1993 and increase both the number of the channels and their duration as and when software and hardware facilities are available.

"It is proposed to devote these channels to the following:

i) Primary Channel - the present format of Doordarshan

ii) Metro Channel

iii) Enrichment and Cultural Channel

iv) Sports Channel

v) News, Current Affairs and Business Channel."

The government's thinking was actually getting finalised and what ultimately emerged a little later when DD came out with a fulfledged scheme was five new channels, apart from the primary channel, the main DD. They were:

Entertainment Channel (also known as the Metro or Metro-Entertainment Channel);

Sports Channel;

Business news and Current Affairs Channel;

Enrichment Channel; and

Music Channel.

This was announced by DD in a pamphlet called "Detailed guidelines for Time Slot Allotment on the Satellite Channels of Doordarshan". The booklet priced at Rs.50 (about two dollars) sold like hot cakes among a class of people and in a country where publishers find it hard to sell even good books. So high was the popularity of the Metro channel which was by now in fine fettle as more than a dozen producers had booked slots for their programmes with enthusiastic response from the sponsors and other advertisers. DD set up a separate office in Delhi's Tolstoy Marg to run the Metro and other channels and to cope with the rush of the seekers of time slots.

The DD pamphlet made it amply clear that news and current affairs would continue to be a DD main channel programmes and, what is more important, a government monopoly. Some people had been misled by the loosely worded ministerial statement and believed the time slot scheme would also cover "news, current affairs, and business news." The pamphlet removed any doubt and dashed the hopes of those who thought that they could buy time and present news also. Only business-related news and discussion and interviews were covered by the channel devoted to that subject.

The enrichment channel was meant for presenting programmes on agriculture, health, science and so on, while the music channel was assigned to present music of all kinds and sports channel was meant to deal with sporting events at home and abroad.

Meanwhile the Metro channel was making the waves in the media world and its phenomenal success was spurring the producers to rush to queue up before the office in Tolstoy Marg to be the first, or among the first few, to put in their claim. The queues which were formed from June 23, days before D day, July 5, when the applications were to be received and disposed of on a first-come-first served basis, shortened to FCFS by the newspapers. Not unusually the English Dailies took considerable interest in the queues and what they signified, but those who knew the undercurrents were aware that this was more out of self-interest because four of the leading English dailies were themselves applicants.

How the FCFS issue went to court and how the time slot scheme could not become a reality is dealt with in a separate chapter later.

To continue with the narration of the developments affecting the emergence of a national alternative as opposed to private business and purely commercial alternatives, the scheme had several attractive features. Like the programmes on the Metro channel in those days, the time slot programmes on all the satellite channels were to be free of the rigorous DD scrutiny. Serials on DD's primary channel had been subjected to a detailed scrutiny of the script after which the producer had to show the DD bosses a complete first episode, called a pilot, as it would appear on the TV screen (if approved). Again, after the approval of the scheme and the scheduling, the remaining episodes would have to be presented to DD for a possible scrutiny. There was thus a complete screening and even censoring of the programmes, apart from the right of selection which vested in DD.

But the producers who got the time slots on the Metro and other channels, through the FCFS or any other viable scheme of allocation, would have been free to bring in their programmes, subject only to a general code of good taste and an advertisement code. What followed in episode two or three or thirteen was not DD's headache as in the first one. The Metro producers were, in fact, availing of the freedom to the fullest extent possible. How this situation resulted in some socially harmful programmes being presented and how decency and good taste were violated even by highly rated producers is dealt with later.

But now DD, for the first time, was letting the producers do practically what they liked. In fact, DD did not have at that time nor does it have even now, a machinery to monitor the programmes on the Metro and other channels. The reactions comes only when enraged viewers whose sense of decency has been offended by any programme, busybodies, or the rivals of the programme producer take up the issue with DD.

In order to make a success of its satellite schemes DD was inclined to turn a blind eye to display of sex or violence and the frivolities being committed by some producers. Kissing scenes were shown as also the *Choli* song or even the "Sexy" songs of which there was a rich crop by the end of 1993. The freedom from preview of the sponsored programmes and DD's open door policy became almost a licence in the eyes of some.

DD found itself in a kind of fix when its FCFS scheme was challenged in court and the English print media, many of them interested parties, gave what they considered an expose of the weaknesses of the scheme, the lengthening queues and the goings on to corner time slots. On the one hand, there was the official announcement that the five satellite channel would be introduced from August 15 while, on the other, the entire time allotment was before the Delhi High Court which finally struck it down on September 21, 1993.

The Metro Entertainment channel was a continuing one and only four new channels were offered, although time slot were to be had and all slots had to be bought anew even on the Metro channel and there was no guarantee that the same programmes would continue after August 15.

The entire software was to come from the private producers who would have got the time slots allotted to them. The Indian viewers could possibly have been able to see interesting sports and musical events, among other things, and, of course, see a variety of lively entertainment programmes if the FCFS had gone through. How was DD now to go ahead with the five satellite channels, for which the hardware was in position but the software was lacking, except for the entertainment channel to an extent.

But go ahead it did. The five channels were set in motion on the due date but in the absence of viable programmes which could interest the viewers and thereby fetch sponsors and advertisers DD had to fall back on old serials and used programmes of its primary channel, feature films, and only a limited, very limited direct coverage of sports.

Once a channel is opened you have to have a series of relevant programmes. With its primary channel already in full force and the five satellite channels now on the air everyday, DD was reminded of the trite saying that the TV medium is an inexorable consumer of programmes. Feature films were laid on in each channel but, except for the highly attractive Metro-Entertainment channel, there were few takers for these programmes. The cable people were not relaying them and commercial sponsors were giving them the go-by. DD tried the trick of plugging the same programme on different channels at different times, without much success.

Feature films cost money to hire and the producers of the latest movies are not willing to let their films be shown on a wide network like DD's because that spoils their chances of making more money in the cinema circuits. DD's terms for acquiring the rights of films for telecast are also not attractive enough for good producers to sell these rights. All the same, the Metro channel attracted large ad revenues for its film programmes, possibly because it was a known channel and some of the films were also good in the sense that they had a popular appeal. Even a three decade old movie like *Teen Bahuranian*, for example, got one afternoon 12 sponsors, *plus* other advertising. Cable viewers, as we have seen, can watch the latest movies because the cable is a limited, fragmented business, although in totality it is sufficiently big.

DD's appeal to producers to let it have the more recent films did not evoke the required response and, of course, there were no takers for the scheme of letting private parties sponsor entire films. There were some other problems too. The cable operators found the need for a bigger dish antenna for relay of DD's programmes a serious difficulty. Although a number of operators were either ready with the large antenna or acquired one to meet the viewers demand for the Metro channel, the other channels were not favoured and the dish antenna problem thus became a real obstacle.

So, what could DD do? The time slot had gone awry and its policy of rushing with satellite channels, although justified, had created a situation of paucity of programmes to feed as many as five different channels at the same time. DD was in the position of the typical large Indian family which finds itself without the wherewithal of feeding many mouths at a time when the little ones are not able to stand on their feet, much less engage themselves in productive work.

From October 1993, DD used much of the time available on the channels for relay of the regional programmes, or programmes in major Indian languages, instead of Hindi and some programmes which are the mainstay of the primary and satellite channels. This was a good move but again the problem was one of attractive programmes in those languages.

Some of the regional stations have built up a praiseworthy repertorie of serials and plays and some also earn sizable revenue for DD by way of ads. Even votaries of cable in cities like Ahmedabad turn to DD to watch serials and films in Gujarati. Some of the serials are household names.

But unless a proper viewership is built up and a series of attractive new programmes are put on the air even the regional channels cannot become viable propositions. The idea is excellent: as a Bengali or Tamil anywhere in India you can see Bengali or Tamil programmes, but they should be attractive to make you sit up and wait for them and your cableman to relay the channel over which the programme is telecast. Some new programmes were also televised but without attracting any serious attention.

The major Indian languages, miscalled regional languages by the official as well as the English print media, in which the DD programmes were put out on its satellite channels were:

Assamese, Bengali and Oriya, from the eastern region of India, Gujarati and Marathi from the western parts, Kannada, Malayalam, Tamil and Telugu from the south of India, and Punjabi and Kashmiri from the northern part.

The programmes were on the air in each of these languages for two and a half hours each day. The government also expressed a pious hope that "these new channels, besides introducing a greater variety of programmes for the viewers will in time open up outlets at the national level for the vast pool of hitherto untapped talent available in the country, especially at the regional level."

DD also made arrangements for viewers in Hindi to see these programmes in the regional languages on their sets terrestrially without joining any cable, which may relay the satellite channel, or going in for a dish antenna of their own. They were available to the capital's viewers on their sets through the terrestrial channel in the capital. Similar facilities were to be provided to TV owners in the other three metros too at some future date.

While the Enrichment, Sports, Music and Business News channels were virtual non-starters, the Metro-Entertainment channel, the fifth satellite channel, was going great guns. It offered the Indian viewers a variety of options by way of entertainment programmes many of which were certainly superior, in respect of their power to entertain, to any they could get during the evening prime time hours. As we have seen it was the startling success of the channel in May-June 1993 which made prospective buyers of time slots queue up days before the scheme of first-come-first-served was to become operational.

For the first time, the principle that competition is the soul of good entertainment was thus recognised, although the equally important one of competition in news and current affairs was not. But competition is a double-edged weapon and DD Metro posed a threat to DD's primary channel also while it sought to beat off the competition of Zee, Star and other foreign-aided channels. In the metro cities and some other towns and cities many in the audience in the evening hours would switch on the Metro channel and not even bother to watch the news.

At first DD's reaction was peculiar. Instead of recognising that competition can be sustained by making both competitive offerings attractive and improving the entertainment content of the primary channel, it resorted to some other means to meet the competition from within. In the process, the time slots scheme was scrapped from November 1993 and the producers were asked to pay higher rates for the half hour (or a full hour in some cases) they had booked. The sponsorship rates and rates for commercials were yet lower than those on the primary channel but the producers could not now avail of the earlier scheme of buying time at the fairly cheap rate and taking away all the ad and sponsorship revenue generated by their programmes.

The film and film-based programmes were made to pay even higher charges than paid by soap operas, detective and comedy serials, games and other programmes. Some of the affected producers got their grievances aired in the English media through friendly writers adversary to the official media. DD Metro had, however, acquired a status of its own and since the programmes were popular DD could not be faulted for hiking up the charges. The popularity of the channel went up instead of declining and the new scheme of charges failed to drive either the viewers or producers to the primary channel. Even the high-profile video magazines like *Newstrack* and *Eyewitness* which were so far selling only their cassettes to VCR owners who could view the news clips in their homes now turned to DD Metro and booked time even late in the evening (in the early stages) for a weekly presentation.

More and better serials were coming on the channel as time passed and the really creative talent got an opportunity to display their ability (like Ravi Basvani's Manch Masala) while the more organised and financially stronger ones like the makers of *Kanoon* and *Kismat* also turned to this channel.

Meanwhile there was speculation whether the four unsuccessful satellite channels would be scrapped altogether. DD was also undergoing yet another bout of self-introspection to consider the future of these channels and ways to butress its flagship, the primary channel, which had fetched Rs. 360 crores ($120 million) in advertisement revenue in 1992-93. DD Metro, on the other hand earned Rs. 18 crores in just half year's operation. The channel could be expected to earn even more in the remaining months of 1993-94 (The Indian fiscal year is from April to March).

The obstacle of the bar to the FCFS scheme had been bypassed by giving up the time slot scheme altogether in November 1993. But the situation of the primary channel had not improved and not only the revenue had to be increased but the huge domestic audience in the small towns and villages as well as the viewers in the Metros and big cities, many of them still watching the primary channel, had to be kept happy. The satellite channels had to be equipped with viable programmes so that the plans for more satellite channels, with the lanuching of Insat-2C, due in the near future, could also be fulfilled.

The "agonising" thinking led to the recasting of DD's programmes on all channels and restructuring of the channels themselves. On February 1, 1994, nearly a year after DD had launched the Metro channel in a small halting way, the government medium announced that there would be six DD channels, the same as before, but with new nomenclatures - DD 1, the faithful old primary channel, DD 2, the new resurgent and outgoing Metro entertainment channel, DD 3, a new satellite channel with a good mix of programmes, now seeking to win fresh laurels, and three channels to carry regional language programmes, called DD 4, 5 and 6.

The Enrichment, Sports, Music and Business News channels were thus given a decent burial, only five and a half months after they were hearlded with some fanfare, thanks to the FCFS scheme being frustrated by some English newspapers with ambitions to pitch into the TV medium.

It was not just the new names that was the most important part of the restructuring venture. The primary channel now was given the importance it deserved and several new serials written or produced by known TV and film personalities were to be first telecast in this channel and some from DD 2 were to be repeated a few days later. There were other attractions too and the total duration of the channel was also increased. There would be more commissioned or sponsored programmes instead of the weak inhouse programmes.

DD Metro, now rechristened DD 2 but still called by the more popular name, had several programmes during the day and more particularly from early in the evening until late at night, although the restructuring meant that there would be no Hindi feature film in the afternoon or weekdays. The difficulty of getting the TV rights of latest releases and generally of the more popular films has been referred to earlier. That combined with the need to enable DD 1 to get access to these films first and to make the audiences watch the reruns of some of the hit serials of DD Metro in the afternoon hours on the primary channel led to the dropping of the film programmes in the midday transmission.

In fact, repeating programmes from one channel over another is a feature of the restructured DD.

As before the satellite channels, now DD 3 and the regional services of DD 4, 5 and 6, were available to the viewers in Delhi terrestrially but when these would also be shown in the other three metro cities as promised earlier was not announced.

The most important aspect of the entire exercise was the recognition on the part of the DD bosses that they must no longer be content with having a huge network but also make it the vehicle of attractive programmes and make the viewers feel happy. The old paternalistic attitude seemed to have given place to a more competitive and positive programme-oriented approach but whether this would last long and the politico-bureaucratic set-up would always be responsive to the challenges emerging almost daily remained to be seen.

Cosmetic changes are useful only upto a point. They have also to be accompanied by substantial improvement in contents and presentation. The restructured DD programmes from February 1994 also provided for a half hour newscast, in both

English and Hindi, in the prime-time evening hours. The new presentation looked attractive, which could have been accomplished even without any fanfare and earlier; all the same it was welcome. There were, however, no visuals except those, as before, relating to government-oriented (non-) news items.

Much of the bulletin looked like a stock exchange and general market report which has some interest for the investing public but little or none for the lay viewers. There was no effect to find out what the people were thinking about the series of new steep price hikes by the government. Cosmetic changes, alas, are not enough. They cannot hide the underlying ugliness.

The lethargic and time-wasting ways must also yield place to a new regimen of no-nonsense mostly graphic-based announcements. There is no need to announce every programme and some of the aging announcers had better be taken off the screen, like air hostesses being grounded after a certain age.

On the very first day of restructuring, when people would be on the look out for the changes and the new-look channels the afternoon Hindi bulletin was announced a clear five minutes before time. Even a five second pause on radio or TV seems like an endless wait to the audience. (DD should not forget it makes Rs. 100,000 by selling ten seconds at prime time.) In the present case, when the bulletin failed to materialize, quite naturally, an announcer appeared and in a supercilious manner said there was a 'delay' in the news. The straightforward course of apologizing for the faulty announcement and interruption of the feature film which was then on the air, full five minutes before time, did not appeal to her. Instead after the false statement that the news was being 'delayed' the feature film was resumed.

This is only an example of what good broadcasting requires but which is still lacking in DD. There are frequent wrong cues, and at regular intervals the caption *'Rukawat Ke Liye Khed Hai'* (sorry for the interruption) appears on the DD screen as the tape gets wound up or there is some technical fault somewhere. Sports relays are often interrupted because of breaks in transmission. Sometimes the visuals are missing although the voice is there and sometimes the audio is missing, sometimes both are gone, while a wicket fails, a goal is scored or a six is hit. When the power in the mains fails, it takes DD inordinately long to switch on the generator and continue with the transmission

There is no apparent striving for excellence. Spelling mistakes in graphics and captions are galore. (There is no excuse for DD to do it because the same number or more appear in the stories in leading English dailies.) DD gets a bad name and the knowledgeable viewers (they are many) think poorly of the literacy level among DD's key personnel. A graphic was repeatedly screened after the Maharashtra earthquake appealing to the viewers to contribute to the relief fund, a laudable activity. But it spelt 'P.M.'s secretariat' as 'secretariate'. It took DD some days to know that secretariat does not take an 'e' at the end. That the PM's office long ceased to be a secretariat, without losing any of its clout, dawned on DD even later.

Everyone has to be on his toes and a complacent attitude has to give place to keen, competitive broadcasting approach. If DD has to make a success of the restructuring effort and build on the success of its Metro channel a "whole new" outlook (to borrow a phrase from its publicity gimmick) has to inform its performance.

The political masters must lay down the parameters, choose the right men and women for the right jobs and then sit back and watch TV, leaving DD to its devices. The broadcasters must have enough freedom and lattitude to carry out the assigned job. Key personnel must not be shifted too frequently. A highly competent and senior man, thoroughly imbued with the spirit of broadcasting, was summarily shifted to AIR from DD, luckily to find himself one fine morning in Mandi House again after three years.

It is equally necessary not to change and chop the programme schedules and contents. What happened in 1993-94 when six satellite channels were introduced and "restructured" was unavoidable under the circumstances and perhaps the speed was also justified. But can you imagine that in the course of just two years or a little more the main Hindi and English bulletins in the evening have been shortened from 20 minutes to 15 minutes and then again lengthened to half an hour.

The English bulletin now comes on the air at 10 p.m., when most Indians, specially those advanced in age, have retired for the day. Time was when Sardar Patel, then Deputy Prime Minister, used to go to bed after listening to AIR's 9 p.m. news bulletin (Thank you, AIR, for not shifting this bulletin, by a minute backwards or forwards, although radio has to reschedule all news bulletins soon.)

Now you must keep awake until 10.30 p.m. if you wish to watch what the government would like you to see as the news of the day. Even the advertisement rates fall steeply after 10 at night in recognition of the fact that people prefer the comfort of their beds to the pleasure of watching TV at that hour.

A little bit of pressure by the MPs or some other powerful group and the time of the newscast could change. And DD's standing among the viewers could take another nosedive.

With a network of 553 transmitters DD is one or the biggest networks of the world, although its standing in terms of commercial revenue earned may not be high. As many as 760 million people in India can now watch DD terrestrially, apart from many who have access to a satellite channel or two. With the restructured new look DD is now on the air for 90 hours a day. Even before 488 hours of programmes emanated from DD transmitters every week.

The surprising part of audience response is not that DD's primary channel has lost some of its shine and appeal to the viewers after the appearance of its own Metro channel but they many people still watch the main channel programmes. On sundays, its film-based *Rangoli* programme of selected hits from the new and not very old movies had an audience rating of 77 per cent in the non-metro cities in January 1994. Even a cultural information programmes like the sponsored *Surabhi,* on the main channel, had a high rating of 51 per cent.

The Metro channel has continued to be a favourite of the urban audiences and, according to the survey, carried out by DD's audience research people, as many as 69 per cent viewers in Bombay watched the Thursday comedy show *Dekh Bhai Dekh,* now a year old. Bombay urban audiences were once wedded to cable or Zee, apart from Star.

All this imposes a much greater responsibility on DD. The issue of the unhealthy character of some of the presentations and the influence of growing consumerism on the minds of the middle classes which are the biggest watchers of TV as well as others will be dealt with in a later chapter.

Finally, will someone in DD pay attention to the wrong term for TV watchers? Doordarshan, or seeing or showing something at a distance, is all right for television, although the Srilankan term, *Roopvahini,* carrier of form (or beauty), would appear to be a better term. But to go ahead and call a viewer of TV as 'Darshak' is an atrocity. The root 'Darsh' in Sanskrit means to show, not to see. The viewers are seeing not showing something. The correct word is 'Prekshak' as used in classical Sanskrit drama and books People are said to be going to a temple for 'darshan' because the deity shows itself to the devotees who see it.

11

The FCFS Fiasco

The five new satellite channels of DD were announced in a pamphlet called "Detailed Guidelines for Time Slot Allotment on the Satellite Channels of Doordarshan" following the successful launching of the Metro channel, formally from April 1, 1993 but actually even earlier. The publication came out in May that year and private producers were out in force to buy up the slots.

The terms were very attractive: a payment of just Rs.54,000 per half hour per metro (Rs.2,16,000 per half hour for the four metros together) in return for which you got five minutes of free advertising time and you could fix your own rates for sponsorship and for commercials. No questions asked about the scripts, no bother of producing a pilot and getting DD's approval for it and every succeeding episode, a great measure of freedom to say and show what you like and what you think your audience would like and so on.

What was more, there was the shining example of the success of these Metro channel slots which were also now on sale *de novo*.

The DD bosses were also offering the other four channels and hoped all the slots would be taken up and the scheme would be a success. There was no reason why it should be otherwise. The terms were all designed to attract the producers who would be lucky to book the slots. All they had to do was to bring it attractive programmes and the audiences would lap up and the advertisers would fill their coffers.

What would be the basis of the allocation of time slots? This, DD said, would be on the basis of 'first-come-first-served', something which the government had often practised in the matter of granting import licences and things like that. Nobody objected when the basis of the scheme was first announced. There was a rush on DD's Metro Office at 4, Tolstoy Marg, close to Connaught Place in New Delhi, to buy the booklet and then be ready to hand in the applications with the earnest money. The allotment was to begin from July 5. Hope, as they say, springs eternal in the human breast and the hard-headed producers were no exceptions.

On June 23, full 12 days before the applications were to be received on the first-come-first-served basis by DD, a small queue of prospective buyers of slots appeared before the Tolstoy Marg office. In no time the number of queuers swelled and at its largest there were more than 250 people in the queue, although some newspapers put the number at 450. This is the time Delhi is lashed by the first monsoon rains, preceded by fierce heat and unbearable humidity. (Delhi should get the first monsoon rains on June 29, the latest by July 9). Those in the queue, mostly surrogates and paid employees or daily wagers, had thus to brave first the heat and then the rain and always the humidity.

Such was the roaring success of Metro, such the attractive rates and such were the producers' high expectations that they were paying at least Rs.100 a day to people who were holding the slots in the queue for them to earn the time slots on July 5, when DD's gates would open to receive the applications.

And who were these people who were queueing up or making others do it for them ? There were some, like New Delhi TV, whose Pranoy Roy is one of the best known TV personalities in India because he has been giving us the election results and analysis, for the past four years, with lightening speed and commendable fairness and does a superb programmes on the Centre's annual budget every year. He is also well known to many viewers through his enjoyable TWTW — The World This Week show—on Friday late in the evening since 1990 on DD's primary channel. (Now shifted to Thursday).

There were others like Nimbus which had already got a lucrative slot on the Metro — the *Superhit Muqabla* — and was angling to keep that and get more if possible. There were others who were already producing programmes for one or the other DD channel. But there were also those who were in the TV business in a small way or who were completely new to it. In this category were four leading English dailies — *The Times of India, Hundustan times, Indian Express*) and the *Hindu*.

The *Times of India* had floated some years ago its Times TV which had been sponsoring a science programmes 'Turning point' on DD's primary channel. The show had failed to catch on despite an array of cinema personalities to compere it. Beginning with Nasiruddin Shah, it had acquired Mallika Sarabhai before getting Girish Karnad without getting anywhere in particular. In between it had promoted the highly appreciated *Mullah Nasruddin* serial by Amal Allana. Television was indeed high in the expansion programmes of Bennet Coleman, the owners of the *Times*.

The *Hindustan Times*, another successful paper with a lot of cash in hand and powerful industrial and financial backing of its owners, the Birlas, had so far been known for only its *Eyewintess* video magazine in the sphere of TV. These two had some TV connection worth mentioning. The other two had not at all, although the *Hindu* came up with a TV company name at least, *Indus Television*. There were also other news media like the *India Today* magazine which had fathered the first video magazine *Newstrack*.

In the western world, specially the United States, the print media have branched out into television business. The TV giant, Rupert Murdoch, spread out in the TV field from his newspaper perch. A king became an emperor. But only in India have the newspapers used their clout to promote their TV business. This fact became evident in the FCFS (an abridgement of first-come-first-served by the dailies themselves) case. First they attacked DD (which they always do) and Pranoy Roy in particular. They could not match his TV skills but their columns tried to make up for their TV inadequacy. When the court began hearing their writs, the papers gave elaborate coverage to their own position while DD was given short shrift.

Others in the queue included experienced TV companies like Mudra Communications, Independent TV, ITV, United Television, UTV, and Samvad Video, Creative Eye, Moving Picture Company, Octave Communication, and the Home Communication Network of the industrial houses of the Modis. There were besides some others and several in the queue would not identify themselves.

There was a strong element of the dramatic as well as comic in the queue and the scene was just ready for a film or TV serial script writer to use his pen but, alas, few people can laugh at themselves. By July 3, the courts began to be approached. The first to do so was the *Times of India* which approached the Additional District Judge, Mr. Sunder Lal Bhayana, and got an order asking the SHO (Station House Officer, police chief) of New Delhi, for clearing the queue. Before that order could be implemented. Roy's New Delhi TV and some other producers rushed to the Delhi High Court's Justice Arun Kumar (on a Sunday). The Judge passed an order asking the Deputy Registrar of the court to prepare a report on the queue.[1]

In the meantime, the *Times* and the other dailies unleashed their men on the queue. The site was already a sight of dirt and half eaten food, empty cartons and even dried leaves, in which many Indians like to eat their food and snacks, lying around. In fact, the newspaper surrogates formed a second queue of their own and later a third queue was formed by some others. We cannot do better than quote from the horse's mouth. The *The Times of India* in a report on July 5,[2] titled "Queue Drama Outside DD", said in parts: "The second queue was formed in a systematic operation in which chairs and durries (floor-spreads) were brought in vehicles. The chairs were placed in a neat row with people occupying them within minutes of the queue being formed.

"A shuttle canteen was also set up to provide those in the second queue with refreshments and tea". You must look after your own men.

At this stage, DD changed its stance and said it would give up the FCFS scheme in favour of random number generation by computers, a virtual lottery pattern, and the date for accepting the applications was also extended. So, the queuists evaporated but soon came back, almost in the old order, when DD switched back to its FCFS Plan.

This switch back and forth cost DD much legal face and was to come in for severe reprimand at the hands of Delhi High Court Judges, Justices D.P.Wadhwa and Vijender Jain, before whom the *Times of India*, the *Hindustan Times, Indian Express*, the *Hindu*, along the some others, filed writ petitions against the DD allotment scheme.

Among the others were cinema actress Sridevi, who was not known to have fathered (or mothered) a TV programme before or after the FCFS drama, and Dr. Arvind Gupta. The Home Communication filed a counter writ petition in the same case which was now to decide the fate of the FCFS scheme as the two judges began hearing the arguments from June end almost on a day-to-day basis.

The queue drama continued to be played for some more time[3], although DD and the government said in the court they did not recognise the queues. A writ was also filed in the Madras High Court.

Justice D.P. Wadhwa and Vijender Jain, constituting a division bench of the Delhi High Court, summoned and scrutinized the government and DD files on the subject of time slot allotment. Learned counsel appeared for both sides and the court finally gave its verdict on September 21, 1993. The *Times of India,* in its edition of September 22, ran a three column story in its National news page: "HC Quashes DD Allotment ways" in which the adverse judgment of the court was reported.[4]

The *Times* report said: "In a landmark judgment, the Delhi High Court has struck down both the first-come-first-served and random number generation methods of Doordarshan for allotting time on the five satellite channels.

"Calling the Doordarshan scheme to be "bad in law" the court has directed them and the government to introduce a proper scheme for allotment of slots on satellite channels after due consideration.

"THE JUDGMENT: The operative part of the judgment reads as follows — The impugned scheme to introduce five satellite channels is bad in law. It is set aside ... The basis of first-come-first-served for allotment of time slots on satellite channels is arbitrary. It is unreasonable, unjust and unfair. The order dated July 3, 1993 of the Central Government in the Ministry of Information and Broadcasting reverting to the allotment of time slots on this basis is set aside ...

"The random number generation method, though it treats all the applicants equally and the allotment would be dependent on chance and not on merit entailing an element of lottery, is not valid as all the methods available for allotment of time slots on satellite channels have not been taken into account and has, therefore, also to be set aside."

"A mandamus is issued to the respondents to introduce a proper scheme for allotment of time slots on satellite channels after due consideration in view of observations in this judgment..... Accordingly, the writ petitions filed by Home Communications Network Ltd. is dismissed and rule in this case discharged. Other petitions are allowed."

The Metro channel had come into being with time slots even before the time slot scheme was announced by DD in the pamphlet on detailed guidelines. The four other satellite channels were launched on August 15, as planned by the national TV network, of courses, without any time slots. But the time slot pattern was abandoned by DD from November 1993 and instead the private producers were charged a fixed rate per programmes and the time allowed. Also DD raised the rates for film-based programmes and at least one producers got the *Times of India* to write about the "injustice" done to him. There was logic in what DD did because serials, game shows and the like involved some effort while the film-based programmes leaned heavily on the popularity of a known product, although some film-based programmes bent over backwards to appear different and added new features, which they called their VAP, value added programmes, like the government's VAT tax.

In February 1994, all DD channels, including the satellite ones, were restructured, as DD 1 to 6. The *Times of India's Timestyle* which had already got a slot on Metro was now given a near prime time slot in the revamped scheme. It had its commercially unsuccessful 'Turning Point' science programmes on the primary channel as before.

The *Hindustan Times* perhaps realised the unremunerative character of its video news magazine programmes, *Eyewitness*, and managed for itself a late evening slot on the Metro. It also had another, more popular programmes, *Manch Masala*, at prime time, with highly competent comparing by Ravi Baswani who is a gifted and hardworking cinema and TV personality and with supposedly improvised acting by talented stage actors and actresses. *India Today's* video news magazine also came on the Metro channel, in another late evening programmes. There were reports in the newspapers earlier that the news magazines were not clicking any longer.

The newspapers perhaps realised the futility of their court venture and could see that if the FCFS had been allowed to go unchallenged the producers would have got time slots at a much cheaper rate until DD hiked up the rates after a year. The courts did what the law required them to do but those who approached them first and later quietly moved into the DD slots showed that they were not fighting for any high principles. All the five Indian satellite channels would have secured sponsorships for their programmes and they would have become a success had the newspapers not acted in haste to protect their TV interests. In a way, DD had the last laugh. It preferred an appeal in the Supreme Court later.

That no high principles were involved was evident when the *Times of India* quietly cornered most of the time slots on AIR's FM service on the same FCFS basis even while it was battling the sister medium of DD in the courts over the basis. Slots on the radio on FCFS were good but not on TV. The bigger you are, you can have own logic and rules to determine your attitude to things and events and nobody dare question you.

At least the illogicality could have been pointed out by DD, but then the electronic media are terribly afraid of the print media who never feel shy to protect their interests. It is not unusual for an editor, executive editor or editor-in-chief as the editor is now variously called, to phone the secretary of the I and B Ministry and flay him and DD for not giving his paper's TV enterprise time on some DD programmes or not allowing it to corner the production of some commissioned programmes. Some secretaries who can hear the self-interest of the paper speak in the complaint would politely say: "I will look into it" and do nothing about the silly complaint. Several others, would lambast their media chiefs and even interfere with the latter's decisions to placate the editor, sorry, executive editor or editor-in-chief.

DD's scheme of time slots was stalled by the queue drama and legal disputes, but AIR went ahead with its. More than a month after DD announced its scheme, the older but by now less popular and much less glamorous medium of the radio had come out with its own slot scheme. AIR went in for FM (Frequency Modulation) broadcasting some years ago and later in 1992 a regular service with classical, film, pop and other kinds of music and news was introduced. Out of its 12 hours of broadcasting time nine hours were put on sale, although it was made clear that the bidders would not be able to beam any news bulletins of their own.

The rates were reasonable — Rs.6,000 per hour against Rs. 54,000 for half an hour of DD (under the scheme which is now defunct). The timings of the slots were: 0700 hours to 1000 hours, 1300 to 1500 hours and 1800 to 2200 hours. The FM channel is disturbance-free and suitable for continuous listening of musical programmes.

With a sizeable number of people fed up with the generally adolescent approach of TV programmes, whether DD or Star, and with people often working late in offices or on the move when they would like the radio to be on and love to listen to music the FM has considerable potential for programmes and sponsors.

The *Times*, which got the bulk of the time in Bombay and Delhi on AIR's FM channel, has been rendering a good service to the medium by using its news and advertisement columns to project its own FM programmes. Apparently, its venture has not proved to be a thundering money spinner but the potential remains. AIR has plans to go up to 20 hours of FM broadcasting in 1994 and may even offer more than nine hours to bidders of time slots.

12

Print Media's Antagonistic Role

The press, now referred to as the print media, has had a glorious record in India's freedom struggle. After British rule was brought to an end and India emerged as a major player in the world community, the press also underwent a big change. Many people nostalgically refer to the shining role of the press during the independence movenent and wrongly accuse it of going commercial. When everything else becomes a business or industrys, how can the press, or print media, help not becoming one itself ? But the media have a higher responsibility to their country, through their readers and listeners or viewers and can't be compared with manufacturers of shirts or even steel. More about it in the chapter on a possible foreign print media invasion of India.

It is also true the press must needs play an adversary role to the government of the day and be ever ready to expose its failures and lapses, scrutinise every action analytically and critically, unearth scandals and lay bare all departures from probity and national interest. Even newspapers which are marked out for their pro-government attitude have to stay credible and keep up a critical stance.

They must not only carry reports inconvenient to the government but also publish stories which some government agencies may not find palatable, although these papers would generally shun stories which reflect badly on the top leadership. For this reason, newspapers, like a family daily (along with its sister papers) of the Indira Gandhi family, which always sing the tune of the Congress(I) party while wiping adverse stories off its pages have never clicked as newspapers, despite the heavy doses of Central and state government advertisements.

But where the two electronic media, AIR and DD, are concerned, several other factors come into play in determining the newpapers attitude, irrespective of their ideological proclivity. Most newspapers have been antagonistic to AIR and DD, firstly because they are government-owned and government-run media. The ruling party and its leaders, who are always in top positions in the goverment, have invariably exploited their hold on the electronic media. This is true of all parties, although the Congress(I), which has been in power for 43 of the nearly 47 years for which India has been a free nation, has been much more guilty of misuse and blatant in its approach.

This naturally evokes sharp public criticism and even anger and most of the papers endeavour to reflect it. But the press attitude to the broadcast media is governed by not only the excesses committed by the party in power but by some other factors—rivalry, the attitude of the staffers in the English dailies many of whom are great admirers of the winds blowing in from the west, the changing mores in the print media, and, last but not the least, by their self-interest specially their involvement, present and potential, in the vastly expanding TV business.

The rivalry has grown with the time. Radio has generally been first with the news and despite the shackles of political and bureaucratic constraints under which it has to operate the evening bulletins have generally managed to steal the thunder of the morning papers, in terms of hard news, as opposed to speculative stories and scandals. The same goes for DD after it began to overtake the older medium and even put it in shade.

That the government media could do so is a measure of the devoted, professional work of the news personnel in both media, even as their failure to rise to the occasion several times has to be attributed as much to their failure to function as newsmen as to the official constraints. Newspapers are not entirely free of constraints, apart from the business interests of the proprietors, but that is a different story and we shall not enter that area.

AIR went commercial in 1967 and DD in 1976 and have gradually taken away a sizeable share of the total advertising cake in India. It was never large enough but lately it has grown, what with the growth of the economy and the large presence of the multinationals who became the biggest users of the media.

Even in DD alone[1], four of the top five advertisers in 1992, accounting for 21 per cent of the total ad revenue, were multinationals — Hindustan Lever, Procter and Gamble, Nestle' and Colgate, with only Godrej, coming third among them. (HL was, interestingly, more than four times larger than Goderj in spending.)

The share of DD[2] has grown over the years in inverse proportion to the decline in the share of the print media as the following figures would show.

MEDIA SPEND SHARE

	Press	*Television*	*Radio*	*Cinema*	*Outdoor*
1985	75	12	4	3	6
1992	67	20	2.5	0.5	10

(Figures in percentage)

Out of the TV revenue, video/cable had a one per cent share and Star took away another one per cent, leaving DD with 18 per cent of the total TV revenue from ads. Along with the 2.5 per cent of the radio going almost entirely to AIR the share of the government media has become a sizable 20.5 per cent while that of the press decline from 75 to 67 per cent.

That the press has become less of a favoured medium is also evident from a study made on behalf of the well organised Indian Newspapers Society, INS "Impact of TV and Video on Press", generally ignored by the print media. The study was conducted by Mediasearch, a division of Marketing and Research Group, Bombay. The study was probably carried out for the perod 1977-87, after which, if anything, TV has come up even in a bigger way.

The study arrived at the conclusion that most advertisers feel that TV is the ideal medium irrespective of the target group and scores over the press in reach as well as cost-efficiency. In fact, manufacturers of fast moving consumer goods rate it significantly better than the press on both counts. The impact of the audio-visual message is seen greater. The press, particularly the English language press, will continue to have some uses but only a later study would show how the press has withstood the juggernaut of TV. Video, according to the study, is not seen as a major source of competition. Cable is also perceived to be a medium with a potential only.

The point about rivalry need not be laboured further. In fact, the big newspapers which have been trying to acquire a niche for themselves in the growing TV sphere recognise the great strength and potential of TV. Otherwise they would not have queued hp at 4 Tolstoy Marg even while they invoked the authority of the courts. (See chapter 11).

The adversary role has become somewhat complicated because the TV medium has been viewed as both a rival and a fertitle, happy hunting ground for all media magnates including the newspaper owners (and why not). One can't help viewing the favourite TV channel in one's spare hours even if you are a tycoon or a mere reporter but few newspapers can hope to entertain you. Now rivalary reaches the point of envy and you can let yourself go if you have a newspaper at your disposal. That brings us to the second point of the gushing admiration which some of the English mediamen showed (and several are still showing) for Star, MTV and even Zee.

We have shown that the appeal of Star and its MTV channel has been primarily to the English speaking homes and Star came up at a time when DD's contribution in terms of entertainment had somewhat declined. After the emergence of DD Metro and the revamping done by the national network a lot more has been offered by way of entertainment and even pop music is being telecast on both the entertainment and primary channels for a considerable time. There are now more English programmes and English films on both these channels and the craze for Star, a completley foreign channel, has considerably diminished.

The approach of the English speaking reporters and writers in the dailies and weeklies, some of whom are also drawn from the advertising agencies or migrate to work for them, created a kind of simulated Star explosion in these papers in 1992. That was the time, as we have seen, when the I and B minister and his officers spoke bitterly of the forgein invasion and took a number of steps to open DD to the private producers and make it an effective competing medium.

These mediamen fell for the Star programmes and made their personal reactions the basis of highly exaggerated reports of the spread of Star and its different channels. Star was no doubt making inroads but the extent was blown up by the subjective reactions of the media. At a time when Star viewing was confined to only three or four per cent of the urban TV homes the English media made a big hulabaloo about the foreign broadcasts because many of the writers and reporters were themselves viewing these channels and their children or the young people whom they knew were its fans. They now spoke of an MTV generation.

Their sense of partriotism was warped beacuse while in some other stories they attacked politicians or others for being "anti-Indian" they became unpaid (hopefully) publicists of Star. To defend their action they even said the foreign media were not vulgar, the display of sex and violence was more in the Hindi or Tamil, Telugu films and the viewers would not become corrupted by the fixation with foreign channels.

The Hindi films have always been looking out for material from foreign films which they could copy in terms of the story, scenes and sequences, and in music. Now the film people also watched the MTV and other Star channels and lost no time in reproducing the sex and violence scenes in the Hindi movies, in song and dance sequences and thus making the films more sexy.

In the earlier days, people like Gulzar borrowed themes from Japanese and other foreign movies for memorable films like *Koshis*. Now nobody was bothered about good films as the producers fell over one another in reproducing the pop songs, rap tunes and scenes of the MTV. If ever there was an MTV generation it was in the films. Nobody has seen in real life young boys and girls teaming up and singing rap or dancing in groups but you can see them in the Hindi movies so that the English media can write of an MTV generation.

From this distorted view, there was only a step to trenchant criticism of DD for not showing such programmes not in so many words but indirectly attacking it for churning out boring programmes, losing its audience and so on. One editor of a magazine of TV and video even said "DD was collapsing". Rupert Murdoch became a celebrity and his visit to India was heralded in front page stories and editorials[3].

The proverbial red carpet was rolled out by the print media when he finally arrived on Feb. 7, 1994. A photo session was held at his home and one of the leading papers even published a picture or two out of this session, one leading daily showing Murdoch looking quizically at his wife. His 49.9 per cent investment in Zee was seen as a great event, ignoring the foreign control and intrusion it signified. Obviously the news media now in the TV business were curious if this could mean money for private producers (like the newspapers themselves). As the threat from the foreign print media was developing there was a softening of this hostile attitude in the English press towards DD but some even then could not see that Murdoch acquring Zee was the thin end of the foreign media wedge, whether in the print of TV media.

The newspapers almost singlehandedly flayed DD during the Hero Cup controversy (dealt with in detail in the next chapter) and openly sided with the Trans-World International which was sponsored by the Board for Control of Cricket in India (BCCI). Even a staid newspaper like the *Hindustan Times* of Delhi (and Patna), exulted[4] that TWI had been able to telecast its programmes by uplinking them from Indian soil thus DD's monopoly had been broken. That this monopoly must be broken cannot be disputed but should a commercial multinational company, only interested in making money for its owenrs, become instrumental in breaking this monopoly ? The so-called breaking of the monopoly was only a one-time operation in any case.

The *Hindustan Times* invited Indian companies to "prise open the door that the courts have unlocked". If the door has been unlocked you do not have to prise it open. The courts gave only a "One-time" permission to the foreign company to uplink its signal.

On can only say that the Indian media, specially the English newspapers, are far from being fair and objective in writing and reporting on TV. That they are themselves actual or potential TV businessmen only colours the reporting and writing as in the examples we have quoted. Everything that a newspaper reports or writes need not be taken as gospel truth but on TV and in their evaluation of DD their reports have to be taken with a large pinch of (multinational or other) salt.

The changing mores also affect newspaper coverage. In the old days, films were as popular and as influential or uninfluential as now, but they hardly ever figured in the newspapers exept on the film page, mainly the weekly reviews of the new film releases. Now the films are more often on the first page, on the film page and on any other page.

Pretty girls working as models are written about more than sporting heroes and the ad agencies which were formerly known only to the advertisement managers are now scoured for stories by the reporters (some of them also hoping to migrate to them). Film personalities are the epitome of glamour and their deeds and misdeeds are lapped up by the readers. Earlier they were confined to the films magazines (called mags) but now the dailies are vying with the film mags.

In fact several of the newspapers are in a kind of unstated competition with the films in projecting vulgarity which deadens your taste and sensitivity. If the producer of *Khalnayak* titillated you with his *Choli Ke Peechhe* number these newspapers applauded it and held it up as a sign of liberation. Indian population growth may not show signs of coming down, but the print media must carry any number of stories about a small-time actress in passionate embrace with a man selling a brand of condom. Condoms are essential not only to prevent further population growth but also to arrest the spread of aids. There are several condoms in the market and they are selling without such gimmicks.

The ad agencies are utterly amoral, although they have great pretensions to being modern and concerned about the nation and the citizens. But they can show a pretty young woman in such poses and if they find the prestigious news media hailing their sale gambit they are more than justified if they look upon themselves as leaders of society.

When these papers wrote disapprovingly of the "sexy" songs of some films one was thoroughly amused. Were they really concerned about our morals or were they catering to the kind of clientele which would, relish such writings, embellished with colour photographs if possible.

One of the writers on this theme bemoaned that the "sexy" songes were vulgar, but she found the MTV was not. So the wealthy classs can watch MTV in their homes and swing all night but if the groundlings of the cinema world, who have no access to a TV set and for whom the cinema is the only means of entertainment, watch "sexy" films they are liable to be corrupted. The poor chaps who spend their hard-earned money on the cinema so that Messers Subhash Ghai, Govinda, Nadeem-Shravan and their ilk may be in business must not get to see what the MTV generation sees everyday.

If you are applauding the *Choli Ke Peechhe* song and cavilling at the "sexy" songes you are making a distinction without a difference. One is vulgar in its words and their evocation and the other both in its words and the gestures it portrays. Some of the cinema people are as little concerned about the morals as many of the newspaperpetrons. If one piece goes down with the public more of the same is in order, according to them. The writers in the news media argue there is nothing vulgar about the condom ad, about the kissing scenes, about *Choli Ke Peechhe* because they portray reality. Can bedroom secnes also be portrayes now ? What can be more real than a bedroom scence? Applaud it and a producer or two would come out with it too. If the Censors cavil, bang the censors. Meanwhile your circulation goes up.

It is this level at which several of the print media operate and if DD is 'prudish' they lambast it remorselessly. DD, to make sure, has not banned *Choli Ke Peechhe* and even the sexy songs were seen, on the Metro for some time, until the censors, on appeal, put the scissors to a part of the song and the programme producers thought it prudent to behave.

Finally we have to take not of a kind of writings in the print media which are actuated by some peculiar considerations. That is, writings and reports which are intended to project the private interests of some producers in the garb or laying down a general principle.

If a producer has a grievance against DD hiking up the rates for film-based progammes shown on its Metro channel he can find a writer to voice his complaint. That is perfectly all right but should not the writer also ask DD about its point of view. The *Times of India* phoned Chief Election Commissioner T.N. Seshan at 10.30 one night to ask him about the suspension of a police sub-inspector attached to him for security duty but did not bother to find out the DD point of view when flaying DD for raising the rates of Superhit Muqabla, which has made tons of money, before and after the rates were raised.[5]

Likewise, the same paper and writer espoused the cause of another producer[6] of a serial ignoring the same principle (of presenting both points of view). That DD had thought of providing attractions of more or less the same level in DD1 and DD2 and this was the purpose of a new serial on each of its two channels televised simultaneously was ignored in projecting the private interests of the producer of one of the serials.

If the second serial, first shown on Metro, was to be telecast on the primary later, as was made clear in the programme announcements, what was so wrong with two new serials being put on the air simultaneously on two channels ? Competittion is now the soul of the heightened entertainment contents of the DD programmes. But if a favourite producer feels shaky about the success of his venture you can always use your newspaper column to voice his (commercial) grievances without giving DD a chance to present its point of view.

13

Hero Cup Controversy

A few years ago, in 1987, India staged the world Cup of Cricket which was won by India four years earlier in England. It was actually a joint enterprise of the Indian subcontinent. While a few matches were played in Pakistan, the majority of matches were staged in India including the final between Australia and England at Calcutta's Eden Gardens. All the matches in India were televised live by DD on an exclusive basis and relayed not only by the countries concerned but also by several others.

The world TV media thus took the signal from DD and were satisfied with the quality of the coverage. Some like the BBC, which relayed many of the matches for its home viewers in England, conveyed their pleasure to DD.

There was a dispute over payment for the TV rights between DD and the Board for Control of Cricket in India, BCCI, which had jointly staged the World Cup, also called the Reliance Cup, with its counterpart in Pakistan. The matter was, however, sorted out well in time. The then BCCI president N.K.P. Salve was a minister in the Rajiv Gandhi government in India which perhaps facilitated the agreement.

At a time when radio owners were few and far between crowds used to gather outside shops and restaurants in the bazaars of India, to listen to the exhilerating commentary of the late A.F.S. (Bobby) Talyarkhan. When the TV medium arrived DD televised live matches at home and relayed many others from abroad in which India was involved. The TV coverage of the World Cup won by India in 1983 was watched by some millions in this country as DD relayed it from the BBC. If cricket has become a household affair and names like Kapil Dev, Sunil Gavaskar, Mohammad Azharuddin and Sachin Tendulkar are on many lips DD has made a significant contribution to it.

DD's coverage of the Ninth Asian Games in Delhi in 1982 was another memorable occasion. Many other sporting events of national significance were regularly covered. Whether it was Durand football in Delhi, Rover's Cup in Bombay, IFA Shield in Calcutta, or the Agha Khan, Beighton Cup, KD Singh Babu Tournaments of hockey, or even kabbadi and other indigenous games DD's cameras would be there with its commentators, many of whom, alas, did not enhance our enjoyment of the game and had better not be heard. There was considerable amateurism but also much professionalism in the coverage and DD came to be associated with live coverage of sports in general.

It was, therefore, a shock that the Cricket Association of Bengal, CAB, a member of the BCCI, sought it fit to hand over the live coverage of the five nation Hero Cup matches in November 1993 to a multinational company, the Trans-World International TWI, ignoring the claims of the national network and ignored the laws of the land which required compliance with the Indian Telegraph Act, 1885, if a signal is to be uplinked.

The issue came before the public only when the tournament was only a few days away. Until then the print media had not bothered whether the matches would be seen in India, the land where the tournament was being staged. In fact, the successful Sri Lanka tour of the Indian Cricket team in June—August 1993, had not been covered by DD but not a word had been said by the daily press. It was an unpardonable lapse on the part of DD.

In the controversy that ensued, the print media were almost entirely on the side of CAB and its foreign contracted TV company, TWI. As soon as the controversy erupted the media accused DD of not negotiating a proper coverage deal with the CAB well in advance. This was totally contrary to facts and what are the facts?

On March 18, 1993, the Bengal cricket body informed DD that it was organising a six nation one-day international tournament to mark its diamond jubilee. It asked[1] the national network to make its offer on the basis of (*a*) DD creating the "host broadcaster signal" and also undertake live telecast of all matches; or (*b*) DD purchasing the rights from any other party which may create the signal. In either case, the CAB said, the foreign TV rights would be with it.

The DD reply was forthcoming in three days. It asked the CAB what it expected by way of rights fee payment from DD exclusively for its Indian coverage without the Star TV getting the rights. Star was pinpointed because it was (and still is) beaming its signal to India *via* the satellite.

The CAB reply was also prompt. It told DD that the Indian network could create the host broadcaster signal and have the exclusive right to it in India on a payment of 800,000 American dollars. The CAB would sell the worldwide rights excluding India and Star.

Normally, government organisations take their own time, what with the Finance ministry and other agencies having to be consulted, but DD replied in two weeks saying it would buy these rights and create the host broadcaster signal and pay the

CAB Rs. one crore (about $330,000). It was stressed that as the national network it should get the right to create the signal and telecast all the matches for the Indian viewers.

Although the CAB had planned an ambitious six-nation tournament, Pakistan frustrated its efforts by withdrawing at the last moment after first accepting its invitation. The Hero Cup thus became a five-nation affair—West Indies, South Africa, Zimbabwe, Sri Lanka and the host nation , India.

On May 4, DD again reminded the Bengal cricket body of its offer of paying Rs. one crore and sought the latter's decision. This was important because DD had to organise workshops for its camera crew and other staff to help them to upgrade and update their skills in the next few months. The CAB now took the stand that it wished to sell/allot the worldwide TV rights to a single party and asked the TV network to quote on the basis of

(*a*) outright purchase of TV rights; and

(*b*) purchase of these rights on a sharing basis.

DD reiterated its offer on May 14. What followed was astounding.

Not only the ground had now been shifted but to its utter horror DD learnt, in a couple of weeks, that the rights had indeed been sold to a multinational, the TWI. It was obvious that the CAB was looking at the TV coverage from the point of view of making the maximum money out of the tournament which was a perfectly legitimate object. But in the process it completely ignored the vast Indian audience of DD and cared little what happened to the national network. The contract was entered into with the World Production Establishment, WPE, which handled the affairs of TWI, a London based company, in this regard.

Not suprisingly, DD informed the CAB in June that it would not be able to cover any of the Hero Cup matches since it was being made to take the signal from a foreign company for matches played in India. When a Hong Kong based company, a marketing organisation, IMG possibly action for WPE, asked DD about the purchase of the rights held by WPE, DD informed the HK middleman that it was not covering the matches and was not interested in buying the rights.

The CAB thus knew, both from the direct communication from DD and from the HK middleman who must have apprised it of how DD had reacted, that the Indian national network was not going to play second fiddle to a multinational chosen by the cricket body. But the Cricket Association just took no notice of DD for four long months form June.

Apparently, having struck what it considered a big deal contract the CAB was not bothered, then at least, about what would happen to the vast Indian audience. As we have seen in earlier chapters, Star had at best a 7.278 million household audience who were able to view Star programmes, *courtesy* the cable. Even if the Star claim is taken at face value, what would happen to the remaining 33 million TV homes, served only by DD. Out of some 40.337 million TV sets in India at the end of 1993, these vast majority of viewers would have been totally deprived of the pleasure of watching live the action in the Hero Cup.

"What do I care ? I am happy with the foreign money coming to me and surely the Indian print media would be flaying the national network once they knew that DD was not covering the matches ?" could well describe the mental state of the cricket body at that time.

Its parent body, BCCI, had an old score to settle with DD for not paying it enough during the Reliance Cup matches in 1987 and later when interesting cricket events, staged under its patronage, were televised by the national network. There is no dispute that the cricket body must get adequate recompense for such coverages from DD. But that issue has to be settled as between two Indian organistaions, not by seeking the intervention of a multinational and ask DD to go to ......, go to the multinational and pay it in foreign exchange for the pleasure of covering matches played on Indian soil. If DD's offer of Rs. one crore was too little you could ask for more and use the same print media and other influence at your disposal to squeeze more out of it.

Cross commercialism and an attitude of "let the Indian viewer go to hell" was the essence of the cricket body's approach. In Indian history, examples are not lacking of one group striking a deal with a foreigner to spite the other indigenous group. You have every right to ask for and get more but to smuggle in a foreigner to help you fight DD is not a shining exmple of patriotism.

Partly, of course, the CAB's attitude was governed by what happened early in 1993 when the England test team toured India. Possibly under the powerful influence of the then BCCI chief, Madhavrao Scindia, who was also a cabinet minister is the Narasimha Rao government in charge of Tourism and Civil Aviation, (he resigned subsequently following an air crash) DD was pressured to accept the position of allowing a foreign company, the same TWI, to become the host signal generator. DD was put to the shameful state of paying for the signal on Indian soil while the TWI gloated over it. There were, of course, a set of different commentators on the DD signal which most Indians saw while the Star-crazy limited audience saw it on the Prime Sports channel (of Star), with the help of the local cable people. The Star team of commentators were mostly British or Australian, with Sunil Gavaskar the sole Indian.

Usually, Star has only British or Australian commentators, as was the case in the live coverage of the football World Cup qualifying matches among Asian nations played in the Gulf. Certainaly Asia does not lack good football commentators but Star is a western-dominated outfit which many in India do not realise. It plugs now and again some golf tournament or American football and British or Australian Rugby, games which are not terribly popular in this country. This should be enough to show the partisans of Star that their channel has doubtfull credentials in sports also.

What the Scindia pressure had done in January-March 1993 was presumably expected to be done by the CAB, although Scindia was no longer the boss of the BCCI nor a member of the Rao government. Those who expected the India-England series to become a precedent for all time were disappointed because DD, which to its shame had played second fiddle to Star then, was no longer prepared to remain in the back seat. There is no law that once a wrong deed is done under arm-twisting it must always be done, although some of the Indian print media did not shrink from quoting the precedent. It is a mystory why they did not recall the 1987 Reliance Cup Coverage.

The newspapers failed to realise that what was happening to DD could well happen to them. Now the danger of foreign print media coming into India has become more patent but even at that time, October-November 1993, such a possibility could not have been ruled out. In that event if one of the foreign newspapers in India were to acquire the sole rights to the coverage of an Indian event, not an imaginary situation, how will the dailies who were running down DD react? Will they not try to tear to pieces the organisers, whether the Indian government or some international agency, for placing the Indian media at a disadvantage ?

Coming back to the narration of events, after DD informed it in June 1993 that it would not cover the Hero Cup matches since it was being denied the host broadcaster status the CAB slept over the matter for four long months. Only three weeks before the tournament was to get under way, on October 18 it woke up to the possibility that the vast majority of Indians would not be able to see the matches on their TV sets, except those who were Star crazy and submitted a new proposal to DD.

The CAB told the national network that it should share the matches with TWI, nine matches being covered by each. The cricket body also wanted four minutes of free commercial time which it proposed to sell to the advertisers or their agents. The DD reaction came on October 27 when it told the CAB that it was not prepared to take the signal from a foreign agency. It also pointed out to the CAB that the latter was trying to make money at the cost of DD.

Some more exchanges took place between the two in the next few days but no agreement could be arrived at. Interestingly, in the subsequent matter in the courts the CAB made in issue of the sanctity of its contract with the TWI (or the WPE, its parent body) but in making an offer to DD in the end of October it must have been aware that it could have resuulted in the contract being treated as a piece of paper or materially modified.

By November 8, the CAB went to court, first with a writ petition before a single judge of the Calcutta High Court. After some legal arguments and orders by the Judge the matter came up before a division bench of two judges of the same high court on a counter writ by DD. The court passed orders that DD and AIR should cover the matches live for Indian viewers and TWI for the outside world but facilities should be provided to TWI subject to "reasonable restrictions."

This was perhaps interpreted by the DOT (Department of Telecommunications) as enabling it to grant the permission to TWI to transmit the coverage through the Videsh Sanchar Nigam, the government corporation for external communication (earlier known as the Overseas Communication Service), subject to DD generating the signal and TWI not upliking it direct.

The court also directed the CAB to pay Rs. 5 lakhs to DD per match telecast by it and said the ad revenue realised by DD during the match telecast be held in a separate account until further orders. The matter went to the Supreme Court which heard a petition of the CAB at a late night sitting at the residence of one of the two judges, Mr. Justice J.S. Verma and Mr. Justice P.B. Savant, on November 15. The petition challenged the DOT order that the facilities of the Videsh Sanchar Nigam must be used and the DD signal be taken by TWI. This order was set aside by the two Supreme Court judges.

A PTI report published by the *Times of India*, Delhi, on November 17, headlined "TWI told to focus cameras only on field" said, in parts :

"NEW DELHI, November 16, (PTI) The Supreme Court has permitted Transworld International to generate their own signal for telecasting the ongoing five-nation Hero Cup Cricket tournament but with the condition that they focus their cameras only on the ground as directed by the Home Ministry.

"The order was passed late last night by a division bench comprising Justice J.S. Verma and Justice P.B. Savant staying the order of the Telecommunication secretary permitting TWI to use the signal from Doordarshan.

"The order was passed on a petition by the Cricket Association of Bengal (CAB) challenging the order of the Communications Secretary, T.N. Vittal, yesterday".

Obviously this was only a one-time order although the print media held it up as a victory for the cricket body and a "jolt" to DD. In fact, the DOT order showed the entire government was involved and not just DD. From November 15, DD covered all the matches including the two semi-finals and the final at Calcutta as India emerged a convincing winner. The TWI cameras were also there and given generally a better position by the cricket authorities which ignored the fact that DD would always be there and TWI would pack off to London or Hong Kong after the tournament was over. When the Sri Lanka cricket team visited India in January-February 1994, the cricket people quietly let DD cover the matches and the TWI was not interested, although some newspapers wanted to create a controversy over the coverage. They did not succeed. The court matters had not come to a close, however, even by February 1994 (when this was written) and some residual issues would perhaps come up later unless both sides see reason and good sense prevails.

In the circumstances then prevailing and the fact that the Hero Cup tournament had already begun the courts took the view that they did. The government did not take a rigid attitude although it said the law was on its side and the uplinking facility given to TWI to transmit its signal direct from India (to be flashed back by Star for its Indian lovers) was objected to by many.

A press release issued by the government's Press Information Bureau on December 3, 1993, said in parts :

New Delhi, *Agrahayana 12, 1915*
December 3, 1993

"Members of Parliament expressed serious concern over the permission given to a foreign company to set up an earth station and send out signals directly from the country in contravention of the existing statutes. At a meeting of the Consultative Committee attached to the Ministry of Information and Broadcasting here today, the members said that it impignes on the sovereignty of the nation and raises serious security and other issues".

The press release was titled : "MPS" CONCERN OVER THE UPLINKING BY A FOREIGN COMPANY

I & B CONSULTATIVE COMMITTEE MEETS"

During the Hero Cup controversy the official point of view was expressed by a spokesman. *The Times of India* reported, this in parts, on November 12, under the heading "CAB row takes dramatic turn":

"A senior government Spokesman here charged TWI of (should have been 'with') violating the laws of the land in trying to telecast the Hero Cup. He wondered if the Cricket Association, the organisers of the Hero Cup, had done the right thing by entering into an agreement with a foreign agency when the government's policy was not to allow any private network to use uplinking facilities from India to transmit a programme outside.

"The spokesman said there was no question of giving uplinking facilities from India to a foreign company. He, however, admitted that allowing TWI to telecast the India-England series earlier this year was a mistake and the government does not want to compound it.

"He said that applications of a number of foreign networks, including CNN and Asianet (not really foreign) seeking uplinking facilities were pending with the government. Since it involved a major policy decision, even domestic networks were not allowed the facility.

The question of allowing foreign networks to unload tons of equipment, including mobile earth stations, could create security problems as it was physically impossible to cheek everything. Moreover, once the network was in there was no control on what it could shoot.

"The spokesman reiterated that just as in every country, Doordarshan and Akashvani should also get the status they deserve as host broadcasters. In fact , in the case of the Hero Cup, Doordarshan offer was very reasonable but the organisers refused to negotiate with it. Doordarshan had asked CAB to pay Rs. 5 lakhs for production and telecast fees and take 15 per cent of the time slots it sells. The terms were same for the Reliance Cup five years ago. (should be six years).

"Sources in the (I and B) ministry pointed out that Akashvani had to pay broadcasting fees to the Srilankan Broadcasting Corporation for airing the running commentary in the recent India-Sri Lanka cricket series in the island nation.

"As an example they also cited (the) Seoul Asian games in 1986 when the Korean Broadcasting Corporation as the host broadcaster laid down the ground rules for foreign networks who had no choice but to accept them. Similarly the rights of video and audio signals should rest with Doordarshan.

"They stated that it was misleading to claim that the country was earning foreign exchange through TWI. If Doordarshan had been given the rights it also would have earned foreign exchange. In the case of Doordarshan the money would have gone into the Central revenue while CAB benefitted by selling the rights. Doordarshan's interest is to maximise state revenue, they claimed ".

The government's case could not have been put across with more telling arguments. But even at that stage DD could not come out, for reasons best known to it, with the long correspondence that had gone on with the CAB, which we have referred to earlier in this chapter. That would have convinced everyone that DD had been trying to impress on the CAB that the national network was the host broadcaster and its status must be recognised and the terms offered by it were reasonable.[2]

The CAB is a wealthy organisation like the BCCI, its national body, which is also in a position to ask other affiliate bodies to issue a large number of free passes for major matches to the print media, not only for the poor cricket correspondents and the photographers but for the editors and proprietors and their wives. So the CAB had an edge over DD and could brief the press and entertain the writers and reporters.

But the press is basically interested in facts and information (should, at least, be) and the truth of DD's efforts to make the CAB see reason should have been brought out. DD has always been poor in its PR and even this late explanation by the government spokesman, reproduced above, was not carried in extenso by the other media. Even the paper from which we have quoted buried this part in the more spicy controversial aspect as signified by its heading "CAB row takes dramatic turn". The heading gives no clue to the spokesman's clarifications.

The spokesman's briefing of the media, however, helped to focus on the host boradcaster principle and the law of the land which some newspapers called "archaic". Archaic or no, the law is law for everybody, inculding a multinational like the British-Hong Kongish TWI.

There was much sensation and the press had a jolly good time reporting the seizing of the TWI equipment (later released on court orders), the police in Bangalore not allowing the much favoured TWI to use its cameras and other equipment, the Bombay Cricket Club of India, in control of the Brabourne stadium where the South Affica-West Indies match was played, not permitting DD on some pretext to instal its cameras in time for the coverage, and developments like that. DD's strong case (in fact, the government's) was not given even a semblance of coverage. DD must shoulder the responsibility for it. Some brave attempts were made to use the DD news to present this point of view at the last moment and an innocent editor was penalised when some DD statement was not carried by the news bulletins. The press, in the meantime, was pillorying DD but neither the network not the PR agencies of government were able to counter it.

About the print media (meaning again the English dailies) the less said the better. The fundamental principle of journalism that facts must be pressented first and treated as sacred, with comments to follow, was ignored. The official spokesman's clarifications, as we have seen earlier, were not properly and adequately covered and some even ignored them altogether. No paper tried to find out what the DD point of view was and the much vaunted investigative reporting was not in evidence at all because the fact that DD had been at it for nine long months and was denied the host broadcaster status by the CAB was never brought to light.

Some of the arguments against DD were just laughable. Several sports writers argued that TWI coverage was better then DD's and the deal should, therefore, go through. While this is factually wrong, as DD had done a commendable job in covering the Reliance Cup, should one go over to a foreign agency simply because it is presumed to be better then your domestic one. In that event, would the news media agree to the *Times* of

London coming out in Delhi and Bombay when it can sweep the prestigious media off their feet? The way the sports writers and some others plumped for the CAB it looked as through the days of good journalism were over.

14

Rivalry Overcome But Consequences Remain

If 1993 began for the Indian TV network on an uncertain and somewhat unsteady note the bold and thougtful changes effected during the year resulted in a much more cheerful mood at the start of 1994. DD's depth and reach in the TV homes in India was never in doubt and whatever the English media said the vast audiences stayed with DD, as we have seen.

But what the network did in 1993 added up to a new dimension in Indian broadcating—the creation of the Metro Entertainment channel and its phenomenal success, the creation of the other satellite channels and their revamping at the end of the year, the heroic Hero Cup coverage despite the cricket bodies' anxiety to make more money and bring in foreign agencies for the purpose at DD's cost and all that. Above all, entertainment and the needs of the viewer were placed on a high pedestal and the importance of competition was acknowleded in a peculiar way. A dynamic, new approach and readiness to face competition were in evidenc

We have reproduced as an appendix the result of a viewer opinion survey on the major programmes of the primary channel of DD now called DD1, and the Metro, or DD2, conducted by DD's audience research set-up and reported briefly in the news media. This would show the high receptivity of the programmes. Actually, the primary channal programmes have a high rating. Even the cultural information programme, *Surabhi*, which has done more than 100 episodes, has a remarkable level of popular following, 51 per cent in the non-Metro areas and 14 in the Metros.

That means that despite the rival attractions of absorbing serials and other programmes on the Metro channel, one in seven viewer households in the metropolitan cities turned to the primary channel. Notwithstanding the modest literacy and low educational attainments of many urban and rural viewers, if *Surabhi* can go on week after week without a single song or dance it means a deep involvement with culture among the ordinary Indians, something the film producers and the print media had better take note of.

The ratings for the two main news bulletins were fairly good. The Hindi bulletin naturally enjoyed a high audience as its language is understood by a much higher number of people than those who can understand English. The viewing of the Hindi bulletin was around 45 per cent and that of English was about 20. These figures relate to the period before the revamped newscasts which began on February 1, 1994, according to which the English newscast comes on the air only at 10 p.m. This, as we have seen, is somewhat too late for most Indians, particularly those in the northeast of India where the sun rises around five in the morning except for two months in winter. That is something DD will have to look into before long. India has only one standard time based on Allahabad city which is actually to the east of Delhi where DD bosses live.

The Sunday morning *Rangoli* programme of songs and dances from the Hindi movies had an abnormaly high rating of 77 per cent. That is a DD1 programme and this popularity level signifies that despite any rival attractions it has a very large body of viewers on a holiday. That figure was for the non-metro areas but even in the Metros 37 per cent viewers saw this programme.

The other serials at prime time of DD1 also enjoyed a high level of popularity, about 50 per cent or more. With more prestigious programmes in these slots coming in after the revamp, the primary channel viewers had several major attractions and to a great extent their grievances were removed.

That *Rangoli* had an exceptionally high rating of 77 per cent did not mean any decline in the popularity of *Chitrahaar* which is a DD innovation copied by others. Some in the print media wrongly headlined the story on the rating as "a drop" in *chitrahaar's* popularity but the facts speak otherwise. As many as 64 per cent of the audience in the non-Metro area watched this programme on Wednesdays and even 39 per cent of the Metro audience switched back to the primary channel to be able to see their favourite programme.

The popularity of DD's film pogrammes on the primary was also seen in the high ratings of the Saturday Hindi film in the early evening hours. Despite the day's film being an 'art' film, *Suraj Ka Satwan Ghoda* by Shyam Benegal, featuring none of the accepted stars of Bollywood except Amrish Puri who plays the villain's role, and without a single song or dance, the percentage of viewers was 65 in the non-Metro areas and 47 in the Metro cities. According to a leading English newspaper, at Zee TV one has to leave "one's chappals and art films at the door".[1]

The high audience for an art or non-commercial film shows again that people of this country are not sold on the kitsch that comes out of Bollywood in the name of box office hits. But art films must have a gripping story.

Unfortunately, there are still many people in this country who have no access to a TV set. With 40.33 million sets and an audience of five to ten people per set the total TV audience could not be more than 220 million going up to 440, leaving more than 50 per cent of India outside the purview of the TV medium. (The population now could be more than 900 million). If this large body of people also had access to TV they could be watching the entertaining programmes of the Metro or other channels and skipping a visit to a stuffy cinema. Then the films being shown in our cinemas would lose some of their shine and the Bombay film industry would be compelled to turn out more interesting and relevant films.

That DD made a big impact in 1993 cannot be denied. Even those in the media who were out to denigrate it and boost private channels linked to foreign satellite media and foreign channels, *via* the cable, had also something to think about. Not that the propaganda against DD in the English newspapers ceased but even they had to take note of the large following captured by DD's new programmes and channels among hitherto cable or Star and Zee-hooked viewers.

The Metro or Entertainment channel attracted more and more viewers as well as producers of note turned to it and those who had opted to go with it at the start remained so even after a year. Their faith in the new channel had been borne out by the big profits they made. The fact that the prime time now began early and ended late was itself an indication of the success of the channel.

By February 1994, when DD had done the revamping exercise, there were as many as three weekly programmes of an hour's duration. These were: the *Superhit Muqabla*, of top 10 hit songs of the Hindi movies, *Mirch Masala*, a programme of both film and non-film cultural events, and the *Great Maratha*, a pseudo historical serial on the times of the eighteenth century Maratha general Mahadji Scindia who held the north together when the Mughal empire was on its last legs and the East India Company of the British was making inroads.

The family serial, *Junoon* had done nearly a 100 opisodes at the rate of two per week, and was still telecast twice a week, and the comedy show, *Dekh Bhai Dekh* and *Jaban Sambhalke,* were going great guns after being on the air for the better part of the year 1993. Several more family serials and crime or detective serials were becoming household words and those like *Superhit Muqabla* were being copied by other channels. Even the two leading video news magazines had closed shop and come over to DD in evening slots on the Metro channel, the *Newstrack* of *India Today* on Mondays and the *Eyewitness* of the Hindustan Times Wednesdays. The newspapers with TV ambitions were looking for more and more time slots.

The channel offered Entertainment with a capital 'E' specially in the evening hours when most people watch TV. It also had a wide variety of entertainment, soaps, sitcom, semi-historicals, family dramas, detective serials, song and dance programmes, games shows, a show like *Manch Masala* with an accent on acting ability. there was a lot linked to the film world of Bombay but there was also a lot not so linked, although the influence of the feature films is so pervasive that a totally non-film entertainment programme is difficult to conceive. Even in programmes like *Manch Masala,* there were a number of film personalities like the incomparable compere Ravi Basvani and cine stars like Shabana Azmi and Utpal Dutt.

The English print media (and, in imitation, some of the papers in other Indian languages too) made much of the Rupert Murdoch visit to this country in February 1994 to study the Indian market for his media ventures. His Star had, of course, been in the field since August 1991 and in December 1993 he acquired 49.9 per cent cent of the shares of Zee which was even otherwise dependent on him because it was (and is) using a transponder sub-leased from Star.

Some of the English papers played up the visit because they that is, their proprietors hoped to win from him benefits for their TV ventures. The media baron was dined and wined or otherwise the red carpet was rolled out) by newspapers which had gone to court in the FCFS case against DD—*India Today,Times of India, Indian Express,* and *Hindustan Times.*

The Murdoch balloon was, however, punctured by one of the successful Indian TV producers, Amit Khanna, whose *Mirch Masala,* has done a year on the Metro channel and who is connected with *Mere Saath Chal* and *Zameen Aasman,* two other Metro programmes and also *Business.Baaten* Khanna said: "Murdoch is just another moneyed guy. Does he know anything about our media?"[2]. According to him, Murdoch's takeover of Star does not affect him at all. Not until Star is able to produce TV programmes that suit Indian requirements.

His observation about the relevance of Star's programmes to Indian viewers is a highly significant one. This is the point we have made in previous chapters. Notwithstanding all the advances of technology and the vast financial resources at the command of the media Moghuls of the west they would still not be able to make really appealing prorammes. That a certain section of Indians would be attracted by their prorammes is not in doubt (and even their requirements have to be borne in mind by DD and the Indian producers) but the bulk of the viewers are not touched by Star's English offerings of American serials.

The views of Amit Khanna or others producing programmes for DD's Metro channel and making good money for themselves cannot be discounted on the ground that they are biased in favour of DD. Their experience of dealing with DD and the year-long effort put in by them are of much importance in this context.

Harish Thawani of Nimbus,[3] another major TV producer (*Superhit Muqabla,* with Irfan Khan, and *Kismat,* with Ramesh Sippy) said the Murdoch takeover (of Star) was a challenge and an opportunity for Indian producers. DD would have to face the new challenge and in his view it was beginning to get things right.

Thawani was quoted as saying: "On February 22(1993) two jokers called Amit Khanna and Harish Tawani started four prorammes on the Metro channel when people were still wondering what this Metro stuff was. Eight months later this channel was a lesson in broadcasting history". According to him, the top five Metro shows had a viewership three times larger than zee's. "The top ten Indian TV Directors are making programmes for the Metro, not Zee".

Thawani also said that the producers needed a free hand to made DD work. "For it is DD which has trimendous reach as a terrestrial channel while Zee has the look of a terrestrial channel without the reach. A satellite channel is merely an add-on channel and can never be used as a primary channel one. If I were DD I would wipe Murdoch out. But I would also say that at this moment there is'nt a single producer who is not dreaming of a call from Murdoch".

That both Zee and Star had been pushed somewhat into shade by DD's efforts as 1994 began is thus undisputed. Not the English media alone were agog with excitement when Murdoch was in India (he visited Delhi and Bombay and that was all that he saw of India). The cable people of the national capital were more than enthusiastic and a group even invited him and his wife to inaugurate them, the Cable Association of India(CAT), a rival to the older one COFI, Cable operators Federation of India.

They perhaps were not fully aware of his plans to introduce pay TV. At present the cable operators have a jolly good time relaying Star (or any other satellite channel) at no cost to them. All that stuff is free for them and they lay it on to add to their major attraction, Hindi feature films (south Indian language films like Tamil, Telugu, Kannada and Malayalam in the four southern states).

The cable regulation bill is still hanging fire although when Murdoch went to see the BJP supreme L.K. Advani and told him he (Murdoch) would not let his own children see the MTV channel (obviously he thinks it is good for Indian adolescents of all ages), Advani seemed to have realised that the cable needed to be regulated. Better late than never.

When the cable bill was introduced in Parliament, his BJP MPs were the loudest in opposing it for the possible reason that free cable meant opportunities for the BJP tp propagate its point of view through the local channels, something which the government-owned and controlled DD was denying them. Now Advani looked as though he was convinced that unregulated cable was a danger to the nation, although again he blamed the I and B ministry (over which he once presided in the Morarji Desai government, 1977- 79) for lack of a broadcast policy.

Of course, DD has many ills and the government is guilty of many media sins but if it has now woken up and the chaotic cable situation is being brought into order what is the harm? Simply because this is being done by the Congress(I) party is no reason for ;the BJP to prevent the bill's passage.

The Murdoch visit, however, brought to surface a lobbyst of the media boss in New Delhi and one of the dailies hinted that he was influencing some MPs, including those of the ruling Congress(I), to ensure that roadblocks were put in the path of the bill's passage. That the government could not get it through the monsoon or even the winter session of Parliament in 1993 after its introduction in the Rajya Sabha in August that year, would lend some credence to this observation. This is a sinister development and shows how the foreigner was trying to manipulate our media to suit his financial interests. Those welcoming Murdoch with open arms could take note!

Interested people may read the *Times of India* of January 20, 1994 "Murdoch planning recce visit to India in Feb." (front page) but the following (uncontradicted) part of it may be reproduced here:

"Mr. Murdoch's company, News Corp., has retained the services of Amalgmated Consulting Unit (ACU) based in Connaught Place (in New Delhi) and headed by Mr Iqbal Chand Malhotra as consultants. According to Mr Malhotra : 'We have been consultants for News Corp for more than a year. While the exact relationship is confidential broadly speaking we provide News Corp. with advice on business strategy. We help them assess the market and identify sources of programming. We are not enaged in public relations or lobbying on their behelf.'

The newspaper failed to point out the existence of a fullfleded PR outfit serving Star, deliberately or out of ignorance (more likely the first, since a newsman would not like to antagonise a source of information). Not only such an agency exists but its key person is also mentioned as a media specialist. And why not ? If you are doing PR for Murdoch you must be a media specialist. Were not the caged birds in the house of the great poet Kalidasa known to recite Sanskrit verses composed by him? "With a fullfledged Star TV office almost next door to ACU (on the fifth floor of Ambadeep building in New Delhi's Kasturba Gandhi Marg, close to Connaught Place), it is not known what extra "business strategy" advice can be provided by the latter outfit, unless, of course, the former is headed towards redundancy.

"REMITTANCES : In the latter half of last year ACU received at least $125,000 in legal foreign exchange remittances for services rendered to its Star client. While much of this must have been surely payment for business strategy advice, what is curious is the payment of around Rs. 6 lakhs which ACU itself made to Mr Rohit Bal Vohra, who is associated with the Congress party and is a familiar figure to Parliamentarians cutting across party lines. When asked whether he had received payment from ACU, Mr Vohra chose not to comment".

The newspaper was, however, wrong in its implication that the cable bill had been delayed by its reference to the parliamentary committee when it said :

"With or without a little help from Mr Murdoch's well—wishers, the Cable Television Network (Regulation) Bill of 1993 was eventually referred to a parliamentary committee for review following suggestions by opposition members in Parliament last August").

As we saw in a previous chapter the committee, actually the Standing Committee on Communications, had returned the bill to the presiding officers ot the two houses on August 25, in just three weeks after it was first introduced in the upper house, on August 3. Nothing could have been quicker and more of a slap on the face of any lobbyist, ACU, Star or any PR agency working for it (See Appendices for Standing Committee's Report.)

In any case, Murdosh played it cool while in India and allowed the newspapers to build him up as someone who has already become a star in the Indian TV World. How limited is the reach and appeal of Star and its various channels and how DD has faced the challenge with much success has been thoroughly analysed in previous chapters.

If any newspaper is so ignorant as to call him an Australian, one can only say that a fourth of the Narasimha Rao cabinet is Pakistani, because some of his ministers were born in Pakistan or had their ancestral homes in that country.

The cable people hung to his coattails because they are looking for support at a time when they feel that their existence is threatened by the cable regulation bill, DD's new role and other developments. They are a small industry, a typical cottage industry, having to pay *hafta* to the local police and at the mercy of the feature film cassette distributors who make the latest Hindi movies available to them.

The movies constitute the mainstay of their fare and the public craze for the films make their existence possible and lucrative. Some misinformed writers have tried to read into the cable prorammes proof of a TV identity, and a medium bringing programmes of relevance to the viewers. Yes, they do it in an amateurish fashion making these local prorammes even worse than what DD doles out.

Make no mistake, the cable business is vitally and inextricably linked to film business and secondly to the satellite channels which the operators lay on for their subscribers as an added attraction in most cases. The Cable people are so subscriber-dependent that some of them relay even Pakistan for such of their clients as want to see the Pakistan TV programmes. Among the latter are a few who are interested in the Pakistani plays which have come asthetic appeal, some want to see films from Pakistan, but many of those who ask the cable people to relay Pakistan for them are interested in it for reasons which are not praiseworthy.

The government must pursue the cable bill quickly and nail those who lay on Pakistan or such other channels which are openly anti-Indian. Star and its like are interested in the Indian market and in ruling the media waves of this country so that their rivals are kept out. All those interested in preserving the sanctity of the Indian skies must exert their weight in favour of the bill, with such amendments as may be required and excising those provisions which give the bureaucrats unlimited powers.

We have said it before that ours is the only country where the cable business is totally unregulated and is almost in a chaotic state. Any subscriber can see any foreign channel by making the right contacts with the cable operator serving him. The Murdoch visit would have served some purpose if the sinister moves to defeat the cable bill are themselves defeated and the need for regulation is now fully understood.

If Murdoch were to come into the cable business too, as some reports on his Indian journey indicated, that would be a minor disaster. One only wishes the government is alive to it. With all the chaos that prevails in the cable business, most of them are good Indians, many even careful not to air programmes unless they are cleared by some government agency like the Film Certification Board. For example, many cable people did not accept the propaganda videos of the political parties during the assembly elections in October-November 1993 unless these were certified fit for exhibition by the board.[4]

But there are others, whose aggregate number may be big enough and who are not that careful and would do anything for money. They would show uncensored feature films, blue films, or the uncensored parts, and other uncensored programmes or lay on Pakistan for some subscribers if that fetches them money. Those who attribute higher media motives to the cable business and try to read freedom of expression in their work are completely off the mark.

Of course, the cable business has as much right to exist as any other and now that a large body of people are found jobs by it the whole issue assumes a different complexion. But regulation to make the business more orderly is beyond dispute.

All this has been gone into here to make certain points about the cable industry clear. They are carrying on quite happily mainly because of the vast appeal of feature films. Cinemas may have closed and some in the major cities may have been converted into shopping arcades, the video vogue may have become quite widespread, but feature films and the films personalities are exercising a big sway on the mind of the Indian people. The stars are household names and although yesterday's matinee idols like Rajesh Khanna are now seeking shelter on the politician's lap it is mostly the politician who is seeking their company, at election time or otherwise.

Even a former film actor like Sanjay Khan is able to get fiftyfive MPs to support his application to DD for time on the main and Metro channels for a pseudo-historical serial of his, simply because the politicians know that men like Sanjay hold an appeal for the people and through them they can get popular support for themselves as *quid pro quo,* when the time comes. Sanjay is, in fact, an active campaigner for the Congress party in different elections. Such is the close linkage between the cinema people and the politicians who may be otherwise ignorant of many things but know the way their election bread is buttered.

What goes for the politician goes for the Indian film and TV audiences even more. A leading newspaper ones taunted Zee TV that its prorammes were mostly film-based, even the game shows were compered by film or ex-film personalities.[5] Some of the film people have branched out into TV serials, like Ramesh Sippy and even BR Chopra, and many film actors of yesterday are now permanent performers on the TV, like Navin Nischol, Parikshit Sahni and others. Some fine TV actors and actresses would not mind doing bit roles in films, because these for one thing bring much more money than the serials and for another their appearance in films enhances their appeal to the total audio-visual audience in India many of whom also watch TV serials.

Films have thus acquired an all-pervasive influence on the minds of the people and for that reason, while the cinema industry may have suffered considerably in terms of the declining theatre spectators, it has retained its hold through the serials, through the cable showing the latest and old feature films and DD1, DD Metro and to a much larger extent Zee leaning on films.

On DD, there are so many film and film-based programmes, like the feature films themselves almost every day, *Chitrahaar*, *Rangoli* and similar song and dance programmes like the highly successful *Superhit Muqabla* on Metro, the weak *Aamne Samne* programmes which is all about today's and yesterday's film people. Many of its serials are dominated by films whether you take into account producers or actors and actresses, and so on. No doubt, a whole new generation of fine actors and actresses has grown up outside the films, mainly through the TV, but frankly most of them would not mind being called up by a film producer to do even a bit role.

When DD launched its Metro channel early in 1993 and there were not many takers in the beginning it had to lean on the NFDC, National Film Development Corporation, a sister agency in Bombay connected with the film industry. Top performers of the art cinema, like the late Utpal Dutt and Smita Patil, and Naseeruddin Shah all migrated to the commercial cinema because there is more many there and many times more people would see you through these films.

As in the United States and other developed nations, in India too, cinemas may close but films remain. There is nothing inherently wrong in this close linkage between the film world and the TV world since entertainment is the business of both. And if films come, can the influence of films be far behind?

The unabashed commercialism of the Indian film industry leads it to portray, subject to the censors being bent to your will, what they think the audience would welcome and gulp down. If the lover boy image has lost some of its shine, there would be films of violence. Heroes like Amitabh Bachchan, a fine actor otherwise, rose to fill the gap. Men like Rajesh Khanna or today's heroes like Aamir Khan and Shah Rukh Khan cannot be imagined as "he men" and cannot be shown to be knocking out half a dozen tougs of whom the film industry seems to have an unlimited supply through its junior artist suppliers. So only lover boy stories for them or stories in which they kill the heroines they are earlier shown to have been courting, and the so-called action or violence-depicting films for actors like Jackie Shroff, now that Amitabh Bachchan has (temporarily) retired and does not mind appearing in public with a grey beard.

When Bachchan was at the zenith of his career he once justified violence in films with the remark, "We only use tomato sauce for blood in films". The *Times of India* which carried the interview failed to ask him whether the audiences also knew that it was tomato sauce and not real blood. The poor pitclass audiences which cry hoarse "maro, maro" (kill him) are not aware of the blood being tomato sauce. Of course, they know that the same villain will put in an appearance in the next film after being killed in the final act of the previous one. But when the film is on the big screen and a life-and-death fight is in progress they are only concerned with the villain and his goons being cut down by Amitabh or Shroff.

This is mentioned here because the influence of films is reaching our homes through TV medium which brings the violence-laden films (and the sexy ones) to us day after day. There is besides video in the homes which enables their owners to see the films, usually two or three in one session.

Many of the films, except a few ones which are comedies, show us half a dozen or more murders being committed by the villain and his gang until a Bachchan or Shroff puts paid to his depredations and the police are brought in towards the climax to keep the producer on the right side of the law and tell the audience that ultimately the law takes care of everyone.

Policemen and other law enforcement people are shown mostly as corrupt, brutal and also inefficient and the hero takes the law in his own hands, even when he is a cop, because otherwise he would not be able to flex his muscle. Even the courts are shown usually as doling out injustice, sending the innocent hero to the jail (sometimes upto the gallows, but then the hero is saved before he can be hanged) because without the hero being so sentenced the story would not proceed.

All this is written about in great style by film and other media journalists and writers in highly philosophical terms. An actor like Shah Rukh Khan who kills his heroines is lauded as the anti-hero *par excellence,* as though an actor could determine his own script.

The question of the influence of the media on people has been studied by researchers in this country and in many others. This has led to the conclusion that people do not necessarily copy the actions of the heroes and heroines and violence shown in films would not necessarily make people violent. But why portray violence at all, most of it irrelevant and unrealistic? Did not great producers of commercial cinema in an earlier age, like

Mahboob Khan, V. Shantaram, Guru Dutt and Bimal Roy and even today people like Hrishikesh Mukherjee, also make succesful films with a message, without any recourse to violence except to a marginal and relevant extent ?

Media research has alsc shown that while the direct influence of violence or other bad things portrayed in films or other forms of media may not be much they stimulate those with latent tendencies and proneness to violence. After all, why do the pit class audiences cry for the blood of the bad man? The violence in the films brings to the surface the aggressive instincts in them and also helps them to overcome their own helplessness when they see the bad man being worsted by the hero. The fantasy effect comes into play, although no incitement to violence is caused.

The Hindi films or the south Indian ones have always been dealing with smugglers, black marketers, gamblers, pickpockets and other doing such deeds. Titles like *Pocketmaar* (Pickpocket) similar other films *Loafer, Kala Bazar, Gunahon Ka Devta* (God who is a criminal or the other way about) and scores of similar movies testify to that fact. Most people may see the films as fun and applaud the transformation of the hero from smuggler, an employee of one or a pickpocket into a good man, but quite a few with thieving instincts or latent aspirations of getting rich quick by the shortcuts of smuggling would certainly be influenced by them.

Even the moderate element would after repeated portrayals of crime and violence come to look upon such occurences as part of our society which they cannot do much to counter. What is really dangerous is the deadening of people's sensitivities and making them fatalistic, whatever will be, or (*sab chalta hai*) (everything goes)'. The sense of idealism is being eroded.

If there is considerable violence in our society and there are even criminal clements in politics films cannot escape part of the responsibility. They portray violence to make money, the writers call it freedom of expression or the creativity of the film makers while you and I have to gulp down the senseless violence as part of the entertainment we seek from films. How creative are the films can be seen from the fact, testified to by the makers themselves, that there is no set story by a renowned writer but a hodgepodge of a story to which everyone from the producer to the hero and heroine, the director and even the technical hands contribute. The story is hammered out by these various hands who have their own conception of what the audience would swallow, unless they have plagiarised the story with scenario from a foreign film and given the characters Indian names to make it look like a story from India. The myth of creativity is kept up by the critics who know that the films are big business and they have to write about them philosophically.

This is not to deny that the film producer, or writer must have his freedom of expression but only to point out that a film story is seldom the creation of a creative mind. If the producer finds that sex portrayal would go down better with the pitclass (the barometer of the film industry) he would go all out to ask his heroine and other famales to bare their legs, backs, part of the breasts as much of them as the censors would wink at and as much as the audience would lap up.

The display of sex is not confined to the baring of vital parts of the body only. Songs and dances have over the past few years become exercises in pelvic pushes, the hero falling on and rolling on the floor or grass with the heroine, hero and heroine in deep embrace, hero kissing various parts of the heroines's body and so on. All this in the name of the freedom of expression,but custom made according to a box office formula which most producers follow.

Sex in gestures and actions is only matched by sex in words. *Double entendre* has often been resorted to in our films and some of it is just fun. But there is now a growing tendency to insert it in dialogues and even titles of films like Dada Kondke's film, *Andheri Rat Mein Diya Tere Hath Mein* (the light in your hands in a dark night literal meaning or in the dark night I have placed it in your hands, the male organ, of course, the intended meaning.)

In a Bachchan film *Shahenshah,* he was in police uniform and telling the heroine, Meenakshi Seshadri, "Andar Kar-Dunga", the usual Hindi way of saying "I will jail you", quite harmless, until you hear him saying "Dekha Hai Yeh", and showing the baton in has hands. (I will thrust it in).

Even a great star of yesteryear Hema Malini, is made to say in an ad of Tata Tea, "strong, unke jitni" (as strong as he) testifying to the strength of the tea by reference to the man sitting near the woman who next brews the tea. If by strength the advertisers do not mean sexual virility but the physical strength of a man, this must be the first occasion of comparing the strength of a brand of tea with masculine physical prowess.

But these must be dubbed as harmless compared to the open and unbashed verbal sex of some recent songs in which everything possible is called sexy. Earlier only vamps and some actresses like Kimi Katkar, Farah (or now) Mamta Kulkarni and some others were called sexy and even they resented it. Now the hero singing a song in *Dulara* refers to his pants as sexy.

This is promptly picked up by TV. In *Dard* a family serial on DD Metro, a small six-year-looking son of the heroine, who has married a much older man, (so much for liberation) calls her 'sexy' when the old father is also present. She tries to drive some sense into him by asking him whether he knew the meaning of the word sexy and equally promptly the reply comes that he picked it up from Govinda the hero who sang that song in the film referred to. That the actress playing the horoine is also the producer of the serial makes her intention clear; while the sexy craze lasts why not exploit it in one's serial.

But does the producer see the harm that can come to childern by such gimmicks? Already the Indian childern have to bear the cross of Nirodh ads and those of Kamasutra or Kohinoor condoms being telecast at Prime time when they are watching TV along with their parents. Now they may be asking their parents or discussing among themselves in school the next day, what 'sexy' means.

That DD has fallen a victim to the oneupmanship game is clear from several other instances. The DD Metro programmes are not subject to preview which is all to the good but they are expected to conform to a code of good broadcasting and a good advertising code (which should come into play when you have the Hema Malini ad on Tata Tea) and this would not permit the highly popular "Dekh Bhai Dekh" serial to base an entire episode on the love game played by a small boy, almost of the age of the heroin's son in *Dard*. Episode writers cannot cope with the demand of a weekly serial but then the producer (and the promoter who, in this case, is a highly favoured governmental cultural figure, Amitabh Bachchan's wife Jaya) must find good humour writers and pay people well for inventing comic situations and not fall for a mere child indulge in verbal sex.

It is the comedies which are often lapsing into error and cross the point of good taste. Another highly successful Metro sitcom *Zaban Sambhal Ke* made one of the women in the school for adults link V. Shantaram's film *Do Ankhe Bara Hath* with the song *Choli ke Peechhe* and say "Bara Hath" behind the choli (blouse). *Choli Ke Peechhe* is bad enough but if you were to induce as many as twelve hands to go behind the blouse, as the dialogue clearly said, the situation is not one of comedy but much worse.

These are only stray examples of the liberties being taken with people's finer sensitivies by the TV programme producers in imitation of films. The movies are going as far as the law and public opinion will permit them to exploit sex and violence in search of popularity or money. Public opinion is also manipulated.

The films are dominating the entertainment world and how pervasive their influence is we have already examined. While DD has to beat back the competition from the foreign domenated rivals and while there is no need to be prudish about violence which is relevant or sex-some fun being seen as an essential ingredient of entertainment-we have to ask ourselves if producers could be allowed to get away by exploiting childern to serve their commercial ends? How would they like their own childern to utter "sexy" in their routine conversation?

Once more it is a question of the rank commercialism of the serial makers being passed off as creativity and freedom of expression. If a writer claims that a small boy must be made to call his mother sexy, even if the latter chides him for it, there is no freedom involved there, except the freedom to make money by titillating the adults.

So DD has to be careful. If the other channels are not that careful about the sensitivities of the people and are trying to attract business in such despicable manner and if Star and other foreign channels are playing ducks and drakes with Indian cultural values and some Indians, particularly the English media, are applauding it, DD must not swerve from its path.

People like Swami Agivesh[6] and several other organisations who think about the ill effects of the rivalry among the entertainment media leading them to such crudities have to exert themselves more. People have to be awakened before their sensitivities are completely dead. Social action, rather than law, is the answer, although law cannot escape its reposibility.

The foreigner is out to exploit the Indian market and some elements are bound to hold it up as altruism, examples of which we have seen. They try to conceal their own personal interests and ignor the mercenary interests of the foreign media. This is the real danger to Indian values. This is a much more dangerous invasion than the fact that some of the foreign invaders are held up as examples of technological perfection. Indian should not close their eyes to what is happening outside in the world but there is no justification in blindly copying it in the hope of making as much money as the foreigner.

The invasion is real. That some people do not perceive it is as such is India's tragedy. Ones again we have to say that the foreigner invading India has always had friends, collaborators, admirers, most of them self-seekers, within India.

With some gratification we have to note that despite the studied softness practised in recent times by Murdoch and others of his ilk and their calculated gestures of friendship, the government has not changed its view of the cultural invasion. In a written reply to a quesion in the Rajya Sabha (upper house of Parliament) on February 22, 1994 the I and B minister, K.P. Singh Deo, said, in parts: "The programming of a number foreign channels operating from outside India, the signals of which can be received in the country through an appropriate dish antenna, are considered by many as being alien to Indian culture and lifestyle".

On the same day in reply to another question the minister said: "(the) Government is aware that the programming on a number of foreign TV channels are (is) considered by many as alien to Indian culture and lifestyle".

The similar phraseology would show that the replies were drafted with care and after due consideration of all relevant factors. This would also refute those who have been spreading the view that the government would not be averse to a deal with the foreign channels. But we must keep our fingers crossed.

15

Looking for a Solution

The Murdoch mania which seized our Press during his week long sojourn of Delhi and Bombay reflected the servile attitude of several in the media. In no other country in the world a foreigner seeking more markets for his own product could have received such right royal welcome and coverage in the media. He was invited to Delhi's Press Club, interviewed by some who would imagine that they are media experts, sought after and entertained by the proprietors of several English dailies and periodicals, obviously to find out what is in the Star's possible expansion plans for them, (apparently they did no fear he would gobble them) and generally made much of.

Many come and go and even see the minister concerned and sometimes even the Prime Minister as everybody in India is accessible to a foreigner (in most countries Murdoch would be received by a junior minister without portfolio), but few are accorded such cringing welcome. While the ordinary Indian was least bothered by the visit, the media who would otherwise ignore a foreign tycoon, unless he also has at his disposal a high powered PR agency with unlimited hospitality, were virtually Murdoch-crazy.

If the Star boss was thus made into a minor hero the other rivals were not to be left behind. The CNN outfit was busy denying that Ted (Robert Edward) Turner, the boss of the organisation in New York, and his ex-actress wife Jane Fonda were seeking any publicity for themselves during their forthcoming visit to India. It, however, gave obliging newmen details of their invasion of this country.

We were first told by one daily that they would be in India close on the heels of Murdoch but later the travel plans were altered to make it clear that they were a class apart. Their trail was not in the same category, they were extremely fond of this country. Perhaps, being natural Americans, unlike Murdoch who is only a naturalised US citizen, they would wear a 'I Love India' sign on their coat lapels when they finally land up here in April or August two alternative dates according to a leading newspaper[1].

For Murdoch to pay attention to India is understandable. According to a Star statement from Hong Kong, the satellite channel's headquarters, giving details of "Star TV Viewership", as in February 1993 before Murdoch bought it, India accounted for half the numbers. China[2] where it is now totally banned has to be excluded from the calculations although in February 1993 some Chinese could have been watching Star's Chinese channel. The statement is reproduced here in parts:

(See Table on page 163)

The Star statement is very interesting inasmuch as it is silent on the viewership in Malaysia and Singapore where Star is banned. In Vietnam also it is banned. The viewership statement mentions China but we are not reproducing the claims because in October 1993 China banned viewing of Star or any foreign satellite channel, except in hotels and places where foreigners are resident. There is no mention of Japan also, presumably because thousands of private stations in that country offer enough options to the viewers and they obviously have no need for Star, apart from the language problem which would be serve as the Japanese are extremely fond of their language and know little English.

Star TV Viewership

Market	*Star TV homes (February 1993)*	*% of TV homes*
Hong Kong	304,809	19
India	3,300,500	17
Indonesia	36,211	—
Israel	411,000	41
Korea (measured June, 1992)	18,945	
Kuwait	12,780	5
Pakistan	61,239	3
Philippines	137,141	4
Taiwan	1,980,140	41
Thailand	32,393	—
UAE	72,809	18

Also, while Star always trifurcates its timings in its daily and hourly schedule—HK time, India time and UAE time—the audience in the UAE is less than a quarter of the audience in India. Star claims that the Indian viewership (that is, those homes which can receive Star (*Courtesy* the cable) went up to 7.278 million in October 1993, there could have been an increase in the UAE too, but not as much.

Two other facts must be noted. The star statement refers to India as one of the channel's "markets", which clearly shows its commercial approach. Secondly, some people in India are under the mistaken impression that Pakistan is more advanced in TV than India. The Star figures show that the total TV homes in that country is only slightly above 2 million, its own viewership in that country being 61,239 or 3 per cent of the TV homes there. The comparable figure of TV homes in India in 1992 was 34,858,000 much higher than the figure for Pakistan, even allowing for the difference in population. Pakistan suffers even by comparison with the Philippines which had more than 3.4 million sets, 70 per cent more, for half the population of Pakistan[3].

The Murdochmania fortunately did not grip everyone in the print media and media specialists. The Marathi daily, *Navakal* of Bombay, which has a circulation higher than the *Times* group's *Maharashtra Times* and the *Indian Express group's Loksatta*, as certified by the Audit Bureau of Circulation, ABC, said: "Frankly, he (Murdoch) should be banned from any business venture in India .... The English press has already begun distorting Indian culture. Mr. Murdoch will do it with greater finesse. In that sense, he is a greater evil. "(Notably, the *Times of India*, quoting the *Navakal*, described it as a newspaper of the mill workers of Bombay, but failed to mention that unlike the two other papers mentioned above it is not tied to any English newspaper. In any case, the number of mill workers is much smaller than the circulation of *Navakal* which is more than 200,000 while the prolonged strike of textile workers in the late seventies critically reduced the number of mill workers and left this industry itself much depleted than before.)

Well, you can run down a paper which does not fit in with you scheme of things by calling it names. But what would you say to a former communications adviser to the Planning Commission, Krishan Sondhi, telling a few hometruthes about Murdoch?

In an article in the *Times of India*, Sondhi said: "Mr. Rupert Murdoch's arrival in India should be an early warning signal of the devastation which foreign (particularly western) TV systems are going to cause to developing countries like India. In the euphoria of opening up the economy and other aspects of national activities, particularly the media, we seem to have forgotten the concerns expressed in UNESCO, ITU and the UN Committee for outer space during the past four decades. India, incidentally, was the leader of the movement".[4] So Murdoch is some kind of an early warning radar.

Sondhi forgot to mention that the selfsame Indian government was now going all out to welcome Murdoch and the same ruling party which was behind the various pro-third world movements was now throwing the country open to foreign investors. The English print media interpreted this as applicable to foreign media giants like Murdoch and Turner also.

He made a reference[5] to important doctrines like a New International Economic Order, based on a better distribution of resources and on justice, and ridiculed the west's concept of free flow of information in a situation when the technology is all controlled by the west resulting in a perpetuation of its dominantation.

Sondhi said : "Mr.Murdoch is not innocent of the fact that while most of the countries in the world—the USA and those in Europe—are in deep recession and the economics of Latin America and Africa have all but collapsed, the Asian countries are showing an amazing rise in GNP. What brings Mr.Murdoch to India is its uniquely large consumer market of 200 million affluent persons with high purchasing power which is going to touch 400 million within five years—twice the population of Europe .... Mr. Murdoch's strategy is simple : he is going to tell Indian industrialists that they are wasting time on Doordarshan. For half the cost he will show their advertisements all around the globe and for rural India he may even finance small antenna for every village. This obviously can be termed only as war. Since there is no UN body to protect us, India must rise to the occasion and fight the war".

Thank God, there are sensible people who understand the Murdoch strategy and are willing to speak up and there is a newspaper to let him do it, although the paper has been in the forefront of the Murdoch Istaqbal (welcome) committee. It would appear from some of Sondhi's observations ('he is going to tell') that his piece was written before Murdoch landed in

India but published after he left, by design or for reasons of space.

Some interesting insight into Murdoch is also provided by A G Noorani in an article in the *Frontline* magazine of April 8, 1994. Writing sarcastically of the English Media's servile attitude towards Murdoch he said :

"Incidentally, if such be the abasement of the genuflection in the presence of Rupert Murdoch during his brief days in New Delhi when he has not acquired a stake in the press to what depths will some not descend when he does ? He will acquire much more than the power to line some people's pockets. *He will acquire a voice in India's politics.* (emphasis in the original). What Louis Heren, former Deputy Editor of the *Times* (now owned by Murdoch) (also a former *Times* correspondent in Delhi during the fifties) writes of him in his fascinating book *The power of the Press*? should make advocates of foreign-owned Indian journals sit up and reflect. (also the admirers of Star).

"He (Murdoch) was said to have played a disgraceful role in political manoeuvring which brought about a constitutional crisis in Australia. It began when his newspapers withdrew their support for the Prime Minister and Labour party leader, Gough Whitlam, having helped him to win the 1972 election after many years in the wilderness. Within three years their support was withdrawn because, Whitlam alleged, the new government had not granted Murdoch a license to develop bauxite reserves in western Australia. Murdoch said he could no longer support Whitlam because his government was grossly inefficient".

Grossly inefficient it must have been if it could not even issue a licence to Murdoch. It is not our subject here to go into Murdoch's life history and he may have something to be said in his defence. For the limited but vital purpose of the Indian electronic media let it suffice that Murdoch is not an unmixed blessing that some people have uncritically or selfishly made him out to be.

Murdoch, Turner and the rest of them are interested in our money, in acquiring power over our air space. They know that influential elements in Indian media are promoting the western ways and culture and they know there are quite a number of vocal and influential people who are keen on tieups with a Murdoch and or Turner for their own sake while another lot (a small minority of Indians) is yearning for the culture that the Murdochs and Turners would export to us. In between there are a number of people who have given no thought to it and would take in their embrace whoever brings them lively and absorbing programmes, no matter what that source is.

The large majority of Indians who are content, even happy, with DD are derided by these elements. The majority, as always, is silent and unsuspecting. The leaders of political parties are too busy, except some, to bother about this development. Some, as we have seen, have been influenced by Murdoch's agents. The governments, which has shown some guts in facing up to the cultural invasion, has queered its own pitch by telling everyone, Murdoch, Turner or anyone else, that he is welcome.

Already Murdoch has plans to form an Indian company and has cleverly won the hearts of the government leaders by showing on January 26, 1994 the Republic Day pageantry on his Star channel and the Indian print media were all agog. They did not realise that on a Wednesday which is a holiday neither in Hong Kong or anywhere in East and South east Asia nor in the UAE (which observed Friday as a holiday) there would be few free to watch the two hour parade and cultural show even if the time, 9-30 to 11.30 a.m., Indian standard time suited them, (too early in west Asia and afternoon in the east). Republic day 1994 fell on a Wednesday.

It was still a good gesture provided the government is not going to be taken in by it. More such Indian coverages should only be treated on their merit and not be interpreted as expressions of friendship for India. If the programmes are considered attractive enough for Star of anyone else let them do the programmes and let not anyone interpret them as examples of enthusiastic pro-Indian actions of Star or anyone in that category.

About one thing we have to be very clear. There cannot be any foreign participation in our media. If Star wants to set up an Indian company for software to be shown on its channel let him. But Star or Murdoch controlling Zee which would have uplinking facilities from India would not be acceptable. What goes for a Star-controlled Zee would go for all such directly or indirectly controlled TV enterprises. All foreigners must be out.

We are in a kind of simulated situation, a media make believe, in which some adventurous spirits launch a newspaper from India, the Asian Age for the "South Asian", the term covering Pakistanis as well as the poor Indians NRIs, and some people hail it as a multinational media venture. Do it by all means if you find that you have readership, hopefully among the Pakistanis also, in London and if you find it cheaper and technologically feasible to produce the paper in India. (For example, a British or American editor would cost five times more.)

It is just another paper : Likewise Murdoch wanting to do something in India is no occasion to rejoice. He must be told to leave Indian skies to Indians and Indian companies without direct or indirect foreign influences.

How then should the Indian TV map be drawn? Where would one fit DD into the new scheme of things, a kind of not just idealistic but pragmatic and workable arrangement redounding to the benefit of the Indian audiences, giving them enough options, providing full scope for creative talent within the country, making good use of the hardware and software facilities which already exist, taking full advantage of the technological advances in the world but without letting any foreigners hold them as a pistol to our heads.

We have spoken in Chapter 5 of the broadcasting models from Japan and Canada where the national networks, funded by the respective parliaments, function in competition with scores of hundreds of radio and TV stations. In Japan, the NHK has set high standards and so has the Canadian Broadcasting Corporation in Canada but both countries have any number of private channels for radio and TV.

This peaceful coexistence has conduced to the growth and development of broadcasting and the attainment of great heights in the electronic media. Both excellence and freedom, combined with responsibility, have been displayed and there is no Murdoch to tell them what to do, something which those in India enamoured of foreign carpetbaggers would do well to take note of. The viewers are, of course, the biggest beneficiaries as they have options and excellence without commercialism running riot.

Foreigners have been kept at bay (for Canada the American big brother next door is always looking over its shoulders). The satellites and cable add to the options but there is no craze among the viewers for they have their quota of entertainment anyway. The Japanese, in any case, have developed much insularity, because of the acute language barrier, towards the western ways projected by the foreign channels.

It is all to the good that the Indian government is contemplating allowing privately-owned TV channels to operate by satellite and even terrestrially. Competition, which is truly indigenous, would bring greater options to the viewers and improve continuously the quality and contents of the programmes of the various channels.

To have a situation comparable to the Japanese or Canadian model DD has to be strengthened further on the one hand and efficient and professionally run private channels, as opposed to outfits run by foodgrain and bullion merchants, have to co-exist with it. The private channel must needs conform to legal provisions so that there is no chaos as now obtains in the TV media, with the cable people relaying any foreign channel, and the Indian channels, operating under the aegis of the foreigners, not under any legal provisions and answerable to none.

That situation can no longer be allowed to continue. Legal provisions do not necessarily mean that the TV channels would be subject to control by the I and B ministry or any other agency of the government. Such provisions would require the channels to function within certain parameters, like a broadcasting and advertising code. At present the private channels, for example, show liquor and cigarette ads and the cable people know no law. Both liquor and cigarettes are taboo on DD. The print media, of course, carry ads of both, although some papers stop at cigarettes.

The private channels will have to take out licences under the Indian Telegraph Act or some other legal inactment so that their performance can be subject to a minimum monitoring regime by an agency different from the I and B ministry which would continue to exercise authority over DD (and AIR) until autonomy dawns. Even then, Parliament will have to be given periodical reports and information on the functioning of the two national networks through the instrumentality of the ministry.

The cable bill, already before Parliament since August 1993, must be first put on the statute book.[6] At present even the Zee channel, not to talk of the completely foreign Star and other channels, come to the people through the cable. That situation would continue until terrestrial channels are established by private organisations or a cheap dish antenna comes into the market so that people are able to watch satellite programmes without the intermediacy of the cable operators. (Even now, a dish antenna can be used by anyone provided he takes the trouble to install it and can afford the cost).

In other words, there has to be some regulation of the dish antenna also. If China, Malaysia, Singapore, Vietnam and some other nations including Saudi Arabia can get rid of Star by banning dish antennae there is no reason why the Indian State should be squemish about it even in acquiring the powers to control this activity. The present policy of not banning such viewing, as stated often by the I and B minister while lamenting the foreign cultural invasion, should be reviewed.

Some of the cable operators practice a measure of self-regulation. For example, during the electioneering fever that gripped the Congress(I) and the BJP in October-November 1993, when both used the cable transmissions extensively, many operators insisted on the video cassettes of the two parties being cleared by the Board of Film Certification, although they were under no legal obligations to do so. Possibly, they insisted on the clearance as a measure of abundant caution but the parties were also cautious and got their cassettes certified before telecast by the cable transmissions. However, those who saw the BJP propaganda on the Jain TV channel, specially the recordings of the virulent anti-Congress(I) speeches of some BJP leaders, were amazed at the violation of good broadcasting standards.

Some cable people are known to show pornographic scenes from films which are censored or parts cut by the censors and some are said even to show blue films late at night. Not only there is need for governmental regulation of the cable business but there is equal need for putting the cable business on proper lines through formation of cable networks. This need not take the form of big operators swallowing the small fries (at present the vast bulk are small people) but by the small operators coming together and enforcing a measure of discipline and self-regulation. The cable business is an established fact all over the world but the Indian development has been haphazard and totally unregulated.

The cable will continue to play a significant part in the TV business in future too by bringing the Indian and foreign satellite channels to the viewers and satisfying the craze for movies which will also continue to prevail for many years. Cable should also be allowed and encouraged to develop local coverages and given a chance to become a real community service that some people mistakenly think it has already become. But all this will have to be subject to the provisions of a law requiring them to register and conform to a broadcasting code.

The cable people can also bring many more recorded programmes to their clients than at present. For example, they can get good Bengali, Tamil or Gujarati programmes recorded in the respective states and telecast them for the benefit of the linguistic groups in the Hindi speaking and other areas. The recorded content can thus develop and the film craze reduced to that extent. Apart from relaying satellite channels and showing feature films there is thus much more the cable can do if only the people in the business have the right approach.

If the Indian Telegraph act is found to be obsolete and insufficient to deal with the dish antenna age, it should be amended by Parliament which can also legislate an entirely new law to ensure better and more effective regulation of the various TV channels, whether Indian or foreign. The approach that legislation would only place more powers in the hands of the bureaucrats and the political masters in power for the moment has to yield place to a new outlook, although the freedom of the media must be protected. The government, in fact, controls a vast area of trade and industry. It is the government which has introduced liberalisation and called in multinationals virtually to take charge of Indian economy. Some print media extol this action because they are no longer motivated by idealism. Some at best, would not mind the good of the community being given an equal place with their own interests, while many are only concerned with the interests of their proprietors, self-interest, plain and simple, although what is written may be frequently clothed in rhetoric about freedom of the media.

So, the need for effective regulation of the TV media and placing the entire unregulated and chaotic business into a coherent and orderly shape has to be recognized. The BJP leader L.K. Advani is right in saying the government has no broadcasting policy which is clear from the manner in which they have ostrich-like allowed the Indian TV scene to be cluttered up by foreign and foreign-controlled Indian TV channels and the free-for-all cable business. But then does the BJP have a broadcasting policy? Does, for that matter, any of the other major parties have such a policy?

What obtains at present is a vague pledge of AIR and DD's autonomy while out of office and rigid control and partisan use of both in office. Combined with it is a kindly tolerance of the mushrooming growth of the cable industry and the satellite channels which they purvey. To redress the situation the political parties have so far done pretty little. They have to wake up.

There has to be a reorientation among our political masters sitting in Parliament and the top leaders of the political parties— the outlook that TV is useful only as a vehicle for their views to be aired and for their faces and names to be projected in the news and other programmes has to go, the total good of people has to be considered and the control of the foreigner, direct or indirect, has to be completely eliminated. The law makers have to allow the media to develop in a free atmosphere but within the framework of a broad-based and liberal law so that the vital interests of the Indian State are protected.

That would surely mean that sooner the Prasar Bharati act of 1990, put on the shelf by the Congress(I) government for the past four years, is implemented the better for the national media. Both AIR and DD have to be allowed to function free of government control and the shackles imposed by the political masters, together with the bureaucrats, have to unlocked.

Those in the two electronic media have also to realise that they are performing a vital national task and not waste their time and energy fighting one another and engaging in futile and often ill-informed controversy. Many in different formations which are the constituents of AIR and DD have been guilty of cowtowing to the administrators and politicians from time to time for favours received, sometimes only in the hope of receiving them. But some of them snipe at their colleagues in the other cadres and boast they are more concerned about media freedom. Should one delve deep into it and tell the people of how a top AIR man put across a pro-ruling party message in the morning religious 'Vandana' Programme, a couple of days before the casting of votes in the 1977 general election, and then proudly reported compliance to the secretary of the I and B Ministry, who had heard a similar programme on Radio Pakistan (his family obviously listened to Pakistan regularly)? I refrain from naming him and giving more interesting details of this and other incidents because I am concerned with the betterment of Indian broadcasting, not the betterment of the prospects of some individuals or groups of individuals.

The people who would be invested with freedom have to deserve it, both in AIR and DD. Along with a free DD, operating as India's national network, there should be a number of private channels operating on their own but with due regard to a code of good broadcasting and advertising. A minimum of legal restrictions will have to be enforced in the national interest.

The foreign channels can be regulated by telling the cable people not to relay then if, for example, they carry liquor ads or cigarette ads. The governments must have powers to ban foreign TV channels altogether by banning dish antennae if necessary. There should also be an attempt to tell the countries from whose soil the networks beaming TV programmes to India are operating that this would not be taken as a friendly act. With Hong Kong becoming part of the Chinese Republic in the not distant future (1997 is the date) there could be a question-mark on the future of Murdoch's Star TV and with the British Empire losing its last vestige (forget about Falklands) the Murdoch TV empire may also have to shift to a more hospitable home.

Not only the politicians in India have to reorient their thinking about the TV media but influential sections of media opinion stand in need of such reorienting. We have on the one hand the advocates of Star, MTV, Zee, and anything which can hit DD, no matter whether all that is good for India or not, (as we saw in the Hero Cup tussle) and on the other we have media specialists who would want only sensitised AIR or DD, pure and serene, almost lilywhite, and nothing else. Of course, they are for freeing the electronic media of government control but they cannot see beyond the two national networks. They, in short, have not understood the real nature of the media, with competition and entertainment as essential ingredients of a proper TV structure for India.

The government was also in the grip of these media experts for long. It appointed one committee after another, a group after another consisting of eminent men and women of good intentions, but very few of whom had any first hand experience of working with either medium of broadcasting.

In most of 1993 and early 1994 DD showed much resilience and capacity to modify its approach and changed its personality substantially. This has resulted in the big producers in the private sector flocking to it, enriching its programme contents and helping it to win back substantial numbers of urban viewers who had deserted DD in the past few years. There were many obstacles in the way and the English dailies played a highly negative role as we have seen. But all these roadblocks were removed and DD can afford a feeling of self-congratulation.

But the happy augury of a few good and thinking bureaucrats at the top, combined with some vital political support, cannot last for long. The number of pressure groups in India is large. If Sanjay Khan can get more than 50 MPs to support his application for time, both on the Metro channel and DD-1, for his serial *The Great Maratha*, anything else can happen. Somebody else, professionally not as competent as Sanjay Khan can commandeer more support for a piece which has half or less TV appeal, and somebody with much greater competence but lacking such political or other support can languish in the suburbs of Bombay, with what could become a masterpiece lying in files or cans.

This is only one instance of pressure groups at work. There can be others and the newspapers with TV interests are an instance of that kind of pressure. They unabashedly use their columns to flay DD so that the government and DD would silence them by giving them TV time for their productions or hire their TV units to produce news clips or stock market reports which have made the TV news bulletins look like bulletins intended only for the 'satodiyas', the players on the stock market. The government, alas, is not strong in will power or moral force to withstand such pressure from within or without.

So, there is an urgent need, on the one hand, to free DD (and AIR) of government control over day-to-day operations and, on the other, to bring into being competitive but responsible private channels which must eventually become terrestrial, although they could, to begin with, use Indian or foreign satellites.

Way back in 1976 DD went commercial, so it is impractical to expect it to go 18 years back in time or for the government to reintroduce TV lincences which were abolished in 1984. The national network will have to stay the way it is financially. In any case, competitiveness in revenue earnings is an indicator of your popularity. If the Indian viewer is to get all the fare which private channels can bring to him as well as the fare dished out by DD, it would only be fair that all of them earn their keep and a slice of the advertisement cake.

For those who are sold on foreign channels let us cite here the most recent instance of vilification of India by an old established and respected network like the CBS of the United States. If showed a one hour programme in February 1994 just to prove that Indian nuclear reactors are health hazards as the radioactivity released by them threatens the people living nearby. The timing of the programme gave a clue to its real character. It came at a time when the United States had mounted pressure on India amounting almost to blackmail (Kashmir, human rights and all that) to make India sign the nuclear non-proliferation treaty. The United States is the only country in the world to have used nuclear weapons and still has a huge stock-pile of them but it is working hard to denuclearise the rest of the world.

This is what an independent observer, Morris Rosen, International Atomic Energy Agency (IAEA)'s Assistant Director General, had to say to the Bombay press on February 21: "In India there is a well knit group with a lot of morale, which has worked together for long years, has good experience - an advantage over other countries .... It is very easy to take a camera into people's homes and point out the dirt".[7] Rosen was in Bombay when the CBS aired the anti-Indian programme. Bombay is the headquarters of the Indian Atomic Energy Commission.

Dr. R. Chidambaram[8], Chairman of the Commission, commented: "The report (in CBS) purports to expose the ill-effects of radiation due to our reactors by focusing on some villages ten miles away from the (Tarapur nuclear) power plant. It seems a deliberate campaign to misrepresent our nuclear programmes". He described the CBS programme as "malicious, mischivous and a deliberate misrepresentation of facts".

Not CBS alone but most of the foreign networks are periodically taking potshots at India, sometimes motivated by their rulers who would gladly place secret CIA or similar material at the disposal of the TV people. There is close liaisonbetween the western media and their respective diplomatic missions or governmental agencies. Those like the BBC, which is now brought to India by Murdoch's Star, regularly carry anti-Indian programmes showing this country as backward where child marriages take place as a routine, not as an aberration, where girls are not wanted and infanticide is practised.

How would they like London to be portrayed as a haven for harlots and dimly lit strip tease joints or New York as a city where you can get mugged in the subway or accosted more by prostitutes than anyone else on Broadway after dark. Indian mediamen in these august cities have little time for such bad things to comment upon (some of them are in pursuit of the green card or its equivalent because they would like to settle down there after their term of duty ends).

Of course, India has a variety of social and other problems to solve and the evil practices so often highlighted by the BBC exist, although not in the immensity misleadingly portrayed by the programmes. The BBC programmes also ignore the fact that millions of Indian couples welcome the girl child and even in traditional homes girls have a respectable place. This is hardly ever brought out and the modernisation of India is always kept away from the viewers. The evil social practices exist but so also do the prostitutes of Soho.

The cruelties and abuses which are perpetrated by many people in the west on their own fellow citizens ought to attract the attention of the western networks. There was the story of Polly Klass, of Petaluma, California, USA (north of San Francisco), reported in an Indian newspaper in December 1993.[9] She a teen aged white girl was kidnapped, raped and killed by a white man and, despite the efforts of the local police, the FBI (Federal Bureau of Investigation, the American secret police) the pubic spirited actions of hundreds of people who wanted to help in finding out what had happened to Polly and a Hollywood actress, hailign from Petaluma, offering as much as 200,000 dollars for information leading to Polly's captor, it took more than two months to trace her body and nab the killer.

Child abuse is a frequent and widely prevalent practice in the west and this is illustrated best by the case of the pop singer Michael Jackson, about whom the Indian media rave more than his youthful admirers. He reportedly gave away millions of dollars to eye witnesses and the particular child who was his bedmate to silence them and escape the rigours of the law and went into temporary hiding to avoid public attention.

The report in the Indian newspaper about the tragic case of Polly says:[10] "The kidnapping of Polly Klass and the ordeal of her family has unfolded amid increasin public concern in America about a broad variety of issues involving abuse and violence against children. The most prominent case has been that of rock superstar Michael Jackson, who has been accused of having slumber parties (in which young friends are invited to one's home for a good evening's time and then spend the night there) and sharing his bed with young boys ...... Recently a California monastery admitted that some of its religious students had abused a number of children in years past ..... The problem, of course, is by no means confined to the USA. For years Paris was shocked by the case of a church choir director who was found to have drugged some of the boys in his choir and then videotaped them undergoing various sexual acts".

Such fiends can be found in our midst too. The point is that while the foreign networks would promptly pick those cases up, they are never known to have brought the Polly or similar cases to us. The western thinking about its own role in the world of today and tomorrow is epitomised by an article in the London *Economist* in January 1994[11] which advocated European-American hegemony of the world. In the latest version of "1984" by George Orwell the reputed paper said future action in global power politics would be between four dinosaurs, USA, Europe, China and Russia, and the *Economist* plumped for combined Europe-US domination of the world.

India will continue to need the west and its technology, its liberal thought, and its elevating and enlightening literature. There is no need to close our eyes on the west or turn our backs on it and all possible collaboration with it must also be encouraged. What is essential is that we know the west for what it is, its domineering instinct and its paternalistic and exploitative approach, which coexist with all that is good in the western world. To think of it as inherently superior or altruistic is stupidity which some of our media practice. To that extent we have moved away from what Gandhiji taught us—to allow foreign cultures to blow about us without ours being swept off our feet.

16

Invasion of the Print Media

If the invasion of the skies by Star and the growth of the cable business, which facilitated the invasion, was unknown to many for a considerable time the invasion of the print media was even more incipient. We should call it a potential invasion because so far no foreign newspaper or a newspaper owned by a foreigner on Indian soil has seen the light of the day. That does not mean that behind the scenes efforts have not been made to induct the foreign print media, mostly at the instance or with the connivance of some Indian newspapers.

While TV came in because of big technological changes, the comparative failure of DD to rise to the occasion and face the foreign challenge, made almost good later, and the helping hand of the cable people, the print media's possible invasion has been occasioned by the government's liberalisation policies.

The policy of opening up the Indian economy to foreign capital and dismantling the public sector built up since the time of Jawarharlal Nehru, euphemistically called "disinvestment", devaluation of the rupee to meet the stringent conditionalities of the International Monetary Fund, IMF, and the World Bank began in June 1991 when the minority Congress(I) government of P.V. Narasimha Rao came to power (since converted into a majority by a process of defections). The liberalisation also meant that a lot of unncesssary bureaucratic controls over setting up of and running industries or over foreign trade would be done away with, a wholly welcome messure.

Whether one likes it or not liberalisation has come to stay and there is foreign capital in every sphere with some multinationals gobbling up indigenous Indian enterprises built up over many years (Coca Cola taking over Parle, Hindustan Lever, Procter and Gamble and others taking over allied Indian units). If Coca Cola could come in why not Murdoch and why not *Financial Times* London, *Time* and *International Herald Tribune,* New York, and a variety of others—so goes the argument of some Indian newspaper publishers. If some of them had their ways Macdonald hot-dogs, Kentucky chicken and other fast foods could be soon coming your way wrapped in *Financial Times,* Calcutta, and *Times,* New Delhi. There is no difference between a soap or toothpaste and a newspaper, according to them. They would flood India with foreign papers published with their collaboration, carrying Indian and, of course, foreign news and news-related articles and comments.

This only goes to strengthen the point we have made in the previous chapters that many Indian newspapers are now principally governed by their own commercial interests although they would like to mask their actions in high-flown journalistic rhetoric and where necessary also seek recourse to the freedom of the press provision in the constitution (actually freedom of expression, under article 19(1)(a) of the Constitution interpreted as freedom of the Press by the Supreme Court to be applicable to the newspapers also) and keep their readers in the dark about their true intentions.

No less a newspaper than the *Indian Express*, which was a party to the court case against DD on the Metro time slot FCFS matter, without having a TV set-up of its own, said : "The editor of a national daily who hinted that the entire dispute has a "mercantile" dimension may not be too far off the mark." The paper was editorially commenting on the Delhi High Court's judgment on a bunch of writ petitions challenging the entry of foreign newspapers on March 3, 1994[1].

The mercantile dimension will, of course, apply to the newspapers which went to court to frustrate the entry efforts of the foreign media as much as to those who are keen on bringing the foreign papers to this country to subserve their business interests.

As the court said[2] in this case the matter had not yet reached the stage where the protection of the court should be sought. The entire issue was premature as far as the courts were concerned. Both parties have been seeking such legal shelter before the time for that has arisen.

What are the facts, apart from the debate that has gone on for banning the foreign media's entry and for allowing them in? India has always kept the foreign media at bay and until recently there was unanimity on the issue. Now that there is liberalisation and the print media have almost become mercenary in their approach some of them have sought foreign collaboration.

Foreign newspapers, whether from far or near, have always had free access to India. Except on rare occasions when the particular issue of a daily or a periodical was banned because it was known to be containing an objectionable piece of writing or a deliberately falsified map of India (showing, for example, Jammu and Kashmir as part of Pakistan or not showing it as Indian territory), foreign papers have had a free run of the Indian market. Journals like *Playboy* or its various equivalents are supposed to be banned but some people walk through the green line at airports with copies of such pornographic stuff tucked under their armpits or away in their suitcases. At one time there was foreign exchange restriction but now there is none.

The issue is not about such papers coming out of foreign publishing centres and seeking entry into India as published journals for sale to subscribers or at newsstands. The current issue is about foreign newspapers seeking to be published in India. Quite early in our career as a free nation the question came up whether India should permit foreign papers to be published *inside India*.

The first Press Commission had reported on the issue and the cabinet, under Jawaharlal Nehru, decided in September 1955 not to permit any foreign media to be published from India. That decision stands and as far as the government is concerned it cannot allow any non-Indian paper to be brought out from within India unless that decision is modified or rescinded.

At the back of mind of those newspapers, individuals or groups who have been seeking recource to courts to prevent the foreign papers' entry is perhaps the fear that the governments would not stand by the old commitment and with its known proclivity for foreign collaboration in diverse areas and what with the Indian Newspaper magnates falling over one another to strike up rich bargains with foreign media putting pressure on a weak-willed government, this decision could be changed before long. How could the courts help even in that case one fails to understand.

Then there was a second decision of 1956 on the limited question of allowing foreign news agencies, like the British *Reuters* and American *Associated* Press (AP), to be able to creed (that is transmit by teletype) their news items straight to the newspapers or other clients like AIR, DD, and commercial subscribers. The Nehru cabinet again decided that foreign news agencies must go through one or the other Indian news agencies. They could not creed their stories direct to the media clients. So, Press Trust of India, PTI, have the *Reuters* and *Agence France Presse*, AFP, services as part of its total news supply of

Indian and foreign stories to its clients and the other national news agency, UNI, United News of India, (agencies are also called wire agencies in American terminology) has the AP newsfall at its disposal. This is apart from a number of other foreign agencies at the disposal of both PTI and UNI.

There are thus two separate executive decisions, not one as mistakenly referred to in some papers, and they are the valid government decisions unless the Narasimha Rao government, unable to bear the pressure of the foreign media or the Indian newspapers eager to enter into a deal with them, wilts. Already, the messiah of foreign collaboration Finance Minister Manmohan Singh is said to be favouring the entry of the foreign media, although lately he has been posing as a great champion of Indianness. Perhaps he has realised that general elections could be held either in 1995 or in the middle or 1996, beyond which they cannot be postponed, and it would not do any good to the ruling party to appear as a keen collaborationist.[3]

The foreign papers realised that they could not enter through the front door but there was a back door, perhaps discovered for them by their Indian friends. They found in the Trade and Merchandise Marks Act, 1958, a loophole they were looking for. The fact that the *Financial Times*, London and half a dozen other foreign media have registered themselves under this act would support the conclusion that these papers and their Indian collaborators in the same fraternity discovered this opportunity to stage a backdoor entry because the Press and Registration of Books Act, 1867, as amended from time to time, was too rigid to permit foreigners to land up in India.

How the Indian newspapers have been vying for the hand of some of the foreign media is aptly illustrated by the case of the *Financial Times*. First it was the *Times of India* group which was about to strike a deal with it and even went to the extent of getting a title cleared by the Registrar of Newspaper for India,[4] New Delhi, in the name of *Financial Times India*.

But at some stage thereafter the negotiations broke down and the rival group of the premier Bengali daily, *Ananda Bazar*

Patrika, the highest circulated single edition Indian daily newspaper, filled the breach. The group has a string of successful, not so successful and losing English and Bengali newspapers and magazines in is fold but the *Ananda Bazar,* truly the flagship, makes so much money it can carry the losing or non-earning members of the group on its shoulders. Now the group became a great champion of foreign media coming into India and its proprietor called *The Times of India* man unprintable names which were, however, printed in another daily paper[5].

Incidentally the *Times* group was among the petitioners before the Delhi High Court seeking to prevent the entry of foreign papers into India. If Manmohan Singh could talk populist jargon after three years of toeing the IMF line way not a newspaper transfrom itself from collaborationist to anti-collaborationist. One's self interest is always supreme.

The registration under the Trade and Merchandise Marks Act is meant only for products and the objects is to ensure that your patented product is not copied by unscrupulous rivals. Can a newspaper also be deemed a product, although its logo could be legitimately protected from colourable or other imitation. But then who bothers about a logo nowadays as long as the title is safe?

The title cannot be registered except by the Registrar of Newspapers for India, RNI, under the Press and Registration of Books (PRB) Act. Under this the procedure for publishing any newspaper from anywhere in India is that the publisher has to first get the title cleared by the RNI and thereafter a declaration has to be filed with the district magistrate or the Commissioner of Police where the Commissioner system obtains. Once you have a declaration in your pockets you go back to the RNI for registration as a newspaper and for obtaining a registered number which entitles you to send your paper by mail at a highly subsidized postal rate for the press.

All this may sound cumbersome but in actual practice it is not, although it is somewhat elaborate. Getting a title cleared in advance of a declaration with the district authorities is to ensure that newspapers with the same title do not appear in the same state and language and do not mislead the readers. There is protection for your title for which you d not have to have recourse to the Trade Marks Law.

The Press and Registration of Books Act requires that the editor, printer and publisher are "ordinarily resident in India." The annual statement to be filed by every newspaper requires its publisher to make his and his editor's nationality clear. All this could perhaps indicate that only Indians would be allowed to publish newspapers in India, although it would appear that a foreigner could become the editor if he normally resides in the country. There are quite a few Indophiles who could fit this description but there has so far been no case of a foreign owner or editor or a newspaper in India.

The RNI is unlikely to register a foreign-owned and edited newspaper in future, unless the Rao government wilts under pressure as we said before. The law does not specifically prohibit foreign ownership or editorship of an Indian publication, as former Supreme Court Judge and social activist V.R. Krishna Iyer said in an interview.[6] "I do not think there is a ban in the PRE (actually PRB) act on foreigners owning or running newspaper in India". But the RNI has never granted registration to any foreign-owned news media and the provisions about the publisher and editor being normally resident in India are relevant. We may quote here the proviso to section 5(B) of the Press and Registration of Books act:

"Provided that no person who does not ordinarily reside in India, or who has not attained majority in accordance with the provisions of the Indian Majority Act 1875(9 of 1875) or of the law to which he is subject in respect of attainment of majority, shall be permitted to make the declaration prescribed in this section, nor shall any such person edit a newspaper".

It is to be noted that the words "who does not ordinarily reside in India" were added by an amendment of the act in

1960 (the act has been repeatedly amended before and after independence), a good 13 years after India became free. It would not avail some of our English media to attack the PRB act as an archaic law, simply because it was first passed by the British rulers in 1867. They attacked the Indian Telegraph act, 1885, as archaic when the law stood in the way of a multinational, whom they were favouring, ousting DD in the coverage of the Hero Cup tournament (see chapter 13).

Justice Krishna Iyer poured his heart out in the interview referred to above. At a time when commercial minded news media were going all out to bring foreign TV and newspapers into India here was a man with an excellent record as a jurist and a noted champion of good causes mincing no words on the baneful role of the foreigners invading the Indian skies and the nation's print media. Asked, somewhat simplistically by the paper's reporter who thought the TV could somehow become foreign but how could the print media (a case of sour grapes for his proprietors), Justice Iyer reacted strongly :

"And see the results (of the satellite TV signals). Much of the Kashmir problem could have been sorted out if only (the) electronic media from abroad behaved more responsibly. Today they can inflame feelings among (the) Muslims. The power of the media, electronic and print, is so strong that India will not be able to guard against dangers. Moreover, (the) electronic media now entering Indian homes can be legally stopped if there is (*a*) political will.

"The dish antennae, for instance, can be disallowed even by a municipal corporation. However, the elitocracy are mindless and myopic. History will not forgive them".

As we have said before, the Chinese have banned the dish antennae for their people so that no Chinese can (legally) receive the Star channel.

Before we go on to discuss this point further let us take note here of the most recent instance of a ban on the Star and other satellite channels, by Saudi Arabia. On March, 10 1994, the Saudis issued a decree prohibiting the import of dish antennae, banned the manufacture of such equipment within the country and also banned the use of microwaves for such purposes. The following UNI report in the *Hindu*, Delhi, March 12, 1994, quoting a Gulf News Agency despatch, in reproduced here in full :

"Saudie ban

dish antenna

Dubai, March 11.

Saudi Arabia has banned the use of dish antennae for receiving satellite television programmes in the kingdom in a bid to protect its religious and social values.

An official decree issued after a Cabinet meeting yesterday said that as part of the move to regularise the reception of foreign television telecasts *via* satellite, the government would set up a cable network.

The Cabinet decision provided that the Information Ministry would shoulder the responsibility of implementing a reception scheme for foreign television telecasts through international space channels and delivering them to viewers *via* a cable system in the kingdom "matching with its religious and social values", the Gulf News Agency (GNA) reported.

It said the decision was taken in view of the constant increase in the spread of satellites which began telecasting various television programmes to reception equipment wherever these are located.

The decree prohibits the imports of dish antennae and related equipment used for receiving satellite telecasts. It also banned the manufacture of such equipment and their parts in the kingdom and prohibited the use of microwaves for such purposes. UNI".

Why cannot the Indian government do so? If it has the will to ignore the howlings of the small minority which relishes such satellite programmes and some print media which are now in the TV business, the government can put as end to Star at the stroke of a pen, instead of entering into "arrangements" with Star which the English press naturally applauds. The Cable regulation bill, if legislated, would also give the government power to keep Star or BBC out, if it wished. Justice Iyer has rightly put his finger on the role of the BBC in fanning the fires of terrorism in Kashmir by its news bulletins playing up the killers and kidnappers in the name of freedom and pro-Bhutto interviews and, alas, some of the educated Indians who watch these broadcasts are also its victims.

Justice Iyer continued: "The entry of the print medium will be more dangerous than the electronic media because of the credibility and glamour associated with the printed word.... (The) Indian newspaper industry must campaign for protecting not only the Indian media but India's economic independence. Masses must be mobilised in time and Parliament persuaded to enact legislation inhibiting infiltration or foreign intrusion. I see in their (foreign newspapers) eagerness to enter India a powerful political motive because a strong India, a strong China and a strong Russia can be a match for any unipolar imperialist power. Our culture is being bastardised and sex tourism is the vogue of the day. ...... More often these press barons from abroad promote the interests of US not of India. I strongly believe that the prevailing impregnability of India as a sovereign republic will be threatened by the anti-national policy of unbridled entry of the media heavyweights from across the sea. Kashmir is in peril. Punjab militancy can be resurrected".

Asked about the consequence of foreign newspapers forging tie-ups with established Indian newspapers, the learned judge said : "They will dominate policy and control the press. Our government cannot enforce laws against foreigners. Proof is Star TV. Newspapers will act likewise. Rupert Murdochs may buy up small papers or break up bigger ones by strategems easy to practice".

Justice Krishna Iyer, known for his leftist views, spoke frankly and somewhat bitterly because he found the government gutless to defend the Indian media and economic independence. But he, at least in the *Times* interview, did not lash out at the Indian protagonists of foreign media ready to take advantage of government's liberalisation policies to induct their foreign collaborators and clothing the sheer pursuit of their commercial interests in journalistic jargon of freedom of the press and international barriers being broken down and, crumbling. Yes, they are crumbling, but the beneficiaries at least for the moment are the powerful nations and their collaborators in India.

A newspaper is not a product or a commodity. All media for that matter have a bigger connotation because of their power over the minds of men. Even in the matter of products there was nothing wrong with the old view that local production must be protected and jobs for Indians must be the first priority. See the way the United States, the ideal of these collaborationists, has invoked the dreaded Super 301 against Japan in order to protect what it thinks are its vital interests in international economic relations. What wrong would India commit if it also acted to protect vital national interests against the foreign intruders? The latter do not become more acceptable simply because they have found some Indians to welcome them. The story of King Ambhi welcoming Alexander the Great to India is repeated all over again.

A foreign newspaper operating in India and reporting and writing on Indian developments from day to day is basically different from the circulation of such foreign media published abroad and carrying reports on India along with a variety of subjects. When a foreigner reports or writes in India he is seeking to influence Indian readers and (viewers for TV). Whereas when he does that for his newspaper or magazine in London or New York from India he is doing it mainly for his readers in those places.

The Indian newspapers have been freed of all restrictions in respect of import of technology and largely also newsprint and heavy duty concessions have been offered to them at the cost of the poor taxpayers. In fact, they are the biggest beneficiaries of successive populist regimes at the Centre (the seat of the Indian government) and in the States. Among the Indian journalists there are many highminded people striving to uphold values and motivated by basic ethics of telling the truth in reporting and fearlessness in their comments. There are also many in their ranks who are the opposites of these people. In fact, the Indian press is perhaps the most stringent critic of India (not merely the government but India as a nation) and the foreign journalists or the so-called champions of human rights outside find a lot of ammunition for their anti-Indian slant in the Indian print media. Even where these writings and reports are motivated by the self-interest of the proprietors or the personal proclivities of the owners and editors (some of whom are known to be friendly even with the ambassadors and high commissioners of countries openly hostile to India), the government has acted in a weak and servile fashion instead of telling those people where press freedom ends and national interests begin.

Why then do they need foreigners to come and fight their battle when the battle has already been won and not even been joined?

In any case the government has not yet swerved from its commitment to prevent the entry of foreign media, as laid down in the 1955 Nehru decision. In the course of hearing of a bunch of writ petitions by the Delhi High Court, the Central government counsel, G.C.Mittal, denied that there was any change in the government's policy. He said the applications for seeking court's orders on preventation of the entry of the foreign media were premature. The following report in the *Times of India* of February 23, 1994 is relevant.[7]

"The counter-affidavit submitted by the Central Government standing counsel, Mr. G.C. Mittal, said at the outset that the petition was premature and the apprehensions were neither true or based on facts.

"I note that only the *Reader's Digest* and the *Parade* (for five years upto November 1992) had been permitted in view of the cabinet resolution, but no foreigner was involved as the publisher, printer, editor or owner. The application of extension of the *Parade* was still under review.

"*No Approval*: The foreign collaboration division of the Industry ministry had also said on February 2 that no proposal had been approved so far by the Foreign Investment Promotion on Board and the recent tie-up proposal of the *Financial Times* and the *Ananda Bazar Patrika* has not been cleared. They had been informed as such on January 21".

That makes the government position clear and even disposes of the *AB Patrika-Financial Times* deal which has clearly not gone through. The debate continues in the media all the same. On the one hand there are people like N. Ram, practising editor of the *Frontline* weekly (of the *Hindu* group), who are staunchly opposed to any foreign media entry and on the other are some of those who have struck up a collaboration deal or are hoping to enter into one and some who think their interests would not be affected by the foreign media coming it. Among them are some stalwarts like the publisher of the leading Tamil daily, *Dinamalar*, of Madras and several other Tamil Nadu cities and towns[8]. He is under the notion that foreigners would not be involved in Indian language papers but then there are big groups like *The Times of India* and *Indian Express* who have a string of Indian language papers under their belt.

The presumption of some of the papers which are opposed to the entry of their contemporaries (several times more powerful) from abroad that foreigners are all right in TV, in the sense that Star is taken as already here, is wrong. Star is an dangerous to India's freedom and culture as the *Financial Times* or *Time* being published (not merely printed) in India.

Nor is the argument that liberalisation of the economy, meaning in plain and simple language entry of multinationals, must automatically be followed by the entry of foreign media of much avail. Such shining examples of economic growth in Asia—the much touted economic giants of South Korea, Taiwan and Singapore—are not good examples of press freedom or openness to foreign media. In Singapore, a leading Hong Kong based journal, the *Far East Economic Review*, has been banned from time to time and even Star TV has been banned. So, there are good precedents of economic liberalisation unaccompanied by foreign media intrusion.

Singapore keeps its press under the thumb of the PAP government and party (several Indian veterans who have served stints in Singapore papers for the attractive money the assignments fetched them quietly acquiesced in the situation of a subservient press). We in India have our press freedom and that has to be zealously guarded. It is those who want the foreign media to come in and allow this freedom to be endangered may be bartering away a part of it for the higher profits they hope to make by the collaboration arrangements.

The argument that the foreign media would always be friendly and care for our values holds no water. Even an agency like *Reuters* has been guilty of distortion both before and after independence. On March 12, 1948 Jawarharlal Nehru told Parliament that *Reuters* was distributing in India and Pakistan different versions of the same news relating to Kashmir.[9] Following that the Indian government stopped subscribing to *Reuters* service (obviously a legacy from the days when British bureaucrat cousins of the British agency occupied seats of power in the North and South blocks in Delhi) and also discontinued the subscription by AIR. Possibly, this was at the back of Nehru's mind when the major decision not to allow direct foreign agency supply of its copy to Indian newspapers was taken in 1956.

The *Reuters* agency had been guilty during pre-independence days of distorting a pamphlet which Gandhiji had brought out in 1896-97 when he was visiting India from South Africa. The pamphlet was about the conditions of Indians in that country and the distorted version, published in the South Africa papers, inflamed white feelings to such an extent that many whites there had planned to lynch the Mahatma on landing. Fortunately for history, the lynching did not take place as some decent European police officers protected Gandhiji but the leading newspaper, the *Natal Mercury*, said "*Reuters* cable is a gross exaggeration of Mr. Gandhi's statement." Another South African paper, the *Natal Advertiser* said: "A perusal of Mr.Gandhi's pamphlet, recently published in Bombay, leads to conclusion that the telegraphic description of its object and contents was considerably exaggerated."[10]

Speaking or other foreign media, let us recall the case of the BBC which was asked by the Indira Gandhi government to close down its operations in India following the telecast of Louis Malle's objectionable films about poverty in India considered defamatory by India.

Those who advocate the entry of the foreign media also argue that Indian civilization has withstood buffetings by foreigners for thousands of years. So, we should now allow them to buffet us from within! The effects of colonisation by succeeding invaders are still with us. Now a new kind of imperialism is sought to be foisted on us by some publishers interested in higher profits.

A number of journalistis are looking at the entire problem as one of more opportunities for their tribe and of foreign postings for some of them. Expansion of newspapers and more papers being published must be welcomed because that would create greater job opportunities and if in the process some could find the coveted foreign posting nothing like it. Desirable as it is should this be at the cost of India's freedom and honour?

On the other hand, there is no doubt that a few foreign papers could upset many an applecart and unbalance several of our big papers if not throw them out of business. If, for argument's sake, the *Times*, London, could be bought in Delhi or Bombay carrying Indian news and selling at about or a slightly higher price as the *Times of India* who is going to buy the indigenous product which would surely look an imitation product ? If one has to prefer a real Indian newspaper opposed to foreign media invasion there would be others to be patronised, not the Indian *Times.*

If the *AB Patrika* succeeded in its objective to publish the *Financial Times* from Calcutta what would happen to its own *Business Standard*? In that case, could some of the staff lose their jobs? Jobs lost instead of created.

Earlier in this chapter we referred to the first Press Commission. Before we bring this examination of the problem of the possible invasion of the print media to a close, let us briefly see what the first and the second Press Commission had to say on foreign ownership and penetration.

In 1954 the first Press Commission said on Page 272 of its report: "We consider it highly desirable that proprietorial interests in daily and weekly newspapers should vest predominantly in Indian hands. We consider the *Statesmen* a notable exception, which has for long been associated with Indian journalism and has become more or less an Indian Institution. Even so, on general principles, we consider it desirable that there should be Indianisation both of capital and of the staff, specially at the higher levels ...... Similarly we would view with disfavour any attempt to bring out Indian editions of foreign periodicals which deal mainly with news and current affairs".

Nearly three decades later, the second Press Commission said in 1982, on page 83 of its report: "In order to curb the influence of foreign money on the press, we recommend the following five steps, and the enactment of necessary changes in laws for the purpose :

(*i*) There should be specific legal provision under which no newspaper undertaking should have any foreign ownership either in the form of shares or in the form of loans.

(*ii*) Advertisements as well as printing contracts from foreign sources should be on terms no different from those applicable to similar work done for others.

(*iii*) Advertisements rates must be published each year, and on every revision, and there should be no discrimination in their application to foreign advertisers.

(*iv*) Once a year every newspaper should publish its profit and loss account with separate information about foreign and Indian sources.

(*v*) Every newspaper must submit with its annual account the following information to the Press Council. (*a*) Details of revenue obtained from advertisements and printing contracts in respect of foreign sources, countrywise, including advertisements and or printing contracts received from an Indian agency and (*b*) names of the top 100 shareholders with their nationality and address and the number and proportion of shares held."

17

Consumerism Running Riot—Where Are We Going

The predictable calculations of the wise men and women who sat in committees and working groups on how TV software should be structured—more developmental programmes, less emphasis on entertainment, careful watching of the impact of programmes on children and women—have gone haywire. Without these people or those in authority knowing much about it, not in any case before it had happened, the viewers had access to options, thanks to cable, Star, Zee, and other satellite channels. All the options were heavily loaded with entertainment.

To stem the rot DD had no alternatives but to join the race, plug more soap operas and sitcoms, splash the filmish stuff all over the programmes and invite the ingenious private producers to handle that job. Metro was born of this struggle against foreign and foreign-aided Indian invasion. It was natural that DD's main channel would not be left unaffected by this turmoil in the broadcasting sphere. At the beginning of 1994 it was also revamped, restructured to use the official jargon. The essence of the exercise was that entertainment was given the primacy of place, much more than before, while competition, the other ingredient of a good TV policy, was provided by the Metro Entertainment channel and regionlisation of some of the ill-fated satellite channel of DD.

Long ago, the public information men, seeking to interact with the rural people with the help of informative and educational films, used as a bait to attract the rural groups (under the Centre's Field Publicity directorate and in similar state units), realised that their objective could be better accomplished by showing feature films. So, a selection of artistic films was made and some movies were acquired. Among them was *Sujata*, a Sunil Dutt-Nutan starrer with the message that all human beings are equal, irrespective of their caste since the hero was in love with a Harijan girl.

This substantially facilitated the task of the field publicity boys but they soon discovered that the rural audiences also liked more spicy, *masala* films. A feature film has many attractions, a (barely) credible story, good acting, a slick plot and crisp dialogue, a suspenseful climax, humour even if it is somewhat disjointed and unrelated to the story, a professional approach, and, above all, songs and dances. The rural audiences being not much different from their urban counterparts, with many of the latter being recent migrants from the villages, feature films, or entertainment, had a real appeal to them too.

The myth that the rural folks were not affected by the movies was exploded. The traditional theatre like Nautanki, Tamasha, Bhavai, Jatra, Yakshagana and others forms of folk entertainment, hold a special attraction for the rural people, and even for urban. They have, however, had limitations and difficulties. Some of the forms are going out of fashion, the groups which staged the forms find it more lucrative to do it commercially than merely to play along for the sake of their art, the developmental message, put across through them becomes too loud and obvious to attract and hold audiences, good scripts for these troupes are lacking, even as urban theatre groups complain of paucity of good plays, and many actors and actresses are languishing and taking up other avocations.

The spread of TV as a medium and the TV culture, of course, made its own powerful contribution to this situation. Feature films, soap operas, sitcoms and other TV entertainment fare have not only overtaken the traditional media but also have a large following in the villages. More than a quarter of the total TV homes, 12 million out of 40.3 million in India, as a whole are in the villages, add to that those who have access to community sets. In the villages, it is not uncommon for neighbours and friends to come uninvited to your homes to watch some of the more attractive programmes on your TV set.

A visit to a touring talkie (as most cinemas in the rural areas are known) is even more of a strain for the village folks then for the urban family to stand in queue for an hour or pay exhorbitant blackmarket rates for tickets, sold often with the connivance of the theatre staff, and then sit in a stuffed hall for three hours. A small screen right in the home bringing alive Dharmendra, Sanjay Dutt or Aamir Khan, Hema Malini, Sri Devi or Juhi Chawla, which you can watch for years after some solid investment is a much better proposition then going out to a cinema or touring talkie and paying through your nose apart from the discomfort. (There is, of course, an urge for an outing now and then).

So, a TV set is a must in the family budget of the Indian middle classes. The economics have been carefully worked out by the family always struggling to balance its budget. There could be economies in other areas but a TV set must be acquired even at some cost and strain. The feature films being shown now almost every day are a major incentive but the middle class, both in the urban and rural areas, knows it well that there is much more to TV than films, although the idiot box is still identified by most people as a handy means to watch films.

Such is the hold of the medium on the people that in a country where the per capita income is still only Rs. 6,249.3[1] as many as 8.5 million colour TV sets were sold in the first nine months of 1993, the year in which DD set up its Metro and satellite channels as the challenge from the cable and foreign satellite channels become acute. For the whole year the projected sales of sets was upward of 11 million. This is some measure of the sway the medium has on the people whose incomes are by no means substantial and explain a long term investment in a set costing from Rs. 5,000 for a black and white one to Rs. 15,000 or more for colour is made.

When, therefore, we talk of the influence of TV on the minds of the viewers, specially the young and the children, we have to bear in mind that the people are sold on the medium. The Indian lifestyle is changing. There is less time for social get-togethers or the Bengali *ada* or its universal Indian version of *gupsup*. Guests who drop in at prime time are not welcome.

As pointed out in an earlier chapter, the number of the comparatively affluent Indians, who can not only afford a colour set but also have considerable purchasing power to be able to afford toothpaste and brushes, toilet soap and detergents, fast foods, chocolates and toffees for their children, tea, coffee and canned milk, juices, cakes and biscuits, not to mention watches, washing machines and vacuum cleaners, is already 200 million and is going up. Whether poverty will ever be wiped out from our midst can be debated. The effect of the coming in of the multinationals on the poverty line and prices front has been minimal if not negative, but the number of the affluent people is going up.

Earlier we had riches amid poverty, now we will have affluence amid poverty. The rich would always be with us and because of the availability of cheap manpower they will also have a lavish lifestyle with scores of servants attending on them.

All this leads us to the major issue of the rapid growth of consumerism and the boost it has received by the people's fondness for the TV medium. To keep themselves in business, in the short as well as the long run, the various channels load their programmes with commercials and have sponsore for many programmes from the business houses producing and selling the products, some of which we have listed in a previous paragraph. DD went commercials in 1976 and has been earning higher and higher revenues year after year through ads and sponsors and the time slot scheme introduced on the Metro in 1993 is expected to bring in additional revenue.

The other rival channels are all commercial in nature and if they lose they have to go out of business. Some like Star can afford to take a long term view of the vast Indian market and can carry on for some time even if it loses money for some time now. In other words, the viewers are not getting all their messages free of cost. They may not pay any licence fees now and until Murdoch goes in for pay-TV they may not pay for the cable services and the cable people themselves would for the time being get everything free (except the feature films for which they pay through their noses to the local distributors).

The viewers are actually paying a heavy price for the free service rendered to them by their programme channels. They are the targets of the advertisers who want them to buy their bathing soaps, shampoos, detergents, toothpastes and what not. Many of the advertisers are quite blunt about it. They openly tell you to buy their product. Others are clever enough to conceal their message although their purpose and their meaning are both obvious.

There are not only several brands of toilet soap but there is a soap for everyone, there is one or many for the baby for the extravagant male, for the pretty female. The advertisers pander to the vanity of women. they always tell women they are pretty but this special soap would make you prettier, or keep you that way. There is a soap for the working class fellow, there is one for the whole family too—not one but several, mostly produced by the multinationals. Mahatma Gandhi taught us to limit our wants and still live happily. The TV advertisers would like you to unlimit your wants so that you never stop buying. There are offers, price cuts, introductory and offseason price cuts, areas specific offers (in selected cities only, in Delhi only) and as we have seen before there are sometimes sexual innuendos in the message (tea stronger than 'him').

A manufacturer has to advertise his wares to sell them, to boost his sales to stay in business, to outrival his rivals and for all that the consumer is his target. The smart boys and girls in the advertising trade spare no effort to put across the manufacturer's message and in the process no holds are barred for them. The only limitation they know are the advertisers' code which a TV organization may be following, like DD not displaying liquor and cigarette ads, but Zee, Star and others allow liquor. Their approach is to load the message with as much appeal as public opinion will bear.

The ads are not subject to any censorship. But even otherwise, if the *choli* song is fine with the censors and the Indian audiences the advertiser and his agency would exploit it to sell his product whether it is a *choli* or something more or less intimate or even unconnected. The claim of the advertising fraternity that they have a high standards council (there are undoubtedly some bright professionals and public spirited men and women in the ad business) but they could go to any limit to outsmart one another and capture business. Interestingly, the much vaunted professionalism has led to such TV ads like the one in which comedian Asrani asks a shopkeeper (another cinema actor) for six electric blubs and the latter, instead of promptly and gladly selling them, expresses surprise, a most unshopkeeper-like response. There are many errors in other ads too and we can go on to build up a long list but this is not our subject.

The ad makers mercilessly exploit children and women since many of their products are aimed at these classes and also because the husband and father even in a male-dominated society, cannot resist the pressure from his wife and children. Children are shown as mischievous which is understandable and tolerable to an extent but when a toffee manufacturer shows children as dirtying the clothes of a stranger on a rain affected street then silencing him by offering him a few toffees the limit is crossed. The idea may be fun for some people but it has a deleterious effect on the minds of the young people.

Apart from the appeal to the children to make them want more and more of toffees, chocolates, and then toothpastes and brushes to prevent tooth decay, there is an umpremediated effort to encourage them to be nasty and make a general nuisance of themselves to everyone. The manufacturer is in the hands of his advertising agency and the latter think they have to stay in business. There is no advertising code or censorship regulations to impede them here.

While one cannot do much about the promotion of the feeling that one must go on acquiring worldly goods and have unlimited wants or expect ad makers and advertisers to create a climate for simple living and high thinking (the adman would want you do adopt the motto 'simple thinking and high living'), you have to do something about this kind of portrayal of children as nasty and anti-social. The toffee ad is only an example. There are several in which the children are shown as a general nuisance. You laugh while the goods sell and TV charts pick up.

Consumerism is thus a danger not merely in the sense that people are made to increase their wants and thinks of life as one long journey through toothpastes and soaps. But also because children are ruthlesely exploited by the advertiser and the ad maker. That a man like Murdoch would not let his own children see the MTV programmes, part of his Star channel, shows the double approach of such people. They would want the TV coffers to overflow with funds and the ads to get currency knowing that all this is not good for children. Curiosly, some ad makers pick out boys or girls with broken and decayed teeth (which are shown in the ads) for their long and lustrous hair. Do they think the viewers do not notice the oddity of a child having luxurious hair, for which her mother, of course, uses a particular brand of shampoo, coming soon after the toothpaste ad ? Or do they want their shampoo ad to serve the cause of the toothpaste ad made by the brother across the street ?

The child is the loser in either case. By his TV addiction the child is also made to lose a lot of time which could be better utilised in playing and studying, reading books at home or in the school library. The problem of the child sitting for hours before the family set, making by heart the title song and the jingle of every ad (including the one on Nirodh, the government to take note), neglecting his homework and not devoting any or enough time to his or her studies is worrying most parents. They are partly responsible for the phenomenon because they are oblivious of the effects on the minds, studies and lifestyle of their children when they switch on the TV set at any hour of the day or night and keep it on for long. The unreal life portrayed by many of our films may not have that degree of influence on the adults but the children could assimilate the influence and may even believe 'life is like that'.

Do you want some choice quotes about the influence of TV on children? In its report "An Indian Personality for Television", the Working Group on Software for Doordarshan has them in plenty. Here is one:[2] "A young mother in Assam, not identified, lamented : we watch these films with our growing children along with our elders. And we feel ashamed. The children ask us what is going on. We have to tell lies. Adult films being shown to the children, how do people in Delhi allow this? Have they no children about whose welfare they are concerned? Almost all outdoor activity by children and homework has been adversely affected by TV. What is the future of a country whose children are being turned into film addicts" ?

One need not be so pessimistic. The advanced countries of the west have lived with this phenomenon longer than we have done. But the problem remains and some solution has to be found. It is not a question of adult films alone, which are not shown except late at night. Those shown as "U" category films have a regulation rape scene or two, any number of killings by the villain and his toughs before they are all killed by the hero, there are semi-nude dances and the rest of the *masala* of a successful box office or flopped film or any commercial film for that matter.

The portrayal of women as helpless in a maledominated society, as victims of dowry or rape, as a handmaid to man's lust, as entertainers, either as *kothewalis* dancing girls, prostitutes, in most films or even as sophisticated professional singers but having an extra-marital affair, as semi-nude dancers in *choli* songs, which most English newspapers applaud, as often irrelevant objects to attract male viewers in ads raise serious questions. Any number of young girls are, of course, ready to model for money and expose vital parts of their body. The women's group activists protest against this display.

We cannot be prudish and cavil at every ad or film scene and there is no need to extol any past period of Indian history at the expense of the present, each period being bad in then respect, including the Muslim-dominated period when people wanted the women to be covered from head to foot but then held them up as objects of man's lust in *mehfils, mujras* and in the courts of lustful kings. But this is an age in which people think about this issue and there are groups of social activists, so we should expect some results.

Again the report referred to earlier may be quoted. Women participants at several meetings are quoted as asking "Why these advertisements of expensive goods and gadgets, exploiting the female form for attracting attention? Is it not aggravating the dowry problem"?[3] Incidentally, there was at one time a spate of TV ads in which the newly wed girl is asked or made to say, yes, she had brought that brand of *masala* or tea leaves from her father's home (as dowry). Later some of the makers or DD became wise to the meaning and changed the message but even the new bride using a special brand of tea would convey the significance of the dowry message. The evil of dowry is not showing any signs of dying much less declining but should the ads and programmes encourage the evil?

In this regard, the working group's report leans heavily on the findings and conclusions of a seminar organised by the Centre for Women's Development Studies and the Committee on the Portrayal of Women in the Media. It quoted[4] with approval from the seminar's report the following passage :

Middle class ideologies of women's roles as wives and mothers provide the underlying basis for most (media) programmes. In a country where 36 per cent of the agricultural workforce is female, women continue to be projected as predominantly nonproducers and as playing a limited rule outside the home. Women are basically seen as performing a decorative function and as being marginal to national growth and development. Their primary place is seen as being within the home and this value is reflected in the content and setting of most television programmes. The plural nature of Indian culture and the diverse role that women play is neither acknowledged nor communicated. This results in a reinforcing of the stereotyped images and role specifications of women and in a unidimensional projection of their reality.

"This is reflected in its starkest form in the programmes relating to the commercial cinema on which Doordarshan so heavily relies. These programmes are loaded with derogatory images of women and are usually explicity or implicity sexist. They play a significant role in reinforcing negative stereotypes such as

"A woman's place is the home.

"The most important and valuable asset of a woman is physical beauty.

"A woman's energies and intellect must be directed to finding the right man and "keeping" him.

"Women are dependent, coy and submissive, they are masochistic in their response to indignities, humilations and even the physical violence inflicted on them.

"The good woman is the traditional housewife, long-suffering, pious and submissive, the modern woman who asserts herself and her independence is undesirable and can never bring about happiness to anybody nor find happiness for herself.

"Women are women's worst enemies.

"The working woman is the undesirable exception who must be brought into the marriage fold and made to conform to the social norms, etc".

Much of what the Working Group said or recommended has been overtaken by time but these pertinent observations about the portrayal of women in the media, particularly TV, are still valid because the films have, if anything, gone form bad to worse. While the English newspapers acclaim the *Choli* songs and some even the explicity "Sexy" dance and song sequences, the features films abound in rape scenes, cabaret and *Kothewali* scenes, with maximum exposure of the female form or degradation of womanhood. All this is blatantly shown on DD Metro, even the main DD channel and less said the better for the foreign or foreign-aided satellite channels and the cable.

What the Working Group itself said[5] can be found still in a more accentuated form: "Both the commercial films and the film song programmes contain long sequences with semiclad women dancing for men either in cabaret scenes or supposedly rural settings. There is also a trend of growing violence in commercial cinema." Then the Group observes: "The observed rising incidence of violence towards women in real life cannot be delinked from the depiction of such sequences in many of the feature films which are so uncritically projected on Doordarshan".

The villain of the piece here is the censors or Film Certification Board. While the Group, concerned more with Doordarshan deals with the impact of the films shown on TV on the minds of home viewers what about the poor pitclass audience, the real 'mabaap' (patron) of the film industry? In the name of creativity and the freedom of the "writers" of the film—we have seen how the stories are hammered out, rather than written by an eminent writer, how the sequence are manufactured to a set formula and how the so-called creative men of the cinema indulge in the worst form of crudities (laregly plagiarism) like a hero murdering not one but two of his heroines and the critics in the media accalaiming the act—atrocities are perpetrated on their audiences in the cinemas.

What is DD to do? It cannot make the feature films, although it has financed a few, a small fringe of the vast output of the Bombay and Madras industries. If a film is certified by the Film Certification Board as "U-Universal" it has to accept it. If it acts choosy about the films on the ground that violence or sex are portrayed or women are humiliated it has either to do without most of the films or show only weak and innocuous films and lose audiences. DD's culpability cannot, however, be minised because it has a high powered panel to screen films before they are telecast.

The Zee people are not subject to any such restrictions nor are the cable men. The Star which is bringing to you the permissive culture of the west at the drop of a hat and which portrays the western milieu is lapped up by a section of our people.

The situation is, however, not so hopeless. In the west too[6] a large number of peoples, parents, social activists and thinking individuals, are concerned over the ill-effects of TV and films, although the critics are not yet aware of the media's responsibility in this context. There is unrestricted competition in programming and in trying to catch audience in order to attract revenue. The views of the daily media are also coloured to a great extent. Competition is absolutely essential to the growth and fulfilment of the media and should not be hindered as far as possible but there should not be a competition in obscenity.

The solution lies in adopting well considered and enforceable codes of good broadcasting and good advertising which should be applicable to both the indigenous channels and the foreign satellite channels and their Indian component .

That foreign channels can also be subject to some regulation has been seen by us in the previous chapters and China and a few other countries which have clamped bans on dish antenna have shown the way. Even Star TV has lately become aware of the sensitivities of the eastern nations where its viewers live. This American-European enterprise in Asia, so dependent on Asian audiences and their money, has to make some concession to Asian sentiments. Its boss Rupert Murdoch himself made goodwill visits to the affected countries, including India, and sought to assauge hurt feelings. But in the process he also kindled hopes in the breasts of some mediamen and women seeking greener, foreign pastures and they acted as his apologitists in the print media.

The codes we have referred to must be evolved soonest and enforced both on the home grown channels and on the foreigners. The latter's channels should be banned if the codes are violated. Certain programmes, which adults alone can view, should be scheduled later in the evenings or at night. More and more emphasis must be laid on good standards being evolved and followed. The growing permissiveness ought to be ended, without dry and soulless, almost rigid prudishness and conservatism being allowed to hold sway. As we have said so often, the TV media and society need not be squemish and must not show signs of uneasiness at the slightest display of legs or some violence. Everything must, however, be shown within a framework of relevance, akinness to reality and socially acceptable norms. More than anything also we should be conscious of what is going on and where we are going.

18

Zee TV

When the satellite invasion began in 1991 and the cable people acted as harbingers of the new technological and media revolution in this country, some people within the country thought of joining it to see what was in it for them. Among the successful ones in this venture was Zee TV, or Zee Telefilms Limited, to give the full name of the enterprise. Some people in Bombay joined hands with a few Indian in Hong Kong to look after the software and hardware parts of the project and make the new channel a reality.

Since the Indian government does not yet allow any uplinking of TV signals from India, Zee had to find itself a foreign satellite *via* which it could beam its programmes back to India, *courtesy* the cable. The promoters of Zee could hardly have found time to ponder the possibility of being able to put up a transmitter, much less a network of transmitters, to become the first non-governmental TV channel in India operating terrestrially. That would have required a writ being filed before the constitution bench of the Supreme Court for which businessmen in Bombay and NRIs in Hong Kong (or anywhere in the world) have perhaps no time. But, as we have said before, there is no reason why the provision of freedom of expression in the Constitution, as a fundamental right, should not include both the freedom of the press as well as of the electronic media. Businessmen would, however, rather use their time making money by alternative means than going to court to establish a right.

But where was the hardware without which no channel could become operational, much less a moneyspinner? So, the group of NRIs (non-resident Indians) in Hong Kong came together to form a company called Asia Today Limited (ATL) and took on lease an idle transponder of Star's Asiasat satellite for a five-year period. Meanwhile, at the Bombay end Zee Telefilms were getting ready with softward to launch their channel.

As we have seen before, in 1992, even earlier in 1991, there was a vacuum in TV entertainment in India. Doordarshan had not yet shurgged off its insularity and those of its top men who were concerned with the rise of satellite and cable TV did not know as to how to counter the invasion. Interesting serials were lying locked in cans or rotting in files and the CBI, Central Bureau of Investigation, was breathing down on both the guilty and the honest as there were serious charges of corruption in booking serials. Many people who had been watching either the film-fare on the cable or the English serials on Star were meanwhile thirsting of home made Hindi entertainment that a true TV medium can provide for hours on end but which DD was then in no position to provide.

To fill the breach now Zee stepped in with the help of Star. Zee had also to rely on the cable like all satellite channels had done before it or are doing even now. The people who are now at the helm in Zee Telefilms are :[1]

Subhash Chandra (Goel), Chairman of the Company; Digvijay Singh, Executive President (Marketing); Nittin Keni,

Executive President (Programmes) and Rajat Sharma, Director (Programmes), News and Current Affairs.

The NRIs in Hong Kong who had formed the ATL were Rajan Issac, Mohan Tolani, J D R Malhotra (and possibly some others). Zee could not but be successful as private producers were too glad to offer interesting programmes, film-based, film-dominated or film-related, or other programmes, different from the feature films doled out by the cable men.

But hardly had Zee completed its first successful year (October 1992—September 1993) when Rupert Murdoch, now master of Star which he had acquired in July 1993, began to cast his takeover glances at it. The fact that Zee was indebted to him for its transponder enabled him to twist Zee's arm and finally on December 23, 1993 he and Zee signed a deal giving Murdoch 49.9 per cent of the shares. We have seen in chapter 8 how Zee denied there was anything like arm-twisting and said this was a straight forward business deal which left the people in Bombay in full control of the channel.

We asked Zee whether there was no fear at all of Murdoch with his enormous resources (and a lot of print media people in India interested in the resultant transaction) trying to grab the remaining zero point two percent of the shares which would then give him complete control of the channel and its ownership. Zee's reply was that all the remaining 50.1 per cent shares were with Subhash Chandra and his associates. So, there is no danger of some floating shares going Murdoch's way. But then it could also facilitate his task if the shares are all with one individual and his near and dear ones, specially if the individual is dependent on Murdoch for the hardware. Until the government changes its policy and allows private parties to unlink their signal from India Zee cannot use an Indian satellite for which it has applied to the Indian government already. (Engineers say spare capacity is available on Insat-2B, even 2A, and some of the foreign channels are believed to have approached the government to take an INSAT transponder or two on lease).

Zee, however, does not envisage any problem and feels there is no hitch in the relationship with Murdoch. Murdoch himself is planning to set up a Hindi channel or two and several Indian media "moghuls" are said to be keen to get on to the Murdoch bandwagon. If Star's Hindi channel becomes a reality what could happen to Zee is difficult to say but the competition provided by DD's Metro channel should provide some indication.

DD Metro made inroads into Zee's little kingdom and some of the top programme producers gradually flocked to DD. Both the viewers and producers were wary at first and kept their fingers crossed about DD's ability to become a real entertainer but the doubts began to melt by the middle of the year 1993. Despite the setback of the failure of the time slot scheme and the FCFS fiasco, producers' and viewers' faith in DD kept on growing. By the time the revamping was done by DD by February 1994 many of the slots from 7-30 in the evening until 11 at night had been taken up and even the "prestigious" news magazines *Eyewitness* and *Newstrack* had come over to Metro without setting the Jamuna on fire.

Zee, however, refused to be overawed. Asked about the comments of some producers that the top ten serial makers were working for DD Metro, Zee's reply was somewhat non-chalant: "They may say so because they are working for Metro themselves. We have the top ten programmes in any case".

In the course of 1994 we would know who has the top ten programmes and who has left whom behind in the race. There is no doubt that Metro has come of age even in less time than Zee did. It is equally good to know, from the point of view of good competition for presenting entertaining programmes, that Zee has full confidence in its own ability. But the question remains: what happens when Star's Hindi channel comes and the government, soft as it is on the multinationals would do nothing to stop it. More competition would, of course, mean better and more interesting programmes. But would more competition also mean more compromises with good taste and induction of foreigners in Hindi programmes?

In any case, what impact a Hindi channel from the same stable would have on Zee would be an interesting development to watch. As of now, Zee is facing the future without loss of confidence.

For lack of advertisers' response or realising the need to consolidate rather than think of expansion, Zee has not made headway in its declared plans to become a round-the-clock channel. At present it is on the air for 12 hours on weekdays and 18 hours on Sundays. All the programmes, of course, come to you from Hong Kong *via* the Star satellite and *via* your cable and the programme tapes have to be flown out each day from Bombay to Hong Kong to be flashed from there to the satellite. This is also the drill for the other satellite channels from India and it would remain so until the government gives them permission to uplink their signal from within India.

Zee has been projecting itself as a South Asian channel. It has, of course, some viewership in the UAE, mainly in Dubai among the Indians and some Pakistanis working or settled there. The fact that in its routine programme announcements the Dubai timing is repeatedly announced would show there is an audience waiting there for Zee's programmes. That would seem to give Zee an advantage over Metro.

Actually the footprints of the satellite used by Zee fall on a number of countries. These are :

Afghanistan, Armenia, Azerbaijan, Bahrain, Bangladesh, Bhutan, Cambodia, Cyprus, Egypt, Georgia, India, Indonesia, Iran, Iraq, Israel, Jordan, Kuwait, Kyrgystan, Laos, Lebanon, Malaysia, Nepal, Oman, Mynmar, Pakistan, Qatar, Saudi Arabia, Singapore, Sri Lanka, Syria, Tajikistan, Thailand, Turkey, Turkmenistan, UAE, Ukraine, Uzbekistan, Vietnam, Yemen.

It would be interesting to know how many in Azerbaijan and Uzbekistan watch Zee TV.

The Zee people have some figures to show from where they receive letters from the foreign viewers. In a period of 21 days, October 10 to 30, 1993, it received 1,188 letters from outside India, or 56 letters a day. These included 585 from its main thrust area, the United Arab Emirates, UAE, or just about half. Next in order, Nepal and Pakistan sent in 198 and 169 letters. For record there was a letter each from Bhutan and Burma (Mynmar). There was none from Hong Kong or Singapore.

The viewership in the UAE has to be recognised as significant. Besides Dubai, its main base, there are viewers in Abu Dhabi, Sharjah and Al Fujairah, among others.

According to a Zee advertisment folder, the channel is connected to 75,000 TV homes in the UAE and 63,000 in Pakistan. Obviously the UAE viewers are fairly vocal and the Pakistani audience response is, on the other hand, somewhat muted. Zee, however, is careful to say that it principally addresses itself to Indian viewers. "Our language is Indian (Hindi), the audience is Indian, "said a senior Zee personality when asked to comment on their claim of a "South Asian Channel".

Notwithstanding the UAE viewership and some viewers here and there in other countries, Zee is essentially an Indian Channel. There is nothing to show the contrary is true and those in the Indian media who talk of Zee's foreign audience are either ignorant of the facts or are trying to put a fast one across. We should be really happy if an Indian channel is able to find foreign viewers, other than Indians living for livelihood or settled in the UAE, but facts must be faced.

Typical of the myths spread by the print media was a report saying Zee received 100,000 letters a day. We have seen the daily receipt of 56 letters from overseas, including Nepal, and what is the number of letters from within the country? According to the Zee advertisement folder, released in January 1994, it received a total of 102,492 letters for the five days from September 4 to 8, 1993 or 20,498 a day. When we remember that a single programme, the cultural programme *Surabhi,* on

DD-1, receives sometimes as many as a lakh of letters and several other programmes got nearly as many, the lack of truthfulness of the claims made by the champions of private channels becomes all the more transparent.

Of Zee's Indian viewers' letters, as many as 41,489 came from the western zone where a large part of its viewers live. According to a "Zee TV Penetration Key Priority States" study, Zee had a little over 60 per cent penetration in Gujarat and slightly above 40 in Madhya Pradesh. Some 7.002 million TV households in India were said to be linked to Zee/Star in October 1993. (Star, of course, claimed for itself a viewership of 7.278 million in October 1993). (See chapter 8).

One has to remember that in the case of satellite channels (Zee is one) the viewership is limited to the dish antennae of the cable operators. If there is a terrestrial channel you do not have to worry about the cable people's role. DD-1 being terrestrial has all the 40.3 million TV households in India (figure for the end of 1993) at its disposal and DD Metro is also seen terrestrially in Delhi, Bombay, Calcutta, Madras and Lucknow, apart from the satellite channel on which it is available.

In its rate card, Zee calls itself a "South Asian Channel". The rate card is reproduced in the appendices. What is notable is the number of incentives for advertisers, although it claims that the Zee channel "is already the most popular satellite channel in India and Pakistan."

Apart from such benefits as "naming rights" your company's name being attached to a programme, like Highland Tea's Tuesday Bhajans (nobody has, of course, sponsored Bhajans)—there are several incentives like "buy an advertisement spot on a Sunday film and get a spot free on the subsequent afternoon film of your choice" or two spots free for one on an afternoon film. For regional feature films there is even a "Three-for-one" incentive. Considering Zee's high audience level in Gujarat the viewers there were entitled to ask why not a single Gujarati film was scheduled for the whole of January 1994.

Any advertisement code for Zee? In a preface to the rate card, Zee tells you frankly: "Advertising on Zee TV is governed by Hong Kong rules and regulations." So much for the claim to be Indian. The preface makes it clear that liquor ads are in but cigarettes and tobacco are out. On DD both are disallowed. The rate card is in rupees and US dollars and there are three categories of advertisers, Indians (and Nepalese) who can pay in rupees, Indian "exporters" who have to shell out dollars, and all foreign advertisers (expect those in Nepal) have to pay in dollars.

A large number of advertisers have advertised their wares on Zee. The list of its client (fortunately not referred to as "valued") covers 227 firms almost all from India, multinationals, their collaborators and, of course, Indian manufacturers. The liquor ads are of the IMFL (Indian Manufactured Foreign Liquor) variety, by Indians for Indians.

Zee, as we have seen, came in when DD had not laid enough emphasis on entertainment and the Metro did not exist. Metro really got going in the middle of 1993 and thereafter if began to offer competition to Zee in the area of entertainment. As time progressed and Metro's doors were opened widor (and despite FCFS hiccups) Metro has been a kind of thorn in Zee's side.

Zee, to its credit, has made several modifications in its programming to look like a real TV channel, not just a string of sponsored programmes—serials, game shows and all that stuff - not a glorified cable. More health care shows, children's programmes and cartoons (not generally sponsored) to counter DD's successful "Jungle Book" and other cartoon serials, are apparently part of an exercise to give itself the image of a real TV channel.

Zee has not come forward with figures to show that the Metro channel has not affected it in any way. But if the repeated appearance of a number of interesting programmes on DD Metro is any indication (apart from major producers like B R Chopra, Ramesh Sippy, F C Mehra, Ramanand Sagar and others prefering Metro) it would certainly appear that producers and others having something to show are more inclined to prefer DD to Zee. When the makers of Cibaca Geet Mala, the long standing radio programme, began to take a TV form, it chose DD instead of Zee. Even a few episode affair like the *Nataraj Awards* (for the Indians cinema) in the US, chose DD instead of the other channel.

There are other indications but it is not our purpose to show which of the two channels is more popular. In our scheme of things, as we have said before, there is a definite place for Zee provided it would become Indian in all respects and shrugg off its dependence on Star, which, of course, is easier said than done. Even so, in its approach it has to continue to be Indian.

NOTES

CHAPTER–1

1. In the United States, considered the poineer and the ultimate in free enterprise, every broadcasting station has to have a licence from the Federal Communications Commission, FCC, created under the Communication Act 1934. The FCC consists of seven members appointed by the US President and not more than four members can belong to the same party. In the United States you have to declare your party, Democratic or Republican, when you register as a voter. The US Congress has held that the airways belong to the people and broadcasting is deemed inter-state comerce regulated by the Congress.

   See *Broadcasting Around the World,* William E. McCavitt, TAB Books, Ridge Summit, PA, pp. 135-136.

2. *Economic Times,* Delhi, March 6, 1994 "CNN, Pearson Group & BBC seek line-up with DD".

CHAPTER–2

1. *Hickey's Gazette,* published from Calcutta, 1780.

2. Radio station, KDKA, Piitsburgh, USA, came up in 1920 and WWJ, Detroit, two years later. In Britain, the British Broadcating Company, not to be mistaken for the fancied BBC, received its licence from the British government in 1923.

3. Quoted in *This is All India Radio,* U L Baruah, Publications Division, Delhi.

4. Op. cit.

5. *Natural Bent,* Lionel Fielden, Andre Deutsch, London, p.192—93. "I had never liked the title ISBS (Indian

State Broadcasting Service) which to me seemed not only unwieldy but also tainted with officialdom. After a great deal of cogitation—which may seem ridiculous now, but these apparently simple and obvious things do not always appear easily—I had concluded that All India Radio would give me protection from the clauses which I most feared in the 1935 Act, but would also have the suitable initials AIR. I worked out a monogram which placed these letters over the map of India and it is now about the only thing of me which remains in India". Fielden goes on to narrate how the British bureaucrats opposed his novel idea but he got the Viceroy, Lord Linlithgow, to accept it.

6. For these and other statistics about AIR, see the *Annual Report 1992-93* of the Ministry of Information and Broadcating, New Delhi.

7. Facts and figures about Doordarshan taken from *Doordarshan 1994*, published by the Audience Research Unit, Directorate General, Doordarshan, New Delhi.

CHAPTER–3

1. See *Doordarshan 1994*, op. cit.

2. Even as late as the early 1980's, the Sixth Five Year Plan for the period 1980-85 made a total provision of Rs. 122.38 crores for sound broadcasting and considerably less Rs. 86.95 crores for television "emphasis being laid on the completion of the schemes from the earlier plans".

   p.316, Sixth Five Year Plan, Planning Commission, Govt. of India, New Delhi.

   Incidentally the Member Secretary of the Planning Commission, who generally writes the Plan, was none else than Dr. Manmohan Singh who is now hailed as the messiah of liberalisation in India.

3. See *Women, Television and Rural Development,* Binod C. Agrawal and Kumkum Rai, National Publishing House, Delhi.

4. In 1982-83 the Plan provision for AIR was Rs. 13.78 and the actual plan expenditure was Rs. 12.86 crores. As for TV, the total provision was Rs. 14.08 and the actual spending was Rs. 14.20 crores, just slightly more than AIR. Only in the following years DD broke loose and ran ahead of radio. In 1984-85 its Plan provision more than doubled, Rs. 63 crores against Rs. 30 crores for AIR.

   Figures taken from *Annual Plans* of the Planning Commission for the respective years and the *Annual Report* of the I and B Ministry (1983-84). A crore is equal to ten million.

5. See *Annual Report* of the Ministry of I and B 1983-84. "The Special Plan for Expansion envisages setting up of 13 additional HPTs and 113 LPTs at an outlay of Rs. 68 crores to ultimately reach a target of 180(LPT) transmitters in the country by the end of 1984-85". p.2.

6. *Doordarshan* 1994, op. cit.

CHAPTER–5

1. *Broadcasting Around the World,* William E. McCavitt, TAB Books, Blue Ridge Summit, PA, pp.76 ff.

2. *Broadcasting Around the World,* op. cit. pp. 120 ff.

3. *Akash Bharati, National Broadcast Trust,* Report of the Working Group on Autonomy for Akashvani (AIR) and Doordarshan, Ministry of I and B, New Delhi, 1978. It said: "We envisage an autonomous national

trust as the authority under which Akashvani and Doordarshan should grow. This we are naming Akash Bharati—the National Broadcast trust. *By their very nature radio and TV television are in the public domain and must serve public interest". Emphasis added.*

4. Prasar Bharati Act, 1990. Passed by both houses in September 1990, and received the assent of the President (of India) on the 12th of the same month, has yet to be implemented by the government which has not issued a notification to bring it into operation. The act aims to remove governmental control over AIR and DD and set up a Prasar Bharati Corporation to run the two media networks. There is to be a 15-member Board to operate the media, of whom the lage majority will be non-officials appointed on the recommendations of a high powerd body consisting of the Chairman of the Rajya Sabha (actually the Vice President of India), the Chairman of the Press Council of India and a nominee of the President, which would, in effect, mean the I and B Ministry.

CHAPTER–6

1. The author is grateful to P.S. Sundaram, Secretary, Broadcast Engineering Society (India), for some of the information on satellite broadcating.

2. *Aryabhata Astronomer Mathematician*, K N Menon, Publications Division, Delhi.

   Aryabhata The Space Temple, Vladimir Gabarev, Sterling Publications, New Delhi.

3. *Globostar—A New Concept for BSS* (Broadcast Satellite Service), T J Brewer, *Conference Publication*, 1st International Broadcating , Cable and Satellite India'93 Exhibition and Conference, New Delhi, published by the Broadcast Engineering Society (INDIA).

4. *The Conference Publication*, op. cit, has a wealth of information on this and other aspects of satellite technology.

5. *Digital Compression*, the New Standard for Transmission, Thomas C Hunter, *Conference Publicaton*, op. cit. He says :"What is compression? It is means of transmitting and receiving many TV channels using the same amount of radio spectrum (space) as has been used to transmit a single channel.... upto twenty films can be compressed into one channel.... six channels of live action sports per conventional channel ... many programs can be transmitted over a single tranponder".

6. Much of the information on NIC's election coverage was derived from DDG, NIC, Dr N Vijayaditya, and his colleagues. Also see 'Role of NIC in the Election Process' in *Informatics* Quarterly Newsletter of NIC, Vol. I No.1, October 1992 (which obviously covered the events before the state assembly elections 1993).

CHAPTER–7

1. *Doordarshan 1994*, pp. 93-94.

2. This information and some other details on cable operations gratefully received from Mrs Roop Sharma, President, Cable Operators Federation of India, (COFI) Delhi.

3. Siddhartha Ray, Star's Indian representative, New Delhi.

4. Illegal gratification extracted monthly or weekly as protection money or insurance against registration of minor violations of the law.

5. Infromation on the US cable industry is drawn from the keynote address of Michael C Rau, Senior Vice President,Science and Technology, National Associa-

tion of Broadcasters, USA to the 1st International Broadcasting Cable and Satellite India'93 Exhibition and Conference, See *Conference Publication*, op. cit.

6. *Economic Times*, Delhi Dec 14,1993 "Cable operators threaten Zee TV blackout".

7. *Times of India Delhi*, Dec. 6, 1993 "Cong poll video reached 70 lakh people".

8. "Satellite TV in Kerala faces problems", *Times of India Delhi* December 18, 1993. Also the *Statesman*, Delhi June 29, 1993 "Asianet worries cable operators".

9. *Independent*, Bombay, October 12, 1993 "Star TV too dim in Calcutta".

CHAPTER–8

1. King Ambhi of Taxila (Takshasila, 15 km from Rawalpindi, the twin city of Pakistan's capital Islamabad) was the archtypal collaborator. He went to meet Alexander the Great in 326 B.C. at a place near Kabul and invited him to India since he had a score to settle with Porus (called Poros by the Greeks), King of the region between the Jhelum and the Chenab to the east of Taxila. Porus fought bravely against the invading army of Alexander, and asked by Alexander after defeat how he would like to be treated by the Greeks said: "Like a King".

   See *A History of India*. J.C. Powell-Price, Thomas Nelson and Sons, London, New Yark, pp. 31-32.

   "The ruler of the Taxilan Kingdom, called Taxiles by the Greeks, already hard pressed by the Paurava (Porus) and Abhisara from the east and the north, had sent his son Ambhi to Bactria to assure Alexander of his support against any Indian who might resist him".

Advanced History of India, K. A. Nilakanta Sastri and G. Srinivasachari, Allied Publishers, Bombay, Calcutta.

2. See Harvey Stockwin's informative report from Hong Kong in the *Times of India* Delhi, July 27, 1993.

3. "Star Buys Half of Zee shares" *Indian Express,* Delhi Dec. 25, 1993 and "Zee TV denies armtwisting by Murdoch", *Times of India,* Delhi Dec. 25, 1993.

4. See Chapter 18 for more details on Zee.

5. "Star trying hard to twinkle in China", *Observer,* Delhi January 17, 1994.

6. "China to black out foreign TV" *Statesman,* Delhi October 17, 1993.

7. "Impeding the Western intrusion" *International Herald Tribune* report reproduced in *Observer,* Delhi, October 19, 1993.

8. Conveyed orally to author by Siddhartha Ray, Star representative in India, on Dec. 15, 1993.

9. See *Doordarshan 1994,* pp. 32-45.

10. See paper "BBC World Service Television's First Year in Asia", presented at the "Satellite and Cable TV—Opportunities and Challenges" Seminar, November 17-18, 1992, organised by the Indian Institute of Mass Communication, IIMC, in New Delhi.

11. "BBC World Service Television's First Year in Asia", op. cit.

12. "Open Skies for TV" survey conducted by Dr. J. S. Yadava, Director IIMC, Delhi, September-October, 1992.

13. "BBC's Biased Programme", letter to the editor, *Indian Express,* October 27, 1993, Delhi, and "Newsreading", another letter in the same paper, November 4, 1993.

14. "BBC confronts Murdoch", Raymond Snoddy's report in the *Financial Times,* London, reproduced in the *Times of India,* Delhi, October 19, 1993.

CHAPTER–9

1. *Doordarshan 1994,* Chronology pp. 91-95

2. *Gazette of India* Notification, October 1, 1992 "Scheme for Allotting time slots on the Metro Channel of Doordarshan and All India Radio" (the radio's FM channel was selected and became eventually the only one to give time slots to private broadcasters when the slots scheme on DD was frustrated).

   See also the abortive report of the Air Time Committee of India, laying down the procedure for the allotment of slots in DD and AIR, January 20, 1993, which was not implemented.

3. *Proceedings of IIMC* Seminar, November 1992.

4. *Indian Express,* Delhi, Dec. 12, 1993 "Diabolical Invasion from the Sky", being on account of K. P. Singh Deo's address to a seminar on the "Impact of Television on Economic, Social and Cultural Life of Indian Society", organised by the AINEC, All Indian Newspapers Editors Conference, Delhi.

5. I and B Secretary's welcome address to the seminar on New Mass Communication Environment, October 26, 1993, organised by the Press Information Bureau, under the aegis of the Indo-US Sub-Commission for Education and Culture, New Delhi.

CHAPTER–10

1. K.P. Singh Deo's statement of March 23, 1993 reproduced in full in the appendices.

CHAPTER–11

1. *Indian Express*, Delhi, July 5, 1993 "DD slot grabbers seek legitimacy".

2. *Times of India*, Delhi, July 5, 1993 "Queue drama outside DD" and July 7 "Queues swell as producers fight it out".

3. "Eager producers make a bee line", *Indian Express*, Delhi, July 1, 1993.

4. *Times of India*, Delhi, July 22, 1993 "HC quashes DD allotment ways" and *Indian Express*, of date, "HC rejects DD time slot scheme".

CHAPTER–12

1. *Doordarshan 1994*, p.30.

2. Op. cit. p.30.

3. There were news reports of his arrival and doings, inculding meeting governmental and other VIPs, in one of which he was quoted as saying he did not allow his children to watch MTV (a clear admission that he practised double standards), photographs, (fawning) cartoons, interviews and special articles. About the admission that he did not let his offspring watch MTV. See the *Statesman* February 19, 1994, "Murdoch calls on Advani".

4. "Rival for DD on home turf", *Hindustan Times*, Delhi, November 28, 1993.

5. "New DD policy hits many serials", *Times of India*, Delhi, Dec. 10, 1993.

6. "DD fails to live up to new policies", *Times of India,* February 3, 1994.

CHAPTER–13

1. Details of the negotiations conducted by DD with CAB are drawn from a note prepared for Parliament.

2. DD also kept quiet when its silence was liable to be misunderstood. In raking up the issue close to the tournament, CAB was seeking to put psychological pressure on DD, although indirectly there was acknowledgement that any tournament staged in India which was not covered by DD would bring a bad name to CAB itself.

CHAPTER–14

1. "No peep-show ", Letter to the editer, *Times of India,* Delhi, January 15, 1994, by Zee TV's Vice-President Kamlesh Pandey, and *Times* editor's comment thereon.

2. " Murdoch Spells software success", *Times of India,* Delhi February 13, 1994. The hading is somewhat misleading.

3. Op. Cit. " Murdoch Spells Software success".

4. Mrs. Roop Sharma, president, Cable Operators Federation of India, COFI, in conversation with the author.

5. "It is to be hoped, then that the media baron will keep a vigilant eye on Zee TV and rescue it before it becomes just another song and dance peep-show", 'Enter Mr. Murdoch', *Times of India,* Dec. 27, 1993.

6. "Agnivesh for ban on satellite TV", *Times of India,* Delhi, November 20, 1993. See also "Bishops' call to protect Indian family values", *Times,* March 7, 1994.

CHAPTER–15

1. "CNN Chief to visit India in April or August",*Times of India,* Delhi, February 19, 1994.

2. See note 6 under chapter 8.

3. Pakistan's population was 114 million (1991 census) while the Philippines had a population of 60.9 million (1991), according to the *Statesman's Yearbook 1993-94*. The Philippines had 174 TV stations against five in Pakistan where it is a government monopoly (Indian population by 1993 was more than 900 million).

4. "Countering the Threat from Satellite TV" by Krishan Sondhi, *Times of India,* Delhi, February 21, 1994.

5. *Many Voices, One World,* being the report of the Sean MacBride Comission, set up by UNESCO, published by it and Kogan Page, London. The book is subtitled "Towards a new, more just and more efficient world information and communication order".

6. See Chapter 7.

7. "IEA gives clean chit to India on safety norms", *Indian Express,* Delhi, February 23, 1994.

8. *Indian Express,* Delhi, February 23, 1994, op. cit.

9. "Requiem For Polly", Paul Chutkow, the *Statesman,* Delhi, December 14, 1993.

10. The *Statesman,* December 14, 1993, op. cit.

11. The *Economist,* London, January, 8-14 1994 "The New World Order".

CHAPTER–16

1. *Indian Express*, Delhi, March 4, 1994, "My Country, Wrong or Wrong". The paper argued that satellite TV was accessible to all. But only seven million of the over 40 million TV households had satellite TV connections, not *all*. Countries like china, Saudi Arabia, Malaysia, Singapore and Vietnan, had shown that dish antennae could be banned by the government. Only the exponents of foreign media, TV or newspapers, take satellite TV as "inevitable".

2. "Plea against foreign papers entry rejected", *Times of India*, March 3, 1994. "HC dismisses petitions against entry of foreign papers", the *Statesman*, Delhi, the same date.

3. See note 7 below.

4. Information obtained from RNI, Delhi.

5. *Pioneer*, Delhi January 23, 1994, in which Aveek Sarkar, the chief of the *Ananda Bazar Patrika* group, is quoted as saying "Samir Jain is scared shit". Samir Jain is second in command at the *Times of India* and the controlling company, Bennet Coleman and company. Sarkar argues that all leading editors have supported the entry of foreign media. While his list is not exhaustive and there are editors who oppose the entry, one has to say: "A Newspaper is too serious a matter to be left to the editor (and his proprietor)".

6. "Justice Iyer warns of the dangers of foreign press entry", *Times of India*, Delhi, January 17, 1994.

7. "HC reserves orders on foreign media", *Times of India*, Delhi, February 23, 1994.

8. "Media divided over foreign papers entry", *Times of India*, Delhi, February 6, 1994.

9. *PTI story, Origin and Growth of the Indian Press and the News Agency*, G. N. S. Raghavan, PTI, Delhi, P. 117.

10. Ibid. (pp. 35-38). *PTI story*.

CHAPTER–17

1. See *Economic Survey 1993-94*, Ministry of Finance, Delhi, S-3 Appendix.

2. *An Indian Personality for Television*. Report of the Working Group on Software for Doordarshan, Publications Division, Delhi, p. 7.

3. *An Indian Personality*, Op. cit. p.10.

4. *An Indian Personality*, Op. cit. p. 141-42.

5. *An Indian Personlity*, Op. cit. p. 142.

6. A survey of 1,000 adult Americans, commissioned by the US magazine, *Mediaweek*, in 1993 as reported by the *New York Times*, said that nearly two-thirds of American adults say they find violence and sex on television offensive. Nearly half of that number said that they would no longer consider purchasing products that are advertised in programmes featuring sex and violence. The *New York Times*, report was reproduced by the *Indian Express*, Delhi, November 23, 1993.

CHAPTER–18

1. For this and other factual information and for answers to questions, as indicated, the author is grateful to Rajat Sharma of Zee Telefilms who also provided him with an informative folder on Zee primarily addressed to advertisers.

APPENDICES

Appendix I

CABLE REGULATION BILL
Bill No. LXVIII of 1993
THE CABLE TELEVISION NETWORKS (REGULATION) BILL, 1993

A

BILL

to regulate the operation of cable television networks in the country and for matters connected therewith or incidental thereto.

Be it enacted by Parliament in the Forty-fourth years of the Republic of India as follows:-

CHAPTER 1
PRELIMINARY

Short title, extent and commencement.

1. This Act may be called the Cable Television Networks (Regulation) Act, 1993.

(2) It extends to the whole of India.

(3) It shall come into force on such date as the Central Government may, be notification in the Official Gazette, appoint.

Definitions

2. In this Act, unless the context otherwise requires–

(*a*) "Cable operator" means any person who provides cable service through a cable television network or otherwise controls or is responsible for the management and operation of a cable television network;

(*b*) "Cable Service" means the transmission by cables of programmes including retransmission by cables of any broadcast television signals;

(*c*) "cable television network" means any system consisting of a set of closed transmission paths and associated signal generation, control and distribution equipment, designed to provide cable service for reception by multiple subscribers;

(*d*) "company" means a company as defined in section 3 of the Companies Act, 1956; 1 of 1956

(*e*) "person" means -

(*i*) an individual who is a citizen of India;

(*ii*) an association of individuals or body of individuals, whether incorporated or not, whose members are citizens of India;

(*iii*) a company in which not less than fifty-one per cent of the paid-up share capital is held by the citizens of India;

(*f*) "prescribed" means prescribed by rules made under this Act;

(*g*) "programme" means any television broadcast and includes—

(*i*) exhibition of films, features, dramas, advertisements and serials through video cassette recorders or video cassette players;

(*ii*) any audio or visual or audio-visual live performance or presentation, and the expression "programming service" shall be construed accordingly;

(*h*) "registering authority" means such authority as the Central Government may, by notification in the Official Gazette, specify to perform the functions of the registering authority under this Act;

(*i*) "subscriber" means a person who receives the signals of cable television network at a place indicated by him to the cable operator, without further transmitting it to any other person.

CHAPTER II
REGULATION OF CABLE TELEVISION NETWORK

Cable television network not to be operated except after

3. No person shall operate a cable television network unless he is registered as a cable operator under this Act :

Provided that a person operating a cable television network, immediately before the commencement of this Act, may continue to do so for a period of ninety days from such commencement; and if he has made an application for registration as a cable operator under section 4 within the said period, till he is registered under that section or the registering authority refuses to grant registration to him under that section.

Registration as cable operator

4. (1) Any person who is operating or is desirous of operating a cable television network may apply for registration as cable operator to the registering authority.

(2) An application under sub-section (1) shall be made in such form and be accompanied by such fee as may be prescribed.

(3) On receipt of the application, the registering authority shall satisfy itself that the applicant has furnished all the required information and on being so satisfied register the applicant as a cable operator and grant to him a certificate of such registration:

Provided that the registering authority may, for reasons to be recorded in writing and communicated to the applicant, refuse to grant registration to him if it is satisfied that he does not fulfil the condition specified in clause (*e*) of section 2.

5. No person shall transmit or re-transmit through a cable service any programme unless such programme is in conformity with the prescribed programme code. Programme code

6. No person shall transmit or re-transmit through a cable service any advertisement unless such advertisement is in conformity with the prescribed advertisement code. Advertisement code

7. Every cable operator shall maintain a register in the prescribed form indicating therein in brief the programmes transmitted or re-transmitted through the cable service during a month and such register shall be maintained by the cable operator for a period of one year after the actual transmission or re-transmission of the said programmes.

8. (1) Every cable operator using a dish antenna or Television Receiver only shall, from the

commencement of this Act re-transmit at least one Doordarshan channel of his choice through the cable service.

Compulsory transmission of one Doordarshan channel.

(2) The Doordarshan channel referred to in sub-section (1) shall be re-transmitted without any deletion or alternations of any programme transmitted on such channel.

use of standard equipment in cable televison netwok.

9. No cable operator shall, on and from the date of the expiry of a period of one year from the date of the establishment and publication of the Indian Standard by the Bureau of Indian Standards in accordance with the provisions of the Bureau of Indian Standards Act, 1986, use any equipment in his cable television network unless such equipment conforms to the said Indian standard.

63 of 1986

Cable television network not to interfere with any telecommunication system.

10. Every cable operator shall ensure that the cable television network being operated by him does not interfere, in any way, with the functioning of the authorised telecommunication systems.

CHAPTER III
SEIZURE AND CONFISCATION OF CERTAIN EQUIPMENT

Power to seize equipment

11. (1) If any officer, not below the rank of a Group 'A' officer of the Central Government authorised in this behalf by the Government (hereinafter referred to as the authorised officer), has reason to believe that the provisions

used for operating the cable television nework

of section 3 have been or are being contravened by any cable operator, he may seize the equipment being used by such cable operator for operating the cable television network.

(2) No such equipment shall be retained by the authorized officer for a period exceeding ninety days from the date of its seizure unless the approval of the District judge, within the local limits of whose jurisdiction such seizure has been made, has been obtained for such retention.

Confiscation.

12. The equipment seized under sub-section (1) of section 11 shall be liable to confiscation unless the cable operator from whom the equipment has been seized registers himself as a cable operator under section 4 within a period of thirty days from the date of seizure of the said equipment.

Seizure or confiscation of equipment not to interfere with other punishment.

13. No seizure or confiscation of equipment referred to in section 11 or section 12 shall prevent the infliction of any punishment to which the person affected thereby is liable under the provisions of this Act.

Giving of opportunity to the cable operator

14. (1) No order adjudicating confiscation of the equipment referred to in section 12 shall be made unless the cable operator has been given a notice in writing informing him of the grounds on which it is proposed to confiscate such equipment and giving him a reasonable

of seized equipment

opportunity of making a representation in writing, within such reasonable time as may be specified in the notice against the confiscation and if he so desires of being heard in the matter:

Provided that where no such notice is given within a period of ninety days from the date of the seizure of the equipment, such equipment shall be returned after the expiry of that period to the cable operator from whose possession it was seized.

(2) Save as otherwise provided in sub-section (1), the provisions of the Code of Civil Procedure, 1908 shall, so far as may be, apply to every proceeding referred to in sub-section (1).

Appeal.

15 (1) Any person aggrieved by any decision of the court adjudicating a confiscation of the equipment may prefer an appeal to the court to which an appeal lies from the decision of such court.

(2) The appellate court may, after giving the appellant an opportunity of being heard, pass such order as it thinks fit confirming, modifying or revising the decision appealed against or may send back the case with such directions as it may think fit for a fresh decision or adjudication, as the case may be, after taking additional evidence if necessary.

(3) No further appeal shall lie against the order of the court made under sub-section (2).

CHAPTER IV
OFFENCES AND PENALTIES

Punishment for contravention of provisions of this Act.

16. Whoever contravenes any of the provisions of this Act shall be punishable,-

(*a*) for the first offence, with imprisonment for a term which may extends to two years or with fine which may extend to one thousand rupees or with both;

(*b*) for every subsequent offence, with imprisonment for a term which extends to five years and with fine which may extend to five thousand rupees.

C Offences by companies.

17 (1) Where an offence under this Act has been committed by a company, every person who, at the time the offence was committed, was in charge of, and was responsible to, the company for the conduct of the business of the company, as well as the company, shall be deemed to be guilty of the offence and shall be liable to be proceeded against and punished accordingly:

Provided that nothing contained in this sub-section shall render any such person liable to any punishment, if he proves that the offence was committed without his knowledge or that he had exercised all due diligence to prevent the commission of such offence.

(2) Notwithstanding anything contained in sub-section (1), where any offence under this Act has been committed by a company and it is proved that the offence has been committed with the consent or connivance of, or is attributable to any negligence on the part of any

director, manager, secretary or other officer of the company, such director, manager, secretary or other officer shall also be deemed to be guilty of that offence and shall be liable to be proceeded against and punished accordingly.

Explanation.—For the purpose of this section,—

(*a*) "company" means any body corporate and includes a firm or other association of individuals; and

(*b*) "director" in relation to a firm means a partner in the firm.

Cognizance of offences.

18. No court shall take cognizance of any offence punishable under this Act except upon a complaint in writing made by such officer, not below the rank of a Group 'A'officer of the Central Government, as the State Government may, by notification in the Official Gazette, specify in this behalf.

CHAPTER V
MISCELLANEOUS

Power to prohibit transmission of certain programmes in public interest.

19. Where an officer, not below the rank of a Group 'A' officer of the Central Government authorised by the State Government in this behalf, thinks it necessary or expedient so to do in the public interest, he may, by order, prohibit any cable operator from transmitting on re-transmitting any particular programme if it is likely to promote, on grounds of religion, race, language, caste or community or any other ground whatsoever, disharmony or feelings of enmity, hatred or ill-will between different religions, racial or linguistic or regional groups or

castes or communities or which is likely to disturb the public transquillity.

Power to prohibit operation of cable television network in

20. Where the Central Government thinks it necessary or expedient so to do in public interest, it may prohibit the operation of any cable television network in such areas as it may, by notification in the Official Gazette, specify in the behalf.

Application of other laws not barred.

21. The provisions of this Act shall be in addition to, and not in derogation of, the Drugs and Cosmetics Act, 1940, the Pharmacy Act,. 1948, the Emblems and Names (Prevention of Improper Use) Act, 1950, the Drugs (Controls) Act, 1950, the Cinematograph Act, 1952, the Drugs and Magic Remidies (Objectionable Advertisement) Act, 1954, the Prevention of Food Adulteration Act, 1954, the Prize Competitions Act 1955, the Copyright Act, 1957, the Trade and Merchandise Marks Act, 1958, the Indecent Representation of Women (Prohibition) Act, 1986, and the Consumer Protection Act,1986.

Power to make rules.

Gazette, makes rules to carry out the provisions of this Act.

(2) In particular and without prejudice to the generality of the foregoing power such rules may provide for all or any of the following matters, namely—

(*a*) the form of application and the fee payable under sub-section (2) of section 4;

(*b*) the programme code under section 5;

(*c*) the advertisement code under section 6;

---

1. The Indian Express, March 13, 1991

(*d*) the form of register to be maintained by the cable operator under section 7;

(*c*) any other matter which is required to be, or may be, prescribed.

(3) Every rule made under this Act shall be laid, as soon as may be after it is made, before each House of Parliament, while it is in session, for a total period of thirty days which may be comprised in one session or in two or more successive sessions, and if, before expiry of the session immediately following the session or the successive sessions aforesaid, both Houses agree in making any modification in the rule or both Houses agree that the rule should not be made, the rule shall thereafter have effect only in such modified form or be of no effect, as the case may be: so, however, that any such modification or annulment shall be without prejudice to the validity of anything previously done under the rule.

STATEMENT OF OBJECTS AND REASONS

There has been a haphazard mushrooming of cable television networks all over the country during the last few years as a result of the availability of signals of foreign television network *via* satellites. This has been perceived as a "cultural invasion" in many quarters since the programmes available on these satellite channels are predominantly western and totally alien to our culture and way of life. Since, there is no regulation of these cable television networks, lot of undesirable programmes and advertisements are becoming available to the viewers without any kind of censorship.

2. It is also felt that the subscribers of these cable television networks, the programmers and the cable operators themselves are not aware of their rights, responsibilities and obligations in respect of the quality of service, technical as well as content-

wise, use of material protected by copyright, exhibition of uncertified films, protection of subscribers from anti-national broadcasts from sources inimical to our national interest, responsiveness to the genuine grievances of the subscribers and a perceived willingness to operate within the broad framework of the laws of the land, *e.g.*, the Cinematograph Act, 1952, the Copyright Act, 1957, Indecent Representation of Women (Prohibition) Act, 1986.

3. It is therefore, considered necessary to regulate the operation of cable television as the entire country so as to bring about uniformity in their operation. It will thus enable the optimal exploitation of this technology which has the potential of making available to the subscribers a vast pool of information and entertainment.

4. The Bill seeks to achieve the above objects.

K.P. SINGH DEO.

New Delhi
The 23rd July, 1993.

FINANCIAL MEMORANDUM

Clause 4 of the Bill provides for registration of a person who is operating or is desirous of operating a cable television network as cable operator. The application for registration will be made by such person to the registering authority which will be specified by the Central Government under sub-clause (*h*) of clause 2. As there is no reliable estimate of the total number of cable operators in the country, it is not possible at this stage to indicate as to how many applications will be made to the registering authority and the quantum of work involved in the processing authority and the quantum of work involved in the processing of such applications. It is, therefore, not practicable at this juncture to indicate the precise amount of expenditure which will be involved in processing the said applications. However, the expenditure involved in processing the said applications will be met out of the fees which the applicants will deposit along with the applications for registration. Thus no Government budgetary support will be necessary in implementing the provisions of the Bill when enacted.

MEMORANDUM REGARDING DELEGATED LEGISLATION

Clause 19 of the Bill empowers an officer not below the rank of a Group 'A' officer of the Central Government authorised by the State Government, to prohibit, in public interest, any cable operator from transmitting of re-transmitting any particular programme if such officer thinks that the programme is likely to promote, on grounds of religion, race, language, caste or community or any other ground whatsoever, disharmony, feeling of enmity, hatred or ill-will between different religious, racial, linguistic or regional groups or castes or communities or is likely to disturb the public tranquillity. Clause 20 of the Bill empowers the Central Government to prohibit, in public interest, the operation of any cable television network in such areas as it may, by notification in the Official Gazette, specify in this behalf. Clause 22 of the Bill empowers the Central Government to make rules prescribing (*i*) the form of application for registration as cable operator and the fee payable along with such application under clause 4; (*ii*) the programme code which will be complied with by any person while transmitting or re-transmitting any programme through a cable service; (*iii*) the advertisement code which will be complied with by the person while transmitting or re-transmitting any advertisement through a cable service; (*iv*) the form of register required to be maintained by cable operators under section 7; and (*v*) any other matter which is required to be prescribed.

2. The matters in respect of which orders or notifications may be issued or rules may be made in accordance with the aforesaid provisions are matters of procedure and detail and it is not practicable to provide for them in the Bill itself.

3. The delegation of legislative power is, therefore, of a normal character.

Appendix II

Parliament's Standing Committee on Communications' Report on Cable Bill

Introduction

I, the Chairperson of the Standing Committee on Communications (1993-94) to which the Bill to regulate the operation of Cable Television Networks in the country and for matters connected therewith or incidental thereto.

The Cable Television Networks (Regulation) Bill, 1993 was referred by the Speaker in consultation with the Chairman, Rajya Sabha, under Rule 331E(b) of the Rules of Procedure and Conduct of Business in Lok Sabha for examination, having been authorised to submit the report on their behalf, present this Report.

2. The Bill was introduced in Rajya Sabha on 3rd August, 1993 and published in the Gazette of India, Extraordinary, Part-II, Section 2, dated 3rd August, 1993. Considering the time constraint in which the Committee had to work, the committee held only four sittings to consider the Bill.

3. The Committee held its first sitting on 19th August, 1993 and took oral evidence of the representatives of various cable television networks associations, individuals etc. At their second sitting held in the afternoon on the same day, the Committee called the representatives of the Ministry of Information and Broadcasting and sought clarification from them on various clauses of the Bill.

4. At their sitting held on 23rd August, 1993, the Committee considered the Bill clause-by-clause.

5. The Committee considered and adopted the Report on the Bill as slightly amended, at their sitting held on 25th August, 1993.

Kumari Vimla Verma
Chairperson
Standing Committee on
Communications

New Delhi :
August 25, 1993
Bhadra 3, 1915 (Saka)

Report of the Committee

The Committee note that the Cable Television Networks (Regulation) Bill, 1993 has been brought forward to regulate the operation of Cable Television Networks in the country and bring about uniformity in their operation.

2. The programmes that are being put across through satellite channels of foreign television networks and received through dish antenna are at times not in tune with our rich culture and holistic character of Indian tradition.

3. The Committee has considered the principal clauses of the Bill. The Committee would like to highlight a few points to make the proposed Bill more purposeful and effective.

4. In Clause 2 of the Bill, the "cable operator" has been defined to mean any person who provides cable service through a cable television network or otherwise controls or is responsible for the management and operation of a cable television network. The Committee feel that this definition should be suitably amended to signify the commercial motives/intents of the cable operators and accordingly, the Committee recommend that the words "as a commercial activity" may be added at the end of the aforesaid definition.

5. Clauses 5 and 6 of the Bill provide that a cable operator shall not transmit or re-transmit through a cable service any programme or advertisement unless it is in conformity with the prescribed programme/advertisement code which will be notified by the Government under the powers to make rules conferred on it under Clause 22 of the Bill.

6. The Committee are of the opinion that the cable operators show most of the time the programmes available from foreign television networks *via* satellites and have no control over them. As such it will be very difficult for them to ensure that these programmes and advertisements are in conformity with our programme code/advertisement code. The Committee feel that

before holding the cable operator guilty of violation of these two clauses of the Bill, prior knowledge of the programmes being violative of the programme/advertisement code should be established.

7. As far as programmes shown through pre-recorded cassettes on VCR are concerned, the Committee feel that the producers/distributors of the cassettes should also be made equally responsible alongwith the cable operators for adhering to the programme/advertisement codes.

8. The Committee have noted that every cable operator is required to maintain a register showing the details of the programmes transmitted during a month and preserve it for a period of one year under clause 7 of the Bill. The Committee feel that no useful purpose will be served by indicating too many details in the register. The cable operators may keep a note of the chronological list of channels being transmitted or of the cassettes being shown by them through VCR on a particular day and time in the aforesaid register.

9. Clause 8 provides for compulsory transmission of one Doordarshan channel of their choice by the cable operators. If this provision is made mandatory the small cable operators will have to install extra dish antenna for the same. While giving evidence before the Committee, some of the cable operators stated that this clause would cause undue burden on the small cable operators. The Ministry officials on the other hand sought to allay the fears by stating that they had the option to show one Doordarshan terrestrial channel. The Committee strongly feel that when the cable operators are allowed to show the foreign channels, they must also show atleast one of the national channels as a matter of national commitment.

10. In Clause 9, use of standard equipment conforming to Indian Standard has been made compulsory from the date of expiry of a period of one year from the date of establishment and publication of the Indian Standard by the Bureau of Indian Standards. The Committee feel that to mitigate any hardship on

this account to small cable operators in the beginning, they should be allowed a period of three years to phase out their old equipment.

11. The Committee feel that in Clause 11(2), the period of ninety days allowed to the authorised officer for retaining the seized equipment without the approval of the District Judge should be reduced to ten days within which the authorised officer should obtain the orders of the District Judge for retaining it beyond that period. Clause 12 already provides that the seized equipment shall be liable to confiscation if the cable operator does not register himself within 30 days from the date of seizure of the equipment.

12. As regards the notice required to be given for confiscation of the equipment under Clause 14(1) of the Bill, the Committee feel that the time limit for giving such a notice may also be reduced from ninety days to ten days from the date of the seizure of the equipment.

13. Sub-Clause (3) of the Bill states that no further appeal shall lie against the order of the court made under sub-section (2). The Committee feel that the cable operators should be provided the right of second appeal and therefore, Sub-Clause (3) of Clause 15 of the Bill may be amended accordingly.

14. Clause 19 of the Bill gives powers to Group 'A' Officers of the Central Government authorised by the State Government in this behalf to prohibit transmission of certain programmes in public interest. The Committee noted that there were two divergent views of the members on this clause. One view was that the words "or any other ground whatsoever " appearing in the Clause had given blanket powers to the Group 'A' Officers of the Central Government which could be misused by them and it could also be violative of fundamental rights of the citizens. It was suggested that the words "or any other ground whatsoever" might be deleted from this clause. The other view expressed was that the provision as made could not be faulted with as many grounds leading to a situation mentioned therein

may not be visualized today but could crop up when a particular programme is produced *e.g.* on prostitution portrayed not aesthetically as a social problem but crudely and brazenly. If the order of the Officer violates the fundamental right of expression, it would always be open to challenge. At the most the words "any other ground whatsoever" could be qualified by the words "to be recorded in writing.".

Kumari Vimla Verma
Chairperson
Standing Committee on
Communications

New Delhi
August 25, 1993
Bhadra 3, 1915 (saka)

Appendix III

STATEMENT MADE BY THE MINISTER OF STATE FOR INFORMATION & BROADCASTING IN THE LOK SABHA ON MARCH 23, 1993 REGARDING THE INTRODUCTION OF NEW SATELLITE BASED TV CHANNELS IN INDIA

As the Hon'ble Members are aware, Television in India started in 1959 on an experimental manner. During the last 34 years, we have established 546 television transmitters all over the country. These transmitters are capable of giving TV programmes within a fixed geographical area. Initially, these transmitters could not be inter-connected into a national network. With the launching of communication satellites, it was possible to transmit a common programme from one production centre and network the programme throughout the country. At present, two Indian communication satellites, INSAT-1D and INSAT-2A are in operation and are being used for the purpose of television in India. A number of transponders on these two satellites are being used for regional programmes in the States of Maharashtra, Karnataka, Tamil Nadu, Andhra Pradesh, Orissa, Gujarat and West Bengal. Such regional programmes are produced in the State capital studios and are carried by all the transmitters within the respective States from 5.00 p.m. to 8.30 p.m. At other times of the day, the programmes originate in Delhi and are transmitted and networked throughout the country. Government has considered the need for utilising the spare time available in these transponders and introduce a variety of television services to cater to the diverse interests and needs of the country.

2. The Hon'ble Members are aware that several foreign satellite TV channels have started beaming their signals to this country and we are facing what is described by many as cultural invasion. In order to give a befitting response to this challenge, Government proposes to start a few more channels using the spare time on these transponders. These TV signals, uplinked through the transponders on Indian satellites, can be received through appropriate TV receiving equipment, commonly

known as dish antenna and can be further distributed by the cable operators. A large number of cable operators today have installed equipment to receive signals from Asiasat (STAR, BBC & ZEE TV). The reception from the Indian satellite system can be received by the same dish antenna by changing its direction. Individuals can also have their own dish antenna. One of the attractions for such cable operators to reorient the dish antenna to the INSAT system will be that Doordarshan would also be capable of offering a multi-channel option comparable to STAR. It is proposed to start these channels in a phased manner beginning from 1st April, 1993 and increase both the number of the channels and their duration as and when software and hardware facilities are available.

3. It is proposed to devote these channels to the following :-

(*i*) Primary Channel—the present format of Doordarshan.

(*ii*) Metro Channel.

(*iii*) Entertainment and Cultural Channel.

(*iv*) Sports Channel.

(*v*) News, Current Affairs and Business News.

I am reiterating for the information of the Hon'ble Members that while there will be no change in the present method of reception for the primary channel of Doordarshan, the Metro Channel, when uplinked through the satellite, can be received by TV viewers only if they are connected to the appropriate dish antenna excepting in the cities of Delhi, Bombay, Madras and Calcutta where it will be received in the normal manner as at present. The other three channels can be received by the TV viewers if they are connected to the appropriate dish antenna.

4. Government has already announced a scheme of allotment of time slots to private production houses and private producers on the metro channel of Doordarshan. A similar

schemes will be adopted for the three new channels proposed to be established now.

5. Today the transponders used for the existing national channel and metro channel and the proposed three channels are working on two different satellites, *i.e.*, INSAT-1D and INSAT-2A. It is expected that with the launching of INSAT-2B, it would be possible to re-arrange the transponders on a single satellite so that five channels can be obtained on a single dish antenna.

6. It may also be of interest and happiness to the Hon'ble Members that the advertisers who are advertising on foreign satellite channels after paying foreign exchange would now be able to show their products on the proposed five channels. I am sure that those who saw the unfriendly propaganda on the foreign satellite channels would not like the advertisers to go there.

7. I hope the Hon'ble Members would appreciate the steps now being taken by us to optimally utilise the capability of our Indian satellites designed and put in orbit by our dedicated band of scientists.

Appendix IV

DD's New Commercial Rate Card (Effective from 21.3.94)

1. Annexures I, II & III indicate rates for spot buys and sponsorship.

2. The categorisations are as under :

(*a*) *NATIONAL NETWORK (DD I)*

I.	Super 'A' Special	(*i*) Hindi Feature Film (Saturday) (*ii*) Chitrahaar (Wednesday) (*iii*) Rangoli (Sunday)
II.	Super 'A'	(*i*) 9.00 P.M. slot on all days (Hindi/English). (*ii*) 9.30 P.M. to 10.00 P.M. Hindi Serials. (*iii*) Live coverage/highlights of spl. international sports (to be intimated in advance). (*iv*) Before 'Samachar' at 8.30 P.M. (*v*) Any other programme intimated in advance.
III.	'A' Special	(*i*) Various programmes/slots on Sunday morning (9.00 A.M.—12.00 Noon). (*ii*) 9.30 P.M. to 10.00 P.M. (except Hindi serials). (*iii*) Live coverage/highlights of international sports events. (*iv*) Before 'The News' at 10.00 P.M. (*v*) Any other programme intimated in advance.
IV.	'A'	(*i*) 10.30 P.M. slot on all days. (*ii*) Late night/Tuesday afternoon films. (*iii*) Live coverage of National sports events (on Sundays, Holidays and Finals). (*iv*) Highlights/recorded international sport's events telecast after 10.30 P.M.

	(*v*) After 9.00 A.M. on Saturdays only.
	(*vi*) Any other programme intimated in advance.
V. 'B'	(*i*) Morning and afternoon transmission.
	(*ii*) From 11.00 P.M. onwards.
	(*iii*) Regional feature film on National Network (Sunday).
	(*iv*) Live national sports events on week days and matches upto semi-final.
	(*v*) World of Sports/Sponsored sports programmes in the afternoon transmission.
	(*vi*) Any other programme intimated in advance.

(*b*) *REGIONAL CHANNEL—I*

I. Super 'A' Special	(*i*) Films in state regional languages (except Marathi, Gujarati and Punjabi) and film-based programmes.
	(*ii*) Programmes/News in-between Regional Language Feature Films (except Bombay, Ahmedabad & Jalandhar).
	(*iii*) Programmes/News in-between Hindi Feature Films and Chitrahaar on National Network (Lucknow, Jalandhar, Jaipur & Bhopal).
	(*iv*) Before Chitrahaar (Ahmedabad).
	(*v*) Any other programme intimated in advance.
II. Super 'A'	(*i*) Serials.
	(*ii*) Marathi Film (Bombay), Gujarati (Ahmedabad) and Punjabi (Jalandhar).
	(*iii*) Films in Regional Langu- ages other than that of the State.
	(*iv*) Play (Madras).
	(*v*) Chitranjali (Calcutta).

	(*vi*)	Programmes/News in-between Hindi Feature Films and before Chitrahaar (Wednesday) on National Network for Delhi, Ahmedabad, Calcutta and Bombay.
	(*vii*)	Regional News with 10% premium, Madras, Hyderabad, Bangalore, Trivandrum and Calcutta.
	(*viii*)	Regional News at other Kendras.
	(*ix*)	Any other programme intimated in advance.
III. 'A'	(*i*)	Play (except Madras), Saptahiki.
	(*ii*)	6.30 P.M. onwards.
	(*iii*)	Morning transmission on Sundays programmes.
	(*iv*)	Between Hindi Feature Film (Saturday) and before Chitrahaar (Wednesday) on National Network for Madras, Hyderabad, Bangalore and Trivandrum.
	(*v*)	Any other programme intimated in advance.
IV. 'B'		Before 6.30 P.M.

METRO ENTERTAINMENT CHANNEL (DD-II)

1.	Super 'A'	(*i*) 8.00 P.M.—10.00 P.M. (Film-based programmes and serials) (*ii*) Any other programme intimated in advance.
2.	'A' Special	(*i*) 8.00 P.M.—10.00 P.M. (Talk Shows, Quiz, Games Show, English Serials, other non-film based and non-serial programmes). (*ii*) 8.00 A.M. — 12.00 (Noon) (Sundays only) (All programmes regardless of the format and language). (*iii*) 7.30 P.M. — 8.00 P.M. 10.30 P.M. — 11.00 P.M. (*iv*) Any other programme intimated in advance.
3.	'A'	(*i*) 7.00 P.M. —7.30 P.M. (*ii*) Any other programme intimated in advance.
4.	'B'	(*i*) Morning (On All Days). (*ii*) Afternoon and programmes upto 7.00 P.M. (*iii*) After 11.00 P.M. (*iv*) Any other programme intimated in advance.

3. Sponsored Programmes

(*a*) (*i*) Booking is acceptable either of a client or of a product. In the case of a product, the Free Commercial Time (FCT) can be utilised for the ads of that product only.

(*ii*) The Sponsor(s)/Client(s) is allowed to advertise any number of products in the admissible commercial time.

(*iii*) *Commercial Break in Serials* : One commercial break in a 30 minutes slot and two commercial breaks with programme in 45 minutes/60 minutes has been allowed.

In case of outside sponsored programmes, the FCT commercials will be inserted by the Producer.

(*iv*) Ads featuring the artists participating in a particular serial/programme are also accepted for telecast alongwith the same programme.

(*v*) Film song programmes on National Network and Kendras are not open for sponsorship.

(*b*) *Credit Lines*

In addition to Free Commercial Time, the sponsor(s) are allowed credit lines for 10 seconds at the beginning and 10 seconds at the end of the programme only in case of programmes on channel I. In case of Channel II the credit line is part of the FCT.

In case of continuing programmes (*e.g.* feature film, sports etc.) with different sponsors for each 30 minutes slot, the credit lines for 10 seconds each will be superseded over the programme in such a manner that it does not obstruct the viewing of the programme.

The telecast of the credit lines is governed by the following :

(*i*) *Programme sponsored in the name of the client (company)*

The credit line may contain :

(*a*) Visual presentation of the name of the company in any lettering style of their choice and/or name in audio (including accompanying music, if desired).

(*b*) Visual presentation of the standard logo of the company, if so desired; and

(*c*) Any colour scheme of the company's choice for the visual presentation, without special effects.

(ii) Programme sponsored in the name of a product

The credit lines may contain name of the product, spoken or written in any style, with or without accompanying music. There should, however, be no display at all of the product *per se* or any special effects in the visual part of the credit lines.

Note : The procedure for the approval of the credit lines is the same as for ads.

4. Free Commercial Time for Sponsorship of 30 Minutes Programme

(*a*)	Doordarshan programmes (all time categories/all kendras)	40 seconds
(*b*)	Doordarshan commissioned/acquired programmes (National Network) 'Super A', 'A Special' and 'A' Categories.	40 seconds/ 60 seconds

Note : Doordarshan however reserves the right to increase or decrease the FCT from programme to programme.

(c) *Repeats (Primary/Metro to Primary Channel)*

Sponsorship Fee *(B Category only)*

Rs. 70,000/- with 90 seconds FCT (No change)

FROM PRIMARY/METRO OR METRO TO METRO CHANNEL

Spot Buy Rate

'B' Category	Rs. 10,000
'A' Category	Rs. 15,000

Sponsorship Fee

'B' Category	Rs. 20,000 with 90 seconds
'A' Category	Rs. 35,000 with 70 seconds

(*e*) *TELE FILMS/TELE-PLAYS (UNDER 'A' CATEGORY)*

90 Minutes	**4 Minutes (with 2 minutes banking to be utilised with maximum of four programmes of the same category with a period of one month).**
60 Minutes	3 Minutes (with one minute banking to be utilised with maximum of two programmes of the same category within a period of one month).

5. Number of Sponsors Allowed

NATIONAL NETWORK/REGIONAL KENDRAS/METRO ENTERTAINMENT CHANNEL

(*a*)	For a programme with FCT upto 30″	One
(*b*)	For a programme with FCT upto 60″	Two
(*c*)	For a programme with FCT upto 90″	Three
(*d*)	For a programme with FCT upto 120″	Four
(*e*)	For a programme with FCT upto 150″	Five
(*f*)	For a programme with FCT upto 180″ and above	Six

(This will apply to Doordarshan Productions and outside production alike)

6. Other Rates

Film songs programme on National Network and Kendras are not offered for sponsorship.

It has been decided to introduce special positioning and telecast of ads in-between the programme as per premium rates given below :

BEFORE THE PROGRAMME

Positioning in a capsule at premium rate given below :

Last two slots towards the end 10% surcharge premium.

IN BETWEEN THE PROGRAMME

(*i*)	Two capsules-each of 60 seconds at natural breaks for every 30 minutes slot.	25% premium
(*ii*)	*Late Night Films* (Outside Procurers)	
	Afternoon Films Spot Buy	Rs. 25,000/- for 10 seconds.
	Sponsorship fee for 30 minutes	Rs. 1,25,000/- with 90 seconds FCT and two credit lines.
(*iii*)	*Feature film on Sundays (Delhi & LPTs/ Lucknow/Jalandhar/Srinagar/Jaipur*	
	Spot buy	Rs. 60,000 for 10 seconds.
	Sponsorship fee for 30 minutes	Rs. 2,40,000/- with 40 seconds FCT and two credit lines.
(*iv*)	*Film (Tuesdays in the afternoon transmission) (Doordarshan)*	
	Spot buy	Rs. 25,000/- for 10 seconds.
	Sponsorship	Rs. 1,00,000/- with 40 seconds FCT and two credit lines.
(*v*)	*Regional Film on Thursdays (2nd & 4th) Delhi & LPTs (Doordarshan)*	
	Spot buy	Rs. 25,000/- for 10 seconds
	Sponsorship Fee for 30 minutes	Rs. 75,000/- with 40 seconds FCT and two credit lines.
(*vi*)	*Sponsored Songs*	
	National Network	Rs. 1,00,000/-
	Delhi	Rs. 50,000/-
	Madras & Hyderabad	Rs. 20,000/-

Bombay	Rs. 10,000/-
Other Kendras	Rs. 6,000/-

(*vii*) *Tie-up Spot Advertisements*

These ads will be treated as ordinary advertisements with no surcharge.

(*viii*) *Corporate Advertisements*

The restriction on minimum duration of such advertisements has been withdrawn.

(*ix*) *Time Check before News*

Mute ad for 5 to 10 seconds with either the name of the product or the client. *Logo product shot or product advertising is not allowed/acceptable:*

(*a*) 8.30 P.M./10.00 P.M. (Bulletins) : Rs. 25,000

(*b*) Morning/Afternoon (Bulletins) : Rs. 10,000

7. **Banking**

(*a*) *National Network*

Banking of FCT is permissible in the Super A and A Special Categories upto 30 seconds per half an hour for the first 5 episodes. The FCT bank in this manner would however have to be utilised fully in the next five episodes.

(*b*) *Regional Kendras*

Banking of FCT is permissible as follows :

(*i*) 30 seconds, if the duration of FCT is 150/160 seconds and 60 seconds. If FCT is 180 seconds or more.

(*ii*) Banking in any case is within the duration of the programme.

8. **Discount**

Spot booking in excess of 30 seconds would entitle the advertiser to the following discounts :

(*a*) Upto 50 seconds, a discount of 5 seconds.

(*b*) For 60 seconds and above a discount of 10 seconds.

9. (*a*) If at any stage Doordarshan decides to change the category of a running programme irrespective of the telecast, time slot or day of telecast, it may do so after giving a notice of 30 days.

(*b*) The time category of running serial can be changed, irrespective of time and day of telecast.

(*c*) Any programme before its introduction, could be placed in a higher category than the normal time category irrespective of the time and day of telecast.

Annexure-I

RATE CARD —SPOT BUY
NATIONAL NETWORK

Rate for Spot Buy (10 Seconds in Rupees)

Kendra	*SuperA SPL*	*Super A*	*A Spl.*	*'A'*	*'B'*
(1)	*(2)*	*(3)*	*(4)*	*(5)*	*(6)*
National Network	Chitrahaar				
	1,20,000	60,000	40,000	25,000	15,000
	1,30,000 (for last two spots)				
	1,50,000 (in between)				
	Hindi Feature Film				
	1,00,000				

BEFORE SAMACHAR
70,000
THE NEWS

40,000

RANGOLI
Spot Buy
75,000
80,000
(last two spots)
1,00,000
(in between)

BETWEEN CHTRAHAAR
80,000
News : 60,000

Rate Card — Spot Buy

REGIONAL KENDRAS
(10 secs. in Rupees)

Kendra (1)	*Super A SPL* (2)	*Super A* (3)	*'A'* (4)	*'B'* (5)
Delhi	40,000	25,000	7,000	2,000
Madras	30,000	14,000	4,000	1,500
Bombay	26,000	18,000	5,000	1,500
Hyderabad	18,000	11,000	4,000	1,500
Calcutta	18,000	11,000	4,000	1,500
Bangalore	18,000	11,000	4,000	1,500
Trivandrum	12,000	8,000	3,500	1,000
Ahmedabad	12,000	8,000	2,500	1,000
Lucknow	10,000	6,000	2,500	1,000
Jalandhar	7,000	6,000	3,000	1,000
Bhopal/Jaipur	6,000	4,000	2,000	1,000
Srinagar/ Guwahati	—	1,500	1,000	500

Regional News

At Madras, Hyderabad, Bangalore, Trivandrum, Calcutta. : 10% Premium over Super "A" Category

Film Songs Programmes (Regional Kendras)

(*i*) Last two spots — 10% Premium

(*ii*) In-between — 25% Premium

Note : 15 Seconds "ad" is accepted on pro-rata basis.

Annexure-II

RATE FOR SPONSORSHIP OF DOORDARSHAN PROGRAMMES PRODUCED/COMMISSIONED AND ACQUIRED (In Rupees 30 mts.)

TIME CATEGORIES

Kendra	*Super A SPL*	*Super A*	*A Spl.*	*'A'*	*'B'*
(1)	*(2)*	*(3)*	*(4)*	*(5)*	*(6)*
National Network	**Hindi Feature Film**				
	6,50,000 40 sec.	**3,50,000 60 sec**	**2,20,000 60 sec.**	**1,30,000 60 sec.**	
	Sponsored Hindi Film				
	5,00,000 60 sec.	2,40,000 40 sec.	1,60,000 40 sec.	1,00,000 40 sec.	40,000 40 sec.

40 Sec. FCT is common to all regional programmes in all categories.

Kendra	*Super A SPL*	*Super A*	*'A'*	*'B'*
(1)	*(2)*	*(3)*	*(4)*	*(5)*
Delhi	2,10,000	1,20,000	28,000	8,000
Madras	1,30,000	50,000	16,000	4,500
	Tamil Feature Film			
Bombay	—	65,000	20,000	6,000
Hyderabad	90,000	40,000	16,000	4,500
Calcutta	90,000	40,000	16,000	4,500
Bangalore	90,000	40,000	16,000	4,500
Trivandrum/ Ahmedabad	50,000	30,000	10,000	4,000

Contd.

RATE FOR SPONSORSHIP OF DOORDARSHAN PRODUCED / COMMISSIONED AND ACQUIRED PROGRAMMES

(In Rupees)

TIME CATEGORIES

Kendra (1)	*Super A SPL* (2)	*Super A* (3)	*'A'* (4)	*'B'* (5)
Lucknow	30,000	22,000	10,000	3,000
Jalandhar	27,000	22,000	12,000	3,000
Jaipur/Bhopal	22,000	14,000	7,000	3,000
Srinagar/ Guwahati	6,000	5,000	3,000	1,500

Note : (*i*) FCT is 40 seconds except Doordarshan Programmes in Super-A, A-Special, and A-Categories of National Network.

(*ii*) Consequent upon the introduction of capsule in between the film songs programmes (National Network and Kendras), the sponsorship of such programmes discontinued.

Annexure-IIA

RATE FOR SPONSORSHIP ALONGWITH DETAILS OF FCT FOR PROGRAMMERS PRODUCED BY OUTSIDE PRODUCERS

In Rupees — 30 mts. Programme

Super A	*A Spl.*	*'A'*	*'B'*	*Telefilm/ Teleplay*
National Network				
1,40,000 (90 sec.)	1,00,000 (120 sec)	50,000 (120 sec.)	New prog. 25,000 with (150 sec.) (with banking of 30 sec.)	
Mega Serials 1,80,000 (120 secs.)	Mega Serials 1,00,000 (150 sec.)	—	Repeat prog. 70,000 (90 sec.)	50,000 (90 mts) 35,000 (60 mts).

(*ii*) Repeat serials from either the same Kendra or a different Kendra will be in "Super A" category, as per the rates given below :

Kendra	*Sponsorship Fee*	*FCT (in seconds)*
Delhi	Rs. 50,000	40
Bombay	„ 50,000	50
Madras	„ 32,000	60
Hyderabad/ Calcutta & Bangalore	„ 26,000	60
Trivandrum	„ 23,000	70
Ahmedabad	„ 24,000	80
Lucknow & Jalandhar	„ 20,000	100
Jaipur & Bhopal	„ 20,000	120

Note : If the serial is dubbed in any other language, the FCT allowed will be 10 seconds more than indicated above.

Annexure–IIB

RATE FOR SPONSORSHIP ALONG WITH DETAILS OF FCT FOR PROGRAMMES PRODUCED BY OUTSIDERS

(for 30-minute Programme)

(for Regional Kendras)

Name of Kendra/Network	*Super-A*	*Tele-Film/ Tele-Plays*
Delhi	20,000 : 90 Sec FCT	30,000/90 mins. 20,000/60 mins.
Bombay	16,000 : 110 Sec FCT	15,000/90 mins. 10,000/60 mins.
Madras	12,000 : 120 Sec FCT	10,000/90 mins. 7,000/60 mins.
Bangalore and Calcutta		5,000/60 mins.
Trivandrum and Ahmedabad	10,000 : 160 Sec FCT	-do-
Lucknow and Jalandhar	7,000 : 180 Sec FCT	5,000/90 mins. 3,000/60 mins.
Jaipur and Bhopal	5,000 : 210 Sec FCT	-do-
Srinagar and Guwahati	5,000 : 240 Sec FCT	3,000/90 mins. 2,000/60 mins.

Note :

(1) Programmes produced by outside producers (except tele-films/tele-plays will be telecast by the Regional Kendras only in Super-A category.

(2) FCT entitlement for tele-films/tele-plays is :

90 minutes : 4 minutes, including 2 mins. of banking

60 minutes : 3 minutes, including one minute of banking.

Annexure-III

RATE CARD DOORDARSHAN-II METRO CHANNEL

	Super A		*A Special*		*A Category**	*B Category**
	F/	*SS*	*F*	*SS/ C/I/G/Q/*		
Spot Buy Rate (10 sec)	30,000	30,000*	22,000	22,000	15,000	10,000
FCT (In sec)	150	180	150	180	210	210
Sponsorship Fee	2,00,000	1,40,000	1,00,000	50,000(SS) 1,00,000 (C/I/G/Q)	35,000	20,000

SINGLE METRO

	Super A	*A Category*	*B Category*
Spot Buy Rate	8,000	5,800	4,200
FCT (In sec.)	120	150	210
Sponsorship Fee	20,000	10,000	5,000

F : (FILM BASED)
SS : (SPONSORED SERIAL)
C : (CHAT SHOWS)
I : INTERVIEWS
G : (GAMES SHOWS)
Q : (QUIZ)

* In 'A' and 'B' categories there will be uniform rates for F; SS; C/I/G/Q programmes.

1. The Producers will be entitled to book additional FCT (in-between the programmes) as per below mentioned schedule :

(*i*) First 30 Seconds	—	15% Premium
(*ii*) Next 30 Seconds	—	20% Premium
(*iii*) Next 30 Seconds and above	—	25% Premium

2. Doordarshan, programmes will not be available for sponsorship DDII. Ads will also be telecast in-between the programmes at a premium of 20 per cent over the concerned spot buy rate. Two capsules of 90 seconds each will be telecast in a 30 minutes slot.

Appendix V

Zee TV Rate Card

South Asian Channel

Rate Card No. ZINR/October'93, Effective 1-10-93
Valid for Indian Clients paying through
Ambience Space Sellers·Pvt. Ltd.
ALL PAYMENTS IN INDIAN RUPEES

INR

DURATION		*ROS*		*FH*		*FT*	
60	secs	Rs.	1,03,200	Rs.	1,23,840	Rs.	1,44,480
45	secs	Rs.	84,710	Rs.	1,01,480	Rs.	1,18,680
30	secs	Rs.	51,600	Rs.	61,920	Rs.	72,240
20	secs	Rs.	41,280	Rs.	49,880	Rs.	58,050
15	secs	Rs.	33,110	Rs.	39,560	Rs.	46,440
10	secs	Rs.	25,800	Rs.	30,960	Rs.	36,120
5	secs	Rs.	17,200	Rs.	20,640	Rs.	24,080

Odd duration will be charged at 20 sec rate, pro-rata

ROS-Run of schedule rate

Subject to availability, these spots are rotational within the specific day and channel.

FH - Fixed hour rate

Subject to availability, these spots are rotational within the specific day, channel and hour (HKT Clock Hour).

FT - Fixed time rate

Subject to availability, these spots are rotational within the specific day, channel and programme/time slot (+/– 10 minute).

PAYMENT THROUGH AMBIENCE SPACE SELLERS PVT. LTD.

* Eligibility is for existing established exporters only. (Rs. 10 Lakh exports minimum in each of last two years).

* Asia Today Limited (ATL) Invoices will be raised weekly — on the 8th, 15th, 22nd and last day of every month.

* ATL will bill client for 70% ATL component, authorizing client to pay same in Indian Rupees to Ambience Space Sellers Pvt. Ltd. — ATL's collecting agent.

* Client to make payment to ASSPL attaching ADV Form *signed by client* alongwith XC certificate; and storyboard of advertisement.

* ASSPL will separately bill Advertising Agency for 15% Canvassing Agents commission.

* Agency will separately bill client for 30% local commissions, will retain their 15% and pay ASSPL their 15% commission.

* Bills will be sent to Agency via ASSPL, and are payable 45 days from bill date.

South Asian Channel

Rate Card No. ZUSD/October'93, Effective 1-10-93
Valid for Indian Exporters
Using EEFC Accounts
ALL PAYMENTS IN US DOLLARS

$

DURATION		*ROS*		*FH*		*FT*	
60	secs	$	2,670	$	3,200	$	3,740
45	secs	$	2,190	$	2,630	$	3,070
30	secs	$	1,340	$	1,600	$	1,870
20	secs	$	1,070	$	1,290	$	1,500
15	secs	$	860	$	1,030	$	1,200
10	secs	$	670	$	800	$	940
5	secs	$	450	$	540	$	630

Odd duration will be charged at 20 sec rate, pro-rate

Payment Terms

45 days from date of Invoice.

Payment System

Invoice will be raised weekly — 8th, 15th, 22nd, and last day of any month.

— 70% ATL Component - Invoice and checking copy, alongwith Bill of Exchange will be sent direct to client or via his nominated bank. Bill of Exchange and checking copy of Invoice will be given to client by bank with instructions to accept Bill of Exchange within 14 days (checking time). Payment to be made on date Bill of Exchange falls due, in US Dollars.

or (options)

— 70% ATL Component — Invoice in original will be routed thru the agency to the client. Agency will forward original invoice to client for payment in US Dollars.

— 30% local commissions — will be billed by Agency to client. Agency to retain their 15% commission and pay ASSPL 15% being their commission. Payment to be made in Indian Rupees (invoice will convert USD/INR at prevailing rates of exchange — TT Selling Rates as quoted in Economic Times may be applied).

ROS-Run of schedule rate

Subject to availability, these spots are rotational within the specific day and channel.

FH - Fixed hour rate

Subject to availability, these spots are rotational within the specific day, channel and hour (HKT Clock Hour).

FT - Fixed Time rate

Subject to availability, these spots are rotational within the specific day, channel and programme/time slot (+/– 10 minute).

South Asian Channel

Rate Card No. ZUSD/INT/October'93, Effective 1-10-93
Valid for All Markets
Excluding India/Nepal.
ALL PAYMENTS IN US DOLLARS

$

DURATION		*ROS*		*FH*		*FT*	
60	secs	$	2,670	$	3,200	$	3,740
45	secs	$	2,190	$	2,630	$	3,070
30	secs	$	1,340	$	1,600	$	1,870
20	secs	$	1,070	$	1,290	$	1,500
15	secs	$	860	$	1,030	$	1,200
10	secs	$	670	$	800	$	940
5	secs	$	450	$	540	$	630

Odd duration will be charged at 20 sec rate, pro-rata

Payment Terms

Payments are required to be made in advance.

ROS-Run of schedule rate

Subject to availability, these spots are rotational within the specific day and channel.

FH - Fixed hour rate

Subject to availability, these spots are rotational within the specific day, channel and hour (HKT Clock Hour)

FT - Fixed time rate

Subject to availability, these spots are rotational within the specific day, channel and programme/time slot (+/– 10 minute).

Appendix VI

Doordarshan Audience Research Television Ratings

The Audience Research Unit of Doordarshan is obtaining the Ratings for Television programmes on continuous basis in a number of cities through panels which represent a cross-section of the viewing public.

According to these Ratings during the week 9-15 January, 1994, *Vividha, Ek Ghar Aas Paas* and *Sansar*, the serials telecast in the prime time had the highest ratings of 55% in non-metro cities. *Surabhi* had a rating of 51% followed by *Samandar*. However, the ratings for these programmes were considerably less in the metro cities, ranging from 14 to 22. The Sunday morning serials, mostly animated films for children, had ratings of around 35 in the metro cities.

Rangoli had the highest rating of 77 in non-metro cities followed by *Chitrahaar* and the Hindi feature film telecast on Saturday on the National network. These film-based programmes had ratings of around 40 in metro cities.

In non-metro cities Samachar (8.30 p.m.) had ratings from 42-50 on different days and News (9.45 p.m.) had an average rating of 20.

Among the programmes on the Metro entertainment channel *Dekh Bhai Dekh* had the highest rating in Bombay and Delhi whereas the Tamil version of *Junoon* had the highest rating.

(9-15 January 1994)

METRO FILMS

Day	*Films*	*Delhi*	*Bombay*	*Luck-now*	*Madras*	*Av.*
Sunday	Pyari Bahana	64	40	48	21	
Monday	Ek Din Achanak	26	15	34	17	
Tuesday	Madi Da Dva	7	8	6	17	
Wednesday	Salakhen	44	18	39	23	
Thursday	Parmatma	43	21	37	25	
Friday	Ashanti	47	16	38	17	
Saturday	Hum Tum Aur Woh	46	31	6	28	

Table 19 G : Viewing to Metro Channel

Day/Time	*Programme*	*Delhi*	*Bombay*	*Luck-now*	*Madras*	*Aver-age*
Sunday						
8.00 A.M.	Breakfast Show	20	—	10	6	12
7.50 P.M.	Jungle Book	27	9	9	9	14
8.15 P.M.	Shrikrishna	57	42	45	74*	55
8.45 P.M.	Superhit Mukabala	50	66	58	38*	53
Monday						
7.50 P.M.	Metro Dhamaka	24	27	43	15	27
8.15 P.M.	Junoon	56	49	36	70*	53
8.45 P.M.	Family Pride	31	19	23	18	23
9.15 P.M.	Tanhai	54	35	42	14	36
Tuesday						
7.50 P.M.	Hellow Bombay	48	47	40	32	42

Day/Time	*Programme*	*Delhi*	*Bombay*	*Luck-now*	*Madras*	*Aver-age*
8.15 P.M.	Imtihaan	55	39	37	58*	47
8.45 P.M.	Time Style	23	13	29	27	23
9.15 P.M.	Dard	58	42	32	32*	41
Wednesday						
7.45 P.M.	Mirch Masala	36	29	24	24	28
8.15 P.M.	Kismat	38	20	24	21*	26
8.45 P.M.	Ajnabi	58	44	48	57*	52
9.15 P.M.	Nukkad	49	46	44	46*	46
Thursday						
7.50 P.M.	Jharokha	45	32	28	11	29
8.15 P.M.	Dekh Bhai Dekh	59	69	52	33	53
8.45 P.M.	Mere Sath Chal	40	38	43	36*	39
9.15 P.M.	Take-2	36	40	41	27	36
Friday						
7.45 P.M.	Tiger	45	34	19	30*	32
8.15 P.M.	Kanoon	46	37	35	58*	44
8.45 P.M.	Teen Talk	30	17	19	38	26
9.15 P.M.	Junoon	56	50	36	64*	52
Saturday						
8.00 A.M.	Breakfast Show	25	—	12	—	19
7.45 P.M.	World Music Award	8	1	40	6	14
8.15 P.M.	Zaban Sambhalke	52	54	42	24*	43
8.45 P.M.	Mirch Masala	43	46	23	50*	41

Percentages * Tamil Version

Film Based Programmes

Day	*Programme*	*Av Metro*	*Av Non-Metro*
Sunday	Rangoli	37	77
	Mayuri [Assamese F.F]	12	18
Monday	Aap Ki Kasam [H.F.F.]	18	33
	Pyar Zindagi Hai [Tele F.]	8	13
Tuesday	Kanoon Ki Zanzeer [H.F.F.]	18	45
Wednesday	Chitrahaar	39	64
	Nav jeevan [H.F.F.]	6	14
Friday	Gujarati F.F.	9	17
	Endless Love [E.F.F.]	12	19
Saturday	Suraj Ka Satvan Ghoda [H.F.F.]	47	65

News

Day	*Time*	*Average (%)*	
		Metro	*Non-Metro*
Sunday	8.30 P.M.	21	43
	9.45 P.M.	15	16
Monday	8.30 P.M.	22	50
	9.45 P.M.	12	23
Tuesday	8.30 P.M.	22	48
	9.45 P.M.	14	23
Wednesday	8.30 P.M.	24	47
	9.45 P.M.	11	23
Thursday	8.30 P.M.	22	44
	9.45 P.M.	13	19
Friday	8.30 P.M.	19	42
	9.45 P.M.	11	21
Saturday	8.30 P.M.	22	42
	9.45 P.M.	12	17
All Days [AV]			
	8.30 P.M.	22	45
	9.45 P.M.	12	20

Madras Telecasts Tamil News at 8.30 P.M.

National/Network Serials

Day	*Time*	*Serial*	*Average (%)*	
			Metro	*Non-Metro*
Sunday	8.45 P.M.	Int. Film Festival	5	35
	9.15 P.M.	National Games 94	4	20
Monday	8.45 P.M.	Vividha	20	55
	9.15 P.M.	Int. Film Festival	6	25
Tuesday	8.45 P.M.	Ek Ghar Aas Paas	22	55
	9.15 P.M.	Surabhi	14	51
Wednesday	8.45 P.M.	Sansar	9	55
	9.15 P.M.	Int. Film Festival	5	27
Thursday	8.45 P.M.	Sunehere Pal	15	51
	9.15 P.M.	Int. Film Festival	5	32
Friday	8.45 P.M.	Prog On Pongal	7	40
	9.15 P.M.	Int. Film Festival	7	32
Saturday	8.45 P.M.	Samunder	15	47
	9.15 P.M.	Int. Film Festival	9	24

National/Network Programmes on Sunday

Time	*Programme*	*Av Metro*	*Av. Non-Metro*
07.20 A.M.	Rangoli	37	77
07.50 A.M.	Classical Cartoons	13	33
09.00 A.M.	Uphaar (Tele-film)	14	35
09.30 A.M.	Umang Tarang/Cricket	12	28
10.00 A.M.	Guchhe	22	35
10.30 A.M.	Disney Adventure	26	26
11.30 A.M.	Spirit of Unity Concert	10	8
04.00 P.M.	Sports	7	8
10.00 P.M.	Focus	4	11

Percentages

Appendix VII

TELEVISION SETS IN INDIA

TV Licences

1962	41	1970	24838	1978	899,123
1963	58	1971	44855	1979	1,191,311
1964	93	1972	84114	1980	1,547,918
1965	649	1973	1,63,446	1981	1,672,568
1966	4170	1974	2,75,424	1982	2,095,537
1967	6184	1975	4,55,430	1983	2,783,370
1968	7765	1976	4,79,026	1984	3,632,328
1969	12303	1977	6,76,615		

TV HOUSEHOLDS-ESTIMATES*

1985	6,750,000	1990	27,820,000
1986	11,000,000	1991	30,803,000
1987	13,256,000	1992	34,858,000
1988	17,339,000	1993	40,337,000
1989	22,539,000		

(* Estimates made by various agencies.
According to Electronics Industry, 8.5 million colour TV sets have been sold during Jan-Sep. 1993 and the projected sales for the whole year is 11.5 million. After allowing for replacement, upgradation etc. the total TV HHS could be higher than 40 million.).

(Source : *Doordarshan 1994*)

Appendix VIII

TV HOUSEHOLDS
(States and UTs)
(In thousand)

North	
Jammu & Kashmir	123
Punjab	1401
Haryana	946
Himachal Pradesh	116
Uttar Pradesh	4338
Rajasthan	1415
Delhi (NCT)	1726
Chandigarh	61
	10126

South	
Andhra Pradesh	3580
Karnataka	2500
Kerala	1409
Tamil Nadu	3734
Pondicherry	65
Lakshadweep	1
	11,289

East	
Orissa	828
West Bengal	3740
Bihar	2379
Sikkim	5
Andaman	7
Nicobar	—
	6959

North-East	
Assam	692
Arunachal Pradesh	17
Manipur	66
Meghalaya	34
Mizoram	31
Nagaland	30
Tripura	46
	916

West	
Maharashtra	5828
Gujarat	2562
Madhya Pradesh	2558
Goa	91
Dadra Nagar Haveli, Daman Diu	8
	11047

All India 40337

(Estimates of DD AR Unit)

(Source : *Doordarshan 1994*)

Index